A
GOSPEL
of
SHAME

A
GOSPEL
of
SHAME

CHILDREN, SEXUAL ABUSE AND THE CATHOLIC CHURCH

Elinor Burkett
Frank Bruni

VIKING

VIKING
Published by the Penguin Group
Penguin Books USA Inc., 375 Hudson Street,
New York, New York 10014, U.S.A.
Penguin Books Ltd, 27 Wrights Lane,
London W8 5TZ, England
Penguin Books Australia Ltd, Ringwood,
Victoria, Australia
Penguin Books Canada Ltd, 10 Alcorn Avenue,
Toronto, Ontario, Canada M4V 3B2
Penguin Books (N.Z.) Ltd, 182–190 Wairau Road,
Auckland 10, New Zealand

Penguin Books Ltd, Registered Offices:
Harmondsworth, Middlesex, England

First published in 1993 by Viking Penguin,
a division of Penguin Books USA Inc.

1 3 5 7 9 10 8 6 4 2

Grateful acknowledgment is made for permission to reprint an
excerpt from "Among Ourselves" from *The Black Unicorn*
by Audre Lorde. By permission of the publisher,
W. W. Norton & Co., Inc.

The photographs reproduced in this book are from private
collections, unless otherwise indicated.

LIBRARY OF CONGRESS CATALOGING IN PUBLICATION DATA
Burkett, Elinor.
A gospel of shame: children, sexual abuse and the Catholic Church/
by Elinor Burkett and Frank Bruni.
p.   cm.
Includes bibliographical references.
ISBN 0-670-84828-X
1. Catholic Church—United States—Clergy—Sexual behavior.
2. Child molesting—United States.   3. Child molesting—Religious aspects—
Catholic Church.   I. Bruni, Frank.   II. Title.
BX1912.9.B87   1993
261.8'32—dc20   93-3614

Printed in the United States of America
Set in Sabon
Designed by Glen Edelstein

TO MIGUEL CHINCHILLA, 1961–1993, whose story was the genesis of this book, whose personal courage was an inspiration and whose profound faith captured the best of Catholicism.

AND TO LESLIE BRUNI—not just a Supermom, but a super woman, and the greatest, truest friend.

ACKNOWLEDGMENTS

The reporting and writing of this book would not have been possible without the extraordinary cooperation of scores of individuals, many of whom rearranged busy schedules and put other business on hold to share their time and insights.

First and foremost, we would like to thank the dozens of victims who opened their hearts to us, trusted us with some of the most intimate details of their personal histories and put up with what must have seemed a ridiculous number of stupid questions. Special thanks to Dennis Gaboury for his images, dreams and eloquence; for the tours of North Attleboro; and for the introductions to the remarkable men and women whose haunting memories included their abuse by a priest named James Porter.

We would like to thank the law enforcement officials nationwide—detectives, prosecutors and judges—who assisted us. Special thanks to the P.M.S. Club in Phoenix: Laura Reckart, Susan Lindley and Paula Anderson. Next time, the cigarettes are on Frank.

Our gratitude goes as well to the many lawyers across the country who shared their time, materials and recollections. Two lawyers stand out: Bruce Pasternack, who introduced Elinor to the concept of reserved embrace, and J. Minos Simon, who actually let us take three fifty-pound boxes of his files to a hotel room for the weekend.

Portions of this book would not have been possible without the courage and candor of the six priest abusers who granted us interviews, thus providing our work with a unique set of voices. We thank them all, especially Father Ned.

Among the many other priests who talked to us, we would like to acknowledge, in particular, Father Dominic Grassi and Father Kevin Clinton.

Dozens of experts helped us frame the complex issues embedded in the problem of child sexual abuse in the Roman Catholic Church. We give special thanks to Richard Sipe for hours and hours of fascinating conversation and for his grace and wit.

We would also like to thank the bishops who agreed to be interviewed for this book. We asked 188 of them; twelve brave men took the plunge. Their insights were invaluable.

There were friends, family members and professional colleagues whose support and contributions we would also like to mention.

Among fellow reporters, thanks to Karen Springen of *Newsweek* magazine's Chicago bureau for the weekly batches of regional newspaper clippings; to Jeff Hiday of the *Providence Journal* for providing material from that newspaper; and especially to David Crumm of the *Detroit Free Press*. His wisdom, friendship and generosity are all too rare.

Thanks to editors at the *Miami Herald* and the *Detroit Free Press* for granting us the leaves of absence necessary to complete this book.

There are particular editors, reporters and researchers formerly and currently at the *Miami Herald* whose contributions, direct and indirect, are reflected in this book. Thanks to John Doussard, Gene Miller and Bill Greer for teaching Elinor the skills she needed to keep up with her ideas. Thanks to Liz Donovan and Gay Nemetti for running the best and most generous newspaper library in the country.

There are individuals at the *Detroit Free Press* as well whose talents, encouragement and friendship inform this work. Thanks to Ron Dzwonkowski for his countless lessons in good journalism, and his sarcastic asides, Chip Visci for his quirky humor and great advice, Chris Kucharski for going above and beyond the call, Renee Murawski for holding down the fort in so many ways, and Susan Ager for the hazelnut coffee, pine-scented candle and wine-soaked pajamaramas.

Before the *Herald* and before the *Free Press*, there was, at least for us, an old curmudgeon named Blood. After the *Herald* and the *Free Press*, there is still Blood. We thank him.

For helping an idea become a proposal, and a proposal become a book, thanks to Robert Jones, Lisa Bankoff and Dawn Seferian.

Authors usually thank their husbands and wives for making the beds, cooking dinner and putting up with endless discussions of a single topic. Alas, we have neither husbands nor wives. But we have Frank's parents, Frank and Leslie Bruni, who are even better, despite the YMCA dinner. And we thank them.

Elinor would like to give special thanks to Joel Rapoport, Ivan Bernstein and Robin Haueter simply for being there when the going got impossible.

Frank would like to give an extra special thanks to a friend whose constant support, drop-dead gazpacho and shared thirsts kept him sane for so many months. Patricia (Godzilla) Chargot, you're the best.

CONTENTS

PART I

"My hope is that when He comes again, He will still be human enough to shed a clown's gentle tears over the broken toys—that were once . . . children."

—MORRIS L. WEST, "THE CLOWNS OF GOD"

Chapter 1

WHILE GOD WASN'T WATCHING

JUST BEFORE NOON ON A COLD NEW EN-
gland Sunday in 1990, Frank Fitzpatrick sat
staring—yet again—at his telephone.

When the clock strikes twelve, I'll make the
call, he told himself. High Noon, he'd dubbed
it. He'd already run to the toilet four times.

Frank had been planning—and delaying—
the moment for five months. For the six
months before that he had been too busy trying to find the phone number to think about
what he might say. Frank was a good detective. In fact, that's how he made his living. But
James Porter was hardly an uncommon name.
With no middle initial for him, no Social Security number, no help from the Catholic
Church, Frank had started from scratch.

But Frank was a man obsessed. He had begun his search in 1989 when terrifying images
surfaced in his mind, suddenly explaining the

strange mood swings that had bedeviled him, the lingering sorrow and the nagging dread. At forty, he had a solid marriage, a good career, two terrific sons, a pliable cat—and a constant urge to cry.

He had tried Valium, but the tears would not stop falling. He had tried therapy, but could not trace the root of his sadness. He had tried hiding away in the master bedroom of his Cape Cod–style house in Cranston, Rhode Island, but the answers continued to elude him. Then, suddenly, they erupted in a jarring series of images and sensations from a past he had long blocked out.

He saw Father James Porter—the young, charismatic priest at St. Mary's Church in North Attleboro, Massachusetts. He remembered his giddy excitement when his hero invited him to a game at the Boston Garden. He caught glimpses of the strange white house where Porter took him instead. He tasted the strangely flavored mincemeat pie that the priest kept pushing at him. He felt himself awakening in a semidrugged state and the pain of Porter on top of him, pressing hard against him, hurting him.

For three decades, Frank had locked all memory of that night in a sealed vault inside his head. He had done what many child victims of sexual abuse do: he had repressed from all conscious thought an encounter that made no sense to him, that filled his child's world with terror. But with the opening of that chamber came an obsessive need to find Porter. He was not sure what he would do or say or think when he did. He just knew he had to.

He went first to the Diocese of Fall River, in which St. Mary's was located. In October 1989, he told them why he was looking for Porter and asked for their help. But they said Porter had left the priesthood and they had no idea where he had gone. "It may be best to leave it in the hands of the Lord," an aide to the bishop counseled him. Frank tried the Massachusetts Department of Motor Vehicles instead, but Porter did not have a driver's license in that state. He checked out voter registration lists, but could not find Porter's name among them. He sifted through old newspapers in the library, looking for references to the priest. Finally, he found the critical clue: a short obituary from March 1975 for Porter's father. The article said that his survivors included a son named James who was living in Minnesota.

The Department of Motor Vehicles in Minnesota confirmed that Porter lived in the state and gave Frank his address in the St. Paul suburb of Oakdale. Frank called the Oakdale police and told them his story. They seemed puzzled, responding, "What can we do about a thirty-year-old case in another state?" Frank then called the local district attorney in Massachusetts; the response was the same. "What can we do about a thirty-year-old case with no details, no corroboration?"

So Frank started staring at his telephone, memorizing the number he had gotten from Minnesota directory assistance, rolling over and over in his mind how the conversation might go, what good it would do, what his strategy should be. Then, at noon on that Sunday in February 1990, he attached a tape recorder to his phone and dialed Oakdale.

"I have one question," Frank asked haltingly after introducing himself to James Porter. "Why did you do that kind of thing?"

"I don't know," said Porter. "Who knows?" He laughed.

"How many did you molest?" Frank asked him.

"I don't know. There could have been quite a few," Porter answered.

"Do you remember me in particular?" Frank asked, his voice breaking.

"No," Porter responded. "I don't remember names."

That phone call marked the tumbling of the first in a line of dominoes that would end with James Porter's being thrust into the public spotlight; that would provide Americans with the graphic and confounding details of one of the most disturbing cases of mass child molestation to date; and that would expose as never before the crisis in the American Catholic Church of priests sexually abusing children—a crisis the Church had struggled for years to hide or ignore. Porter's case put an end to that, as Porter had put an end to the trusting innocence of Frank and so many other young children who had the misfortune of crossing his path and deferring to his Roman collar.

When his true past was revealed, when the long-kept secret of Frank Fitzpatrick and his schoolmates at St. Mary's Grammar School was set free, the story proved almost too incredible to believe. Father Porter had molested child after child. Many of them had watched it happen to others and sensed that all of them were in danger, yet few of them shared the secret, and almost none of them told their parents. Father Porter had pinched girls' bottoms and given open-mouthed kisses to boys in the middle of crowded classrooms, yet the nuns and other priests who must have seen this did nothing to stop him. The few parents who found out what was happening had reported the abuse to Church authorities, certain that they would do the right thing. But those authorities simply shuffled Father Porter to a new assignment and let him continue to work and play among children.

Decades later, when the truth was revealed, it became clear that the conspiracy of silence and misplaced trust that had allowed Porter to hurt so many children was not at all unique to his case. It was endemic to a Catholic culture that had deified its priests in the eyes of their parishioners and thus rendered children particularly vulnerable to exploitation by those men. Frank Fitzpatrick grasped that, as did the other survivors of Father Porter, who would join forces with him. That chilling knowledge propelled them in a quest for justice that ultimately defied formidable obstacles and odds, and that thrust the Catholic Church into ever-deepening crisis.

"FATHER PORTER'S COMING, FATHER PORTER'S COMING." THE warning flew down the quiet corridors of St. Mary's Grammar School whenever one of the girls saw the priest approaching. Then, as if on cue, dozens of girls in bobby socks and skirts that always covered their knees fled the center of the hallway for the walls, pressing their backs against the hard, cold tile. They knew that if you didn't turn your back to Porter, he couldn't sneak up and grab you from behind. If you didn't turn your back, he couldn't get his hands under your skirt. No one taught the polite parochial school girls the rules: sixth graders didn't warn their younger sisters or cousins—they just knew, they learned from experience.

Patty Poirier huddled next to her best friend, Judy White. The raven-haired Franco-Italian and her blond alter ego had been a matched set—Blackie and Whitie—since they were five. They were so close that when they were eleven, they each told the other the painful secret of how Father Porter was always forcing his fingers between their legs and his tongue inside their mouths. But they told no one else. It was simply too dirty to talk about, too humiliating.

Fran Rotella fled. She had her own special hiding place in a niche on the side of the red brick building where she retreated whenever Porter came around the corner. Like most of the children in the school, she had told no one about her encounter with Porter. It had happened on Columbus Day 1960 when he stopped by the hospital, where she was recovering from an auto accident, to break the news of her uncle's death. So ashamed of what had happened and so certain no one would believe it, she did not tell a teacher, or a parent, or any other adult.

The boys in their ties and pressed pants never guessed what was happening to the girls. Most were too busy watching their own backs. Porter was everywhere. He would show up at baseball practice and grab their crotches as he slapped them on the back. He would appear in their classrooms on their birthdays to give them slobbery French kisses—often in front of the nuns, who said nothing. The sisters were too shocked to know what to do and too uncomfortable with what was happening to even find the language to describe it. Besides, they knew, as did the children, that priests were their superiors. To accuse one of something so vile was surely to invite disbelief, ridicule and censure.

So, in a small town that appeared to be the idyllic community of 1950s mythology, a place where everyone knew his neighbors and neighbors knew each other's business, one secret festered: Nowhere was it safe for the children of St. Mary's. Not on the playground or in the rectory office. Not at the altar or in the vestibule. Not in the corridors, the sacristy, the churchyard or on the green around the statue of the Virgin Mary. Not at the town pool, the nearby beach or the Cathedral Camp. Not even in their own bedrooms.

Pete Calderone tensed every time Porter stopped by for dinner or to visit his parents; the boy knew the priest would come to his room and molest him while his mother and father sat chatting in the living room. Steve Johnson dreaded the summer days when

Porter would take groups of boys to his parents' Rhode Island beach house and creep quietly from one bedroom to another throughout the night. Some boys invented ways to avoid the wrestling matches Porter would organize just so he could watch the boys while he played with himself; others feigned illness if their names appeared on the schedule to serve at his side during Mass. The girls cringed when he called a group into his office. He would place one girl on each side of him and put his hands up their dresses—while their friends played quietly on the other side of his desk.

In 1960, St. Mary's was still a church where the mysteries of the Mass were preserved in Latin, where priests were otherworldly beings in floor-length cassocks and parishioners were worshipful and obedient. No one talked to the working class Irish and Italian children about sexual abuse. No one talked about sex at all. Sex was dirty—unless you were making babies. Children did not dare joke about it. Teenagers were commanded not to think about it, and certainly not to have it.

Enter James Porter, an energetic practical joker straight out of St. Mary's Seminary in Baltimore. He taught the boys to throw curve balls on the baseball diamond. He took his altar boys to play on the rides at Lincoln Park. He took children on outings to the beach, to the church-run Cathedral Camp, to Celtics games in Boston. He organized a sports program and a children's choir. He broke bread with the men and women who ran the parish. He offered to baby-sit for their children.

No one in North Attleboro was aware that the summer before Porter entered seminary he had climbed into the bunk of a twelve-year-old boy at a church camp and straddled him. No church official told them that the year before his ordination, Porter had grabbed the crotch of another sixth grader he was driving home after a game of stickball. So they welcomed the lively priest into their homes and encouraged their sons to begin training as altar boys with him. Excited by the youthful priest, kids followed Porter as if he were a clerical Pied Piper.

Porter repaid that trust and devotion by carefully engineering ways to get the children alone, approaching them with innocuous requests and even appealing to their desire to serve him, then exploiting those opportunities and victimizing them. Within a week of his arrival at St. Mary's he invited Paul Merry—a fifth grader who lived next door to the church and was studying to be an altar boy—into his office for soda and cake. "I'm so stiff from moving furniture," he complained. Paul felt proud to reach behind the priest's chair and rub his sore muscles. He wasn't nervous when the priest lay on the floor for a more thorough massage. Then Porter rolled over, unbuttoned his pants, pulled down the zipper and placed Paul's hand on his groin. For three years, he terrorized the young boy, grabbing and fondling him at least once a week. Paul was North Attleboro's first male victim.

Within a month of his arrival, Porter was pursuing Patty Poirier—leering at her across the playground, touching her in the school hallways. One day he asked the fifth grader to help him prepare the basketball roster. When they got to the rectory office, he locked the door, took off his collar, put the ten-year-old on his lap and fondled her. Patty was North Attleboro's first female victim.

Dozens of other children soon met similar fates. They unquestioningly followed the priest's lead as he ushered them into some private place, told them to sit beside him or on his lap, drew so close to them that they could smell the cigarettes on his breath, then fondled or raped them. They watched him take off his collar before molesting them, thinking that he was somehow becoming invisible to God. With many of these children, Porter came back again and again, until the sweaty touch of his hands and the heavy weight of his body became a familiar sensation, a grim ritual.

While most of them assumed that what Porter was doing was reserved for them alone, a few knew better. One afternoon, a group of John Robitaille's teammates in Catholic Youth Organization basketball found him bleeding on the floor of the shower room. They guessed that Porter had just sodomized him. They never said a word.

A few did try to tell on Porter. Cheryl Swenson, molested by Porter herself, subsequently caught a glimpse of the priest on the altar one day with two boys at his side—and his pants unzipped. She ran to Father Armando Annunziato and blurted out what she had seen. "Why are you stirring up trouble," he screamed, slamming the door in her face. When she told a nun, Cheryl was forced to stand up in class, confess and apologize for saying a bad thing about Father Porter.

Others knew Porter's fellow priests were aware of what was happening; they knew that the priests had witnessed Porter abusing them. Once, Annunziato walked in on Father Porter as he was raping John Robitaille. He caught the boy's eye and left without a word. Once, that same priest knocked at the office door while Porter had Pete Calderone locked inside. "What's going on in there?" Annunziato asked when Porter wouldn't let him in. "It's getting late, time for everyone to go home," Annunziaton told him. When he departed, Porter had Pete masturbate him yet again.

Most of the children assumed from the seeming complicity of other priests and nuns that it must be all right. They should just keep quiet and suffer it. The abuse must be their own fault, most concluded, thinking they somehow must have tempted Porter into these encounters. Priests, after all, were perfect—handpicked by God, in fact. That is what the nuns, and even the children's parents, always said.

That dozens of these children guarded the secret of their abuse for years, despite their pain, is compelling testimony to the extraordinary and well-documented difficulty that children have in talking about being molested, to their fears that parents will be angry and punish them or that their friends will jeer at them. In the 1960s, that difficulty was even more pronounced than it is today because there were no public service announcements about child sexual abuse, no guidance from the schools, no lectures from policemen. But the silence of St. Mary's also bore witness to the lofty, untouchable place that the priest occupied in the lives of these children and their families. A priest brought God into the Eucharist; a priest pardoned their sins.

"How could you tell your parents that God did this to you?" said Patti Kozak after she finally broke her silence. It took her thirty years.

PATTY POIRIER WILSON BLEW UP WHEN JUDY WHITE MULLET READ
her the brief ad in the *Sun-Chronicle*: "Do You Remember Father
Porter?" That's all it said. That was enough.

"Son of a bitch, someone's going to throw that bastard a
party," she concluded. No way, the feisty forty-one-year-old
vowed. No way I'm gonna let anyone honor that rapist. Wilson
marched outside with a pad in her hand to write a letter to Frank
Fitzpatrick—the guy in the ad—and give him a piece of her mind.

"I for one am very familiar with Father Porter and his antics
—or should I say insanity," she wrote. "I lost my faith and dignity
because of this man."

It was October 1990. Patty and Judy had both been married,
and divorced. Patty, a former cheerleader, now a counselor for
the disabled, was still running things in North Attleboro—pizza
night for sports clubs, fund-raisers for civic groups. Judy, a registered nurse, had fled town right out of high school. Now she
was back and the two were inseparable again. Over the years
Patty and Judy had talked about finding Porter. But he had vanished from North Attleboro in 1963. And they had kids to raise
and bills to pay.

Now he had reappeared in the classified section of their hometown paper. Patty was not about to let that kind of opportunity
slip by. She mailed Frank her letter. He called two weeks later
and explained that he was hardly planning a party for Porter.
Rather, he was trying to round up people who could help him
bring Porter to justice.

That night, Frank drove up to Patty's home in North Attleboro and told her and Judy that he had been searching for other
victims, that he had called old classmates who said they had never
been abused and that he had found another guy that Porter had
raped in a different parish—proving that Porter had not changed
even three years after he left St. Mary's.

Then, while Patty and Judy sat nervously on the couch, Frank
played the tapes he had secretly made of his conversations with
Porter:

*"I mean, actually, I've got to look back, how fortunate I was
I didn't get creamed—creamed—by parents, the law, anything
else,"* they heard Porter tell Frank.

"It's funny how things worked out. Marvelous. Especially me, mentally."

Both women froze at the familiar voice, the casual tone. Porter had not changed at all, they thought. Patty still was not sure at this point that she was willing to get caught up in Frank's angry, obsessive quest to make Porter pay for all the pain he had caused them. Then she heard Porter's disembodied voice pronouncing an astonishing lie. Frank said to Porter: *"There were a couple of girls that I heard you molested too."*

"Not that I know of," the former priest answered.

That stunning denial infuriated Patty; it was a challenge to her. She decided at that moment to give Frank whatever help he needed, and Judy, as usual, followed her friend's lead. Patty paused to ask permission of only one person: her seventeen-year-old son. He told her: "Go get that scumbag."

Patty and Frank and Judy set out to do precisely that. At first, they were not sure how they would accomplish it. Frank had already tried the local district attorney's office. This time the women tried, hoping the new D.A. would be more receptive, especially now that there were three people accusing Porter. They were disappointed. They too were told that the charges were dated, the details too vague.

"But there are hundreds of us," said Patty, her statement informed more by instinct than by specific knowledge.

The D.A. responded in a kind voice: "But why now?"

"Because we can," Patty said. "Because we can."

But they could not—at least not yet. They sensed that if they wanted justice, they would need an army of survivors; they were just three. Patty and Judy pulled out their old class pictures and started recruiting. It was an almost impossible task. Some of the people they were certain had been molested denied that anything had happened. Others admitted the abuse but insisted it had done them no harm, so they would just as soon forget it. Still others said that while they knew their broken marriages and empty liquor bottles were legacies of what the priest had done to them, they did not want to go public. Their families, they said, feared ostracism in a staunchly Catholic town. They themselves feared for their jobs.

Frank was afraid too—for his business and his kids. But he was more afraid of the secrecy that had imprisoned him for thirty years. Patty's second husband didn't want her to get involved. But she kept hearing Porter's voice, his simple declaration that he had never touched a little girl. She imagined his taking Communion, a privilege she was denied because of her divorce. She would never back down.

Their plan for bringing Porter to justice was forged by a showy Boston attorney known for his inventive use of the news media in high-profile cases. He told them: Find me nine to fifteen survivors willing to go public and we will splash the story across television screens and newspaper front pages. More will come forward, he said. Pressure will mount. Justice will follow.

Nine became their magic number. For months they combed through old yearbooks. They pressured their friends. They yelled at their friends' husbands.

By the spring of 1992, they had pulled six more men out of the cocoons of silence that the victims had spun and WBZ, the NBC affiliate in Boston, had begun investigating their story. Reporter Joe Bergantino interviewed Porter on the phone. Then, in early May, he arrived in North Attleboro to interview Porter's victims. Eight were to be masked in shadow; only Frank was willing to show his face to the public.

But when Patty began to tell her story, Bergantino cut her off. "Look, you have so much passion in your face," he said. "If you want to get that across to the viewers, they need to see you." Patty's heart was already pounding. Her therapist was the only stranger who had heard her full story. She was worried what her colleagues at Wrentham State School would think. She was scared for her children.

I can't stop here, Patty kept telling herself. There are other girls out there. I have to find them. She knew Judy would follow her lead. She turned to Bergantino and said, "Unmask me."

On Thursday evening, May 7, 1992, the faces of Patty, Judy and Frank appeared on WBZ as Joe Bergantino told their story simply and clearly. Then, with 300,000 viewers watching and listening, he played the tape of his interview with Porter.

"*How many children did you molest?*" Bergantino asked him.

"Oh jeez, I don't know," Porter stumbled. He seemed inexplicably detached and curiously unaware of the gravity of these questions, and of his answers. *"Well,"* he continued, *"let's put it anywhere, you know, from fifty to a hundred, I guess."*

With that stunning admission, the long-held silence of the children of St. Mary's was finally and irrefutably broken.

Dennis Gaboury, a legal administrator in Baltimore, learned that the secret had exploded when his sister called from New Hampshire to tell him about the amazing broadcast she had just seen. "What station?" he asked.

Dennis had been searching for Porter for almost five years. He had gone into therapy. He had told his family about the afternoon Porter placed him on his office floor and raped him. He had hired a private detective to find him. He had recaptured his memories but had given up on locating his abuser in the present.

Dennis frantically dialed WBZ, trying to get in touch with the nine survivors the station had mentioned. Within five minutes, he was talking to Frank Fitzpatrick. Within twenty-four hours, he was back in Massachusetts.

Dennis's was the first of dozens of calls Frank received that night. After Dennis came Steve Johnson, calling from Providence. Then came John Robitaille, who had almost run off the road when he heard the news on his car radio as he drove the back roads of Rhode Island. For thirty years he had repressed every memory of Father James Porter, sealing away the nightmare of his many rapes in the deepest recesses of his mind. That night his defenses cracked. He called Frank.

In less than twenty-four hours, the nine had become fifteen.

All weekend the growing band fielded phone calls from Maryland and New Hampshire, Montana and Rhode Island—from grown men and women who sounded like terrified schoolchildren. Some were from people they had not seen in thirty years. Others were from people they had never met—from other towns in Massachusetts, from other parishes.

As the story erupted, Porter's victims gave interviews at a frantic pace, chasing from Providence to Boston and back to North Attleboro. Giddy with their freedom from secrecy, they talked to anyone who asked questions. The story of James Porter—the priest who preyed on kids—was blasted across the front pages of Boston newspapers, encouraging yet more victims to come forward. National networks broadcast the faces of weeping men and women in their forties to millions of viewers. One Boston anchorman broke into tears after an interview with a victim and his father. *Newsweek, People* and the *New York Times* called. Then "PrimeTime Live" and "60 Minutes," "Geraldo," Oprah Winfrey, Phil Donahue, and Sally Jessy Raphael.

By Monday, the nine had become forty-five.

On Tuesday afternoon, Patty Wilson, John Robitaille and Dennis Gaboury piled into a car and drove to the North Attleboro police station to file complaints. Four satellite dishes surrounded the small building; a dozen reporters lay in wait for one of the victims to appear. The three pushed through the microphones and cameras into the domain of the chief of police, who had been their school crossing guard at St. Mary's. By the time they were finished giving the police their statements, the crowd of reporters was so thick that the police escorted the three out through the garage.

Ten days later, the district attorney sent two investigators to Minnesota to question James Porter. With a video camera rolling, he read the statements of the Massachusetts victims.

"That sounds like what I would do at the time," Porter admitted. With the same strange detachment he had shown in his telephone interview with Bergantino, he was adamant that his predations had ceased when he left the priesthood.

D.A. Paul Walsh announced the opening of a full-scale investigation. By then, there were forty-eight known victims from Porter's seven years in the pulpits of Massachusetts.

FRANK FITZPATRICK IS NOT THE TYPE TO ORGANIZE REUNIONS. Disheveled and disorganized—a sort of latter-day Columbo—he was never the guy who ran the student council or whipped up spirit at football rallies. But on May 20, he gathered the clan of St. Mary's—classes of '61, '62, '63, '64 and '65—at his office.

They were brought together not by nostalgia or enduring school ties, but by a common abuser. With no clear idea of how

many others shared his scars—or what their faces looked like—
Frank had issued a public invitation to all survivors of Porter's
abuse. Will Danny show up—or Mike or Betty? each person wondered. Who else is among the casualties?

One by one, they walked through the door to meet the curious
and horrified expressions of those already present. Bullies who
had terrorized the playground traded sorrowful greetings with the
boys they had terrified. Best buddies from the sixth grade recognized one another after three decades, crying "Not you too."
Brothers met sisters whose pain they had never guessed. Cousins
were reunited: "Oh no, it can't be." The group overflowed
Frank's office into the hallway.

They heard stories just like their own—and some even more
horrifying. Pete Calderone stared in disbelief as one classmate
talked about being locked in Porter's closet after he was molested
so no one would hear his cries. Dan Lyons listened to women
describe their abuse and remembered the way he had teased the
girls in the schoolyard by pulling up their dresses. Suddenly that
prank had sinister overtones. He wandered around the room saying, "I'm sorry."

Patty Wilson suddenly understood why her life had been
plagued by drug and alcohol abuse, nervousness in crowds, a fear
of intimacy. She listened to other victims recite a litany of sexual
confusion, broken marriages, lifelong depression, suicide attempts
and psychiatric institutionalization. And she, like everyone else in
the room that night, began to appreciate, for the first time, the
magnitude of the devastation Porter had wrought.

As the reality sunk in, the men and women rode a roller
coaster from tears to rage. Emotions that had been pent up since
childhood burst forth in a catharsis made possible by the realization, after all those years, that they were not alone, that others
understood. That first meeting turned into a biweekly gathering
that grew so large it had to be moved from Frank's office to an
old Victorian house that the city of North Attleboro used as a
social services center. By mid-June, fifty-four of Porter's victims
had emerged.

On July 2, twenty-two of them and their families appeared in
a special forty-two-minute segment of "PrimeTime Live" devoted

to Porter. Old photographs of young girls in white Communion dresses and young boys in cassocks were interspersed with Diane Sawyer's gripping interviews with the survivors. They described the price of innocence lost to one priest's predations—and their determination to find justice.

The next day, District Attorney Walsh announced that he saw no insurmountable obstacles to pressing charges against Porter, and assigned nine lawyers and three investigators to build a case on behalf of what had become sixty-five victims. His counterparts in Rhode Island, where two former St. Mary's students had allegedly been raped, did not offer good news: the Rhode Island statute of limitations had expired. Even if it had not, by that state's laws Porter had committed no illegal act; in the 1960s, rape was defined as forcible intercourse between a man and a woman who was not his wife. Both of Porter's victims were male.

As their faces were splashed across the nation's newspapers and television screens, the Survivors of Father Porter—as the group came to call itself—still had no idea that their crusade touched men and women who had never seen New England. They had no idea that after Porter left North Attleboro, and then Massachusetts, he had remained a priest—and continued to abuse children. They did not find out until Jim Grimm, a Minnesota bartender, opened his local paper, the *Bemidji Pioneer*, and read their story, which was his story also. A few hours later, Grimm got a call from his old friend Dan Dow, who had been leafing through *Newsweek* and saw Porter's photograph. The two recalled their own abuse in Bemidji more than two decades earlier. It was only the second time they had ever talked about it. The first was the day before their fathers ran Porter out of Bemidji— in September 1970.

Just like the North Attleboro victims, Grimm and Dow had never guessed that there were victims in other parishes, in other states—that Porter had been allowed to hurt children with impunity for years. At a press conference in Minnesota on July 14, Grimm described the weekend Porter took him and a group of altar boys to a Twins game in Bloomington and then to a sleepover in a Hastings farmhouse. All night long, Porter had called the boys into his room one by one.

When footage from Grimm and Dow's news conference was broadcast in Massachusetts, victims there watched in shock. The molestations these men were describing, and the fear in their voices, were sickeningly familiar.

That same day, Porter, who had withdrawn into his tightly curtained house in Minnesota, issued a terse written statement through his lawyer, his first public statement on the matter since the case broke. "I was a very sick man while I was a Roman Catholic priest in the 1960s. As a result of my illness, I sexually abused a number of children." He again insisted his departure from the priesthood had been an absolute cure.

A week later, the survivors in Massachusetts realized that was just another Porter lie: two men and one woman from Oakdale came forward alleging that they, too, had been abused by Porter. None of them knew him as a priest. One had known him as the father of the children she baby-sat, another, as his next-door neighbor.

Then, a lawyer in Albuquerque, New Mexico, filed suit on behalf of three young Hispanic men allegedly abused by Porter when he was in treatment at a church-sponsored retreat center there. Attorney Bruce Pasternack insisted he knew of nine other victims—one molested while in a full body cast in an Albuquerque children's hospital.

At that point there were almost a hundred publicly identified victims in three states. As thirty years of lies and cover-ups washed away in the tidal wave that began in North Attleboro, one burning question led to another. How many children had Porter molested? For how long—and in how many places—had the Church known and allowed him to continue?

UNTIL THE SUMMER OF 1992, FEW PARENTS IN NORTH ATTLEBORO knew about the daily torment their children had suffered at St. Mary's. Those who had learned of it in the 1960s had either been intimidated into silence or persuaded that the church had the matter under control. In the spring of 1963, one mother had confronted two priests at St. Mary's with her twelve-year-old son's accusation against Porter. "There is no way I'm going to receive Communion from that man's dirty hands," she'd insisted.

Both men assured her that Porter was in treatment. When she was not appeased, they had replied angrily: "What are you trying to do, crucify the man?"

A few months later, Henry Viens, one of the parish leaders, went over the heads of those priests after he learned that his nephew, Pete Calderone, had been abused. When the chancellor of the Diocese of Fall River promised to send Porter into treatment, Viens was confident that the leaders of his church would not deceive him.

Only twenty-nine years later did he discover that the chancellor had lied to him, that Porter had simply been transferred to another parish. Only twenty-nine years later did he discover that his nephew Pete was not alone—that one of Porter's other victims was Viens's own daughter, Patty.

As mothers and uncles came forward throughout the summer of 1992, the story of the collusion of the Church in Porter's long history of molestation was pieced together from memories and memos and buried truths. Church officials had received their first complaint about Porter even before his ordination. They had removed him from his parish assignments at least eight times after complaints were filed. But they had never barred him from contact with children, never called the police, never warned parents, never reached out to his victims and never tried to expel him from ministry.

The bishop of Fall River first learned of Porter's predilections in March 1964, when his chancellor—who later became a cardinal and archbishop of Boston—finally informed him that Porter had molested thirty to forty children at St. Mary's.

Bishop James Connolly sent the priest home to his parents to contemplate and pray. A few months later, after Porter was picked up by New Hampshire State Police for molesting a thirteen-year-old boy—a "non-Cath," according to the bishop's notations in his file—the priest was sent to Wiswall Hospital in Wellesley for treatment, including electroshock therapy. By September 1965, his physician declared that Porter had simmered down and he was transferred to St. James parish in New Bedford to work as the chaplain at a local hospital. Within months, he was training altar boys in New Bedford. Within weeks, he was abusing them.

When more complaints were filed, Connolly sent Porter home once more. But a friend running a nearby parish asked the priest to join him at his church. There, Porter molested again, and in April 1967 was sent to a retreat center for troubled priests in Jemez Springs, New Mexico, run by the Servants of the Paraclete.

There was "real hope" for Father Porter's recovery, the head of the order reported to the bishop of Fall River the following July. Three months later, Bishop Connolly wrote a letter recommending Porter to the archbishop of Santa Fe, where the priest hoped to work. He mentioned Porter's "troubles" with boys but wrote at greater length of his kindness and faithfulness to his duties. "I cheerfully endorse his application," ended the bishop, who by then had heard reports of Porter's abuse of children in at least four parishes.

Porter wound up filling in for a priest on leave from Our Lady of Perpetual Help church in Truth or Consequences, New Mexico, where he found at least six more victims. He wound up in Houston on probationary assignment, and molested more children. He was shipped back to New Mexico, and abused yet again.

In August 1969, he was transferred to the Paraclete center in Minnesota, and then given a parish in Bemidji. The bishop of Crookston was told Father Porter had had a breakdown. "During the throes of his illness, he did have some moral problems which were, from all appearances, the result of his illness, something for which he was not really responsible," Church officials informed him. But he was reassured: "Now, having recovered, he gives every sign of having the former problems under control."

He did not. One Friday in 1970, the fathers of Grimm and Dow confronted the church with their sons' accusations that Porter had been molesting them for many months. The priest was gone the next day. Only then was Porter advised to leave the priesthood, and the advice came from a therapist, not a bishop.

In passing his counsel along to Church officials, Father Fred Bennett, of Servants of the Paraclete, warned them not only about

Porter's problems but about the damage that priests who abuse can cause children and the dangers of allowing such priests to remain in the ministry. "The priesthood, especially at the parish level, almost invariably involves some work with youth," Bennett wrote. "Moreover, a priest is able to form relationships with youths while parents and other adults have no suspicion that anything is amiss simply because the man involved is a priest.

"People often suffer psychological difficulties later in life whose origins seem to be found in sexual approaches made to them during their childhood by adults of the same sex. I have reason to believe that the trauma of such experiences may be further intensified when the adult involved is a priest."

These were the very warnings that officials would later vehemently deny having received—about Porter or any other priest—until the late 1980s.

In Porter's 1973 petition for release from his priestly vows, he seemed to concur with Bennett about the dangers of the priesthood. I "used to hide behind a Roman collar, thinking that it would be a shield for me," he wrote Pope Paul VI.

The pope granted that petition, and after fourteen years as a priest—and as many as a child sexual abuser—James Porter lost the right to call himself Father on January 5, 1974.

As this history was revealed bit by bit to Porter's victims, their anger began to focus more and more on the treachery of the Church. They could understand how a single man—even a priest—might be sick, deranged, beyond therapy. But they could not understand how Church officials could protect such a man's reputation and career at the expense of children whose lives would be forever haunted by his crime.

They wanted to know why Father Annunziato had stayed silent even after seeing them abused. He could not comment. The man who had never spoken of what he had seen could no longer speak; he was dying of throat cancer. Most of the other people who had protected Porter were dead. Bishop Sean O'Malley, appointed just months after the Porter story broke, suggested only that Bishop Connolly had suffered from severe depression that might have clouded his judgment. The victims were not moved. They vowed to hold the Church responsible for the damage to scores of children who were molested after the first, the second, even the third complaints.

They demanded financial compensation for years of therapy and drug abuse, medical problems, hospitalizations and marital disasters. The Church insisted victims had the right to no more than $20,000 each because Massachusetts law limits the liability of charitable institutions. In an editorial, the *Boston Globe* asked whether the Church could, in good conscience, seek the protection of that law. They received no answer.

The victims negotiating the settlement with the bishop began by behaving like good little Catholic boys: respectful and polite. The nuns would have been proud. But as Porter's full history emerged—and as Bishop Sean O'Malley pleaded the Church's poverty—their patience was tried. "Cut the shit," Dan Lyons said to O'Malley in exasperation. "How much do you think being sodomized six times by a priest is worth?" he asked bluntly. Dan sent O'Malley samples of the forensics reports prepared by psychiatrists that assessed the damage to the victims in full and lurid detail—and threatened to send these reports to every newspaper, magazine and television station in the country. "Interesting bedtime reading, no?" he asked the bishop.

AS THE SURVIVORS OF FATHER PORTER'S ABUSE HEALED, THEY grew bolder and smarter. Their meetings every other Friday at the Victorian mansion on Elm Street evolved into elaborate strategy sessions. They formed a legislative committee. They formed a legal committee. They formed a media committee. And they kept the pressure on public officials to prosecute Porter with deliberately timed, carefully selected appearances on the evening news and daytime talk shows. The greatest pressure was reserved for the district attorney, who was the target of petition campaigns, phone calls and open threats of political action.

Walsh pleaded for patience, explaining his two legal binds. The first involved the Massachusetts statute of limitations for a felony, which lapses six years after the date of the crime—unless the perpetrator leaves the state before then. In that case, the clock stops running. Walsh had to figure out precisely when Porter left

Massachusetts. He also faced the problem of defining what crimes Porter had committed. In the early 1960s, after all, child sexual abuse was not illegal. No one had thought to make it an offense.

All through July and August Walsh insisted he would make no decision for another week or two. He kept trying to calm the Porter victims, reminding them that the crimes went back to when Ike was still president. On September 8, he said bluntly: "I don't see that time is of the essence here." He insisted there would be "more anguish if we brought the cases and lost them."

Walsh's cautious pace and measured words did not go over well with the Porter survivors, who had already waited decades for justice. Frank Fitzpatrick assailed the D.A. in public, accusing him of holding back for fear of the reaction at the ballot box of "the hard-line, hard-core defenders of priests." Fran Rotella Battaglia fumed to the press: "To have an elected official yank you around like this makes you feel like a victim all over again."

On September 17, 1992, Walsh told the media—yet again—that he still was not ready to seek an indictment.

Five days later, he called his investigatory and legal teams into his office on a Sunday afternoon. They had combed through complaints filed by two hundred men and women and reread their interviews with almost seventy. They had dropped thirty-five for lack of corroboration or because of the expiration of the statute of limitations. That day they spent five hours rehearsing their presentation of thirty-two cases to the secret grand jury that would convene the following morning. No witnesses would be called. No friendly reporters had been notified. No one knew what he planned.

That same day, Walsh sent an assistant district attorney, a Massachusetts state trooper and a member of the North Attleboro police department to Oakdale, Minnesota—to be ready to pick up Porter, just in case.

On Monday afternoon, the grand jury indicted James Porter on forty-six counts of assault, battery, sodomy and unnatural acts. At 3:12 P.M., the Massachusetts legal team went with the Oakdale police to pick up the accused. Porter had been running errands; they arrested him just over a mile from his house. The former priest wept. That night, as he lay behind bars for the first time in his life, Porter's victims in North Attleboro gathered at Pete Calderone's house to celebrate.

By then, ninety-seven people in Massachusetts, New Mexico and Minnesota had filed civil or criminal complaints against James Porter. Walsh said he had received complaints from two hundred people. Minnesota authorities had heard from another twenty-two.

The next day Porter arrived at his extradition hearing in Minnesota with his hair uncombed and his shirt hanging out. Seemingly unnerved for the first time, he signed his extradition agreement on the wrong line. That evening, he was loaded on a U.S. Marshals Service plane for Boston's Logan Airport under tight security and then transferred to New Bedford, where he would be arraigned.

On Wednesday morning, forty of his accusers filled the four rows of the pewlike benches set aside for them in the courthouse. They stared nervously at the door to the right of the judge's bench. "When I see Porter today, I will look at him," Pete Calderone told the others, steeling himself for his first glimpse of Porter in three decades. "I'm going to see him. I'm not going to be afraid of him now. I was afraid of him thirty years ago. I was afraid of him when I was a teenager and throughout my adult life. I'm not going to be afraid of him today."

The courthouse bell tolled nine o'clock. Three minutes later, Porter appeared—handcuffed and flanked by two court officers. He glanced at his victims as the clerk magistrate went through a clinical reading of the forty-six counts of sodomy and sexual assault filed against him. They glared back as he repeated "Not Guilty" forty-six times in a hypnotic echo. He faced a total of 317 years in prison.

Wearing an open-collared blue shirt, gray coat, dark slacks and loafers, Porter was subdued and unemotional, even as Bristol County assistant district attorney Renée Dupuis described how he had assaulted children "in the parish, in the sacristy, in their own homes, in his vehicle and in assorted other places." He sat with his head bowed and his hands clasped as she accused him of forced masturbation, fellatio and sodomy, of silencing the children—some as young as ten years old—with threats of God's wrath.

As Porter was led away, his victims wept and hugged one another. Dennis Gaboury smiled and said: "It's like a rendezvous with destiny."

C h a p t e r   2

REVELATIONS

IT IS DIFFICULT TO OVERSTATE THE IMPACT and importance of the Father James Porter story. As it unfolded like a grotesque soap opera on the nightly news throughout 1992, hundreds of victims of other priests from all across the nation were emboldened by the example of the Porter survivors and, following their lead, came forward to unmask their abusers and demand justice from the Church. They filed suit against their dioceses and berated their bishops in angry—often tearful—interviews on television. The nation's Roman Catholic ecclesiastical leaders held special meetings to prepare their response to the mounting scandal, alternately pleading ignorance and promising swift action.

The Porter story was equally significant for another reason. In pulling back the veil from child sexual abuse by men in Roman collars—

men traditionally accorded the highest levels of respect in society—it gave American parents final, irrefutable confirmation that the latest revelations about the extent and universality of child sexual abuse were true, that their old assumptions about who they could, or could not, trust with their children were false. People reeled from the impact. Was nothing sacred? Was no place—even a church—free of danger and corruption? Was no child—even one dressed in an altar boy's cassock—safe?

This book addresses all three questions. It is the tale of countless American Catholics whose innocence was robbed by the very institution to which they had entrusted their souls. By the 1990s, American children had become too savvy to take candy from strangers or get into cars with odd men in trenchcoats hanging around playgrounds. But few had been told to distrust the embrace of a priest. Their parents were innocents, too, maintaining a fervent, almost desperate belief that at least one institution remained pure. They were proven wrong.

Not only had Catholic priests left thousands of victims in their wake, but the Church that had bestowed on them awesome powers to bless and forgive had protected them for decades. Confronted with a choice between justice for the victims and benevolence toward abusive priests, Church leaders had consistently opted for the latter. Pray, they told offending priests. Repent. And when priests did, they were transferred to new parishes, where they were free to molest and molest again.

Bishops dedicated to following Christ's preference for the weak and vulnerable put aside their pastoral responsibility and behaved like good chief executive officers: they covered up the story. Thou Shalt Not Create Scandal seemed to be the operative commandment. When confronted by parents hurt and confused by their children's wounds, they lied. When lies failed, they stonewalled and intimidated the very members of their flocks they pledged to protect. Church leaders seemed hopelessly trapped by denial—of the charges leveled by the victims, of the seriousness of the damage to them, of the depth of the disorder gripping the abusers, even of the extent of the problem in their ranks.

It was the ultimate betrayal of faith—and it was hardly a twentieth-century phenomenon. Just as grandfathers on the frontier had abused their grandchildren and Southern gentlemen had taken their daughters to their beds, priests had been molesting children for centuries, even before Christopher Columbus landed in this hemisphere. When Pope Alexander VI, the father of Lucrezia Borgia, marked the final victory of Catholic Spain over the Moors, he did so not with a Mass at St. Peter's but with a party in the piazza in front of the church. Flagons of wine flowed among the honored guests, women from Rome's most elegant brothels offered their services and children were passed freely among bishops and priests celebrating Catholicism's latest triumph with a sexual bacchanalia.

For a decade in the mid-eighteenth century, Father Johann Arbogast Gauch, a pastor in the principality of Fürstenberg, Germany, exposed himself to the town's girls and masturbated its boys. It was only when a new monarch ordered him imprisoned that his predations ended. Cases of child sexual abuse by clergy occasionally found their way into the legal arena even in nineteenth-century America, according to Mark Chopko, general counsel for the National Conference of Catholic Bishops.

But public cases like Gauch's were rare. We are most likely to catch glimpses of priests preying on children in veiled references in historical texts or in the works of novelists mirroring reality. In *The Nun*, an eighteenth-century novel, French philosopher Denis Diderot told the tale of a young girl sexually molested by a cleric. In *Birds without Nests*, published in 1889, Peruvian novelist Clorinda Matto de Turner used the sexual abuse of Indian children by Catholic clergy as but one vivid example of the exploitation of indigenous peoples.

But most cases were hidden well into the Renaissance because the Church claimed its priests exempt from civil law. They were judged in secret, in ecclesiastical court. We cannot open the archives and read all the cases. We know only that crimes against children were tried as sins against God, that their victims seemed somehow irrelevant.

Even if the archives were open, the reality might still remain veiled. Child sexual abuse by priests—or anyone else—wasn't discussed because it was rarely considered a crime. Even a century ago, having sexual relations with a child over the age of eleven was not illegal in most of the Western world, as it still is not in some countries. Childhood as we know it, as we conceptualize and fantasize it, is a modern invention. In earlier eras, children were small adults who worked in factories to carry their share of the household burden, went to prison for petty theft and were often used for the sexual gratification of any adult around them who was so inclined. Among the wealthy and powerful, shy young girls still underdeveloped were married off to consolidate family power and fortune. Young boys were taken under the wing of older gentlemen—a practice justified as pedagogical Eros.

Ancient Roman law laid down strict penalties for adultery and sodomy, rape and abduction. But sexual activity with apparently consenting children was no more illegal than sexual activity with apparently consenting adults. It was not until the eighteenth century that children began to be recognized as something more fragile than tiny adults. In the process, children became defined as presexual, almost asexual. Unformed physically, they were assumed to be untainted by desire. But even then, protections were, to modern eyes, inane or inadequate. When Father Gauch was sent to prison, for example, he did not go alone. His victims as well were blamed for what happened and locked in a subterranean cellar for months, where the boys were whipped mercilessly. Queen Victoria was on the cutting edge of reform when she raised the legal age for prostitutes—from nine to thirteen. The first child protection organization wasn't founded until 1884—sixty years after the founding of the Society for the Prevention of Cruelty to Animals.

No one in the United States really began to understand the extent of the sexual abuse that children suffered at the hands of adults until the 1970s, when states began to require that counselors, physicians and other authorities report such abuse to the government. For more than a century, mental health professionals had doubted most victims' accounts of childhood sexual abuse, insisting, as Freud had, that it was a neurotic woman's fantasy. Suddenly, when reporting became mandatory, they were proven startlingly wrong. The trickle of cases recorded in earlier years became a torrent: 12,000 a year in the 1970s, rising to over 150,000 by 1985. Police estimated that only 8 percent of the reports were not credible.

But the fact that men of the cloth were among the abusers remained a secret guarded carefully in the archives of the nation's dioceses—and in the memories of devout Catholics. Bishop Thomas Gumbleton of Detroit remembers two priests who he realizes, in retrospect, tried to groom him for abuse when he was in Detroit's Sacred Heart Seminary High School in the 1940s. The first exposure Archbishop Rembert Weakland of Milwaukee had to the problem also occurred in high school, when a priest was caught molesting children.

Priests knew some of their fellows abused children, but maintained a collegial quiet. Bishops received reports from frantic parents, but hushed them up. In a three-year period in the mid-1980s, 130 priests were evaluated for sexual behavior problems at St. Luke Institute in Suitland, Maryland, and seventy were found to have problems with children. The problem was not reported to the laity who might be in danger.

If today we can glimpse what goes on between some priests and their young charges, it is because of several phenomena, thus far uniquely American, that have turned scores of secrets into public scandals. First, suing has become a national sport as Americans have come to believe that money can compensate for any mutilation, of the body or the spirit. Patients file against their physicians, students against their teachers, employees against their employers. When they were joined by fervent Catholics willing to sue the men who imparted the Body of Christ, the silence was, inevitably, ruptured.

The first crack appeared in the bayou country of southwestern Louisiana. On Thursday morning, February 6, 1986, twelve-year-old Scott Gastal took the stand in the patrician Abbeville courthouse to describe how Father Gilbert Gauthe had guided the boy's penis into his own anus—the first time in the nation's history that the story of a priest's predations were told publicly. By then, all of Louisiana knew that Scott was but one of dozens of victims of the popular priest who had taken parish boys dirt bike riding through the bayous and injected his infectious energy into the

backwaters of Cajun country. Gauthe, after all, was already serving twenty years at hard labor for molesting at least thirty-seven
boys. But Scott Gastal's almost whispered recollections gave testimony to more than the perversions of a single priest. The case
provided the first shocking glimpse of the way in which Church
leaders had responded to complaints of abuse by repeatedly transferring the offender.

Catholic leaders tried to pass off Gauthe and his mishandling
by the Diocese of Lafayette as an anomaly. Just one priest out of
fifty-eight thousand, they argued. But less than a month after
Gauthe's imprisonment, five Native American sisters filed suit
against Father John Engbers, a priest in the same diocese as
Gauthe. Then the truth came out about Father Lane Fontenot:
the Louisiana priest had been sent off to a church center for troubled clergy in 1983 after a family threatened to have him arrested
for child molestation. In the middle of Scott Gastal's testimony,
Fontenot, who was still a priest, was arrested in Seattle for abusing five boys he had been counseling at the Nancy Reagan Care
Unit of Deaconess Hospital.

Just three priests and a misguided bishop, the Church responded. But even that pretense crumbled as criminal charges and
lawsuits were filed against priests across the country, and as a
single attorney, Jeffrey Anderson of St. Paul, Minnesota, began to
specialize in holding dioceses accountable for their failure to remove errant priests from parishes. The Church's defense then collapsed under the weight of an even newer phenomenon, also
distinctly American, that blasted many of the nation's most intimate secrets—including child sexual abuse by priests—into public
view. America had become a nation of self-defined victims seeking
to heal their wounds in public. Victims of rape, incest, child sexual abuse and a host of other predations offered themselves up as
daily fodder for Oprah or Geraldo, Sally Jessy or Phil. Encouraged to think of themselves as proud survivors, they bared their
souls to an enthralled nation hardly aware that the price of an
hour's entertainment was yet another shattered illusion.

For years victims of child sexual abuse by clergy had been too
shy to speak out in public. The first alleged victim to come forward in a public arena other than a courtroom told his story at

an event staged for the news media during the National Conference of Catholic Bishops' 1989 meeting in Baltimore. He spoke from behind a sheet, using the pseudonym Damian de Vuester. When the mother of another victim joined him, she disguised herself with a black wig, blue contact lenses and an alias.

Over the next years, victims began to appear on afternoon talk shows with their faces in front of cameras and their names boldly displayed. The American bishops fumbled and fumed, still insisting that priest molesters were an aberration, too few in number and too sick to merit much attention. But even the Vatican newspaper, *L'Osservatore Romano*, refused to buy the argument. Demanding vigorous action against "the horror, worry and humiliation" of such abuse, they editorialized: "To attribute a whole series of episodes such as these to an occasional outburst of maniacs or sick people would be to exorcise a problem whose dimensions are growing."

Throughout the 1980s and early 1990s, Americans across the country caught occasional glimpses of the problem. In 1985, readers in Illinois found out about Father Alvin Campbell, who had been awarded a bronze star for service in Vietnam but had later been forced to resign from the U.S. Army after he was accused of molesting a boy. Campbell was then assigned to an Illinois parish, where he molested eighth-grade boys and girls for four years before being accused once again. Rather than turn him over to the police, his religious superiors sent Campbell to his mother's house to rest. He was finally named pastor of St. Maurice Catholic Church in Morrisonville, where he molested at least fourteen boys, ages eleven to sixteen, luring them into his waterbed with video games, telephones, watches, clock radios and ten-speed bicycles.

In 1987, Nebraskans heard about Father Paul Margand, who molested two altar boys, including a twelve-year-old taking private religious instruction. Margand had ordered the boy to pray lying on his back, then mounted him while quizzing him about Moses.

Two years later, Polish Catholics in Minnesota discovered a new—and frighteningly contradictory—side to one of their most beloved priests, Father Robert Kapoun. To them he was the guy with the collar who played the accordion in a local polka band, wrote a full polka Mass and recorded eighteen polka albums. But it turned out that in 1973, when a twelve-year-old altar boy confused about his sexual identity had sought his advice, the Polka Padre, as he was widely known, had allegedly helped the adolescent resolve his crisis—in the sacristy before Mass, at his parents' home, in his car and at a local Catholic seminary.

Later that year, North Carolinians heard the sordid secrets of Father Anthony Corbin when the priest confessed to having had sex with an eighth-grade boy. Corbin dressed his victim in a loincloth to resemble Christ headed for the crucifix. Then, in 1990, Georgians caught a glimpse of the Church's handling of priests who molest children, when Father Anton Mowat, a British priest assigned to work in their state, fled the United States after police began investigating him for child sexual abuse. His trial was delayed for twenty-one months while American authorities attempted to ascertain his whereabouts. Although they knew he was hiding in a monastery in Turin, Italy, Church officials in Mowat's home diocese of Northampton, England, told U.S. officials they had no idea where he had gone. They later admitted that they had failed to inform the Archdiocese of Atlanta of the priest's known predilection for young boys.

By the late summer of 1992, no American who watched CNN or the ABC-TV news show "PrimeTime Live" or read the *New York Times* had not met at least one survivor of childhood sexual abuse by a priest or heard one nightmarish tale. A problem that had existed as disconnected images—a rape in New Jersey one year, a molestation in New Mexico the next—coalesced into a coherent picture when the legions of victims of Father James Porter hit the airwaves. The women and men from the Massachusetts towns of North Attleboro, New Bedford, and Fall River were, for the most part, educated and articulate. Enraged by the realization that Church authorities had watched Porter victimize scores of children across four states, they bore stunning witness to the fact that Gilbert Gauthe was more a portent than an anomaly and that the actions of the Diocese of Lafayette were indicative of the way Church authorities throughout the country dealt with abusive priests.

The assault of cases seemed unrelenting. In 1985, there were thirty cases pending against the Church on behalf of one hundred victims. They were handled quietly—discreetly, some might say —by the courts and the news media. By 1992, the trickle had become a well-reported flood:

- In January, Father Wilson F. Smart was sued by a Montana man who alleged the priest had raped him and photographed him in the nude when he was an altar boy. After sex, Smart (who was also a Boy Scout troop leader) would take the thirteen-year-old boy to confession in nearby towns.

- In February, Father Bruce Ball went on trial in Wisconsin for fondling a twelve-year-old boy during counseling sessions in his rectory.

- In March, a San Diego woman filed suit against Father Victor Ubaldi, alleging he had molested her on scores of occasions from the time she was eleven to fifteen years old.

- In April, Father Patrick Kelly was permanently banned from the state of California. The seventy-one-year-old priest had fled to Ireland after being charged with molesting a nine-year-old girl he was counseling at her home.

- In May, the Diocese of Phoenix was sued by a couple whose three children were allegedly molested by Father Mark Lehman, who had been sentenced the month before to ten years in prison for abusing several children at his parish, including one of those three.

- In June, Father Richard Lavigne of Shelburne Falls, Massachusetts, pleaded guilty to twelve counts of child rape after insisting for months that the accusations against him were part of a plot by a local Catholic sect that had broken away from his church. Lavigne was also the principal suspect in the unsolved 1972 murder of a thirteen-year-old altar boy. He was jailed for the abuse, but for lack of evidence was never charged with murder.

- In July, Father James Thomas Monaghan, a retired priest, was charged with sexually molesting a seven-year-old Sacramento girl who he was counseling. The abuse allegedly occurred when the parish priest took the child into the kitchen for cookies.

- In August, Father Myles Patrick White was arrested in Illinois for criminal sexual assault of a minor. Father White was already under indictment in the state of Indiana, where his abuse of boys was discovered after he donated a videotape of a local parade to a Lions Club flea market. When the buyer of the tape watched the parade, he was treated to thirty minutes of White having sex with a boy, a scene the priest had apparently forgotten to erase. When police arrived at the rectory to arrest him, they found the priest using paint thinner and scissors to destroy snapshots of nude boys.

- In September, Father Ronald Provost pleaded guilty to charges that he had taken photographs of nude boys seven to ten years old in order to achieve sexual arousal. When police searched his rectory in Barre, Massachusetts, they found photographs of unclothed boys dating as far back as 1977.

- In October, Father Daniel A. Calabrese was found guilty of sodomizing a minor in his rectory in Poughkeepsie, New York, and sentenced to ninety days in jail. After his sentencing, District Attorney William V. Grady publicly chastised New York archbishop Cardinal John O'Connor for ignoring prior complaints concerning Calabrese's inappropriate behavior and assigning him to run Dutchess County's Catholic Youth Organization.

- In November, Father David Malsch was charged with sexually assaulting a fourteen-year-old learning-disabled boy in Wausau, Wisconsin. The priest allegedly took the boy to a motel for two days, fondled him in the pool, served him alcohol and took nude photographs of him in their room.

- In December, Father David A. Holley became the target of lawsuits for molesting children in New Mexico. In a career pattern reminiscent of James Porter's, Holley had been sent to the Servants of the Paraclete treatment center in New Mexico after he was accused of abusing children in Worcester, Massachusetts. He was then transferred to Alamogordo, New Mexico, where he allegedly molested at least ten youths. Before his retirement in 1989, Holley had worked as a chaplain at St. Anthony Hospital in Denver. Holley was the fifth priest—and alumnus of the treatment program run by the Servants of the Paraclete—to be sued for abusing children in New Mexico.

As 1992 turned into the new year, things went from bad to worse for the leaders of the nation's Roman Catholic dioceses. In late January, members of the Prince Georges County (Maryland) sheriff's department attempted to arrest Father Holley, who had just been indicted in New Mexico. Informed by New Mexico sources that Holley was in treatment at St. Luke Institute, the nation's premier hospital for troubled priests, deputies called the institute but were told he was not there. When they persisted, and were again rebuffed by institute officials, one of the deputies threatened to notify the press that the hospital was hiding wanted felons. Only then were officers permitted to look for Holley, whom they found hiding under a stairwell. It was not the first time the sheriff's office had had problems securing the cooperation of the administration of St. Luke; one priest they had attempted to arrest there had managed to elude capture for two years.

When the story leaked out to the press, Father Canice Connors, head of St. Luke, attempted to shift the blame to the sheriff's department, insisting deputies had driven up to the facility in twenty-two marked cars with lights flashing, sirens screeching—and cameramen from Cable News Network in tow. But no witnesses could be found to corroborate his story.

In early February, the crisis of child sexual abuse by priests reached such critical proportions in the Diocese of Joliet, Illinois, that Bishop Joseph Imesch was forced to send a prerecorded message to be played to the 500,000 members of his flock at Sunday Mass after Communion. "It is deeply distressing for me to have to address you about the tragedy of child sexual abuse," the bishop's message blared over public address systems, "as distressing, I am sure, as it is for you to hear about it. These are times that shake our faith and confidence in our most cherished systems and institutions. It seems that everywhere we go, we hear about sexual abuse and the shattering effect it has on the victims, their families and the community. I am particularly shocked and saddened when I hear allegations that some of our priests have committed these acts."

Imesch had seemingly been shocked and saddened repeatedly in a very brief span of time: In the five years before his taped message, he had removed six priests from their positions after they were accused of molesting children, four in the preceding twelve months. In the preceding month alone, his diocese had been slapped with three lawsuits accusing it of sheltering known child sexual abusers. His message was played just after diocesan attorneys had asked a local judge to issue a gag order against the attorney who had filed two of those suits.

Then, in early March, the Church shocked even many of its most ardent supporters when Father Armando Annunziato, the priest accused of having witnessed—and ignored—James Porter's predations, was elevated to monsignor. Porter's victims and their families wondered openly and in the press whether Annunziato was being rewarded for decades of silence.

Finally, in late March, the child sexual abuse scandal forced the resignation of the Archbishop of Santa Fe. Robert Sanchez, America's first Hispanic archbishop, became America's first bishop to fall to the mishandling of repeated allegations of child sexual abuse by priests in his diocese. For more than a year, Sanchez had stonewalled as one lawsuit after another was filed against the archdiocese, as one accused priest fled the country and two more were indicted. In the end, five women, infuriated at his behavior, went to the press with the stories of their own sexual relationships with Sanchez. The archbishop disappeared on retreat and resigned just before the lurid details were broadcast to the nation by Mike Wallace on "60 Minutes."

"WHY US?" CHURCH OFFICIALS RESPONDED TO THE MOUNTING publicity about molesters in its ranks. Why not talk about doctors who abuse, scoutmasters who molest and teachers who fondle? Roman Catholic clergy are not the only men of the cloth to molest their youthful parishioners, leaders of the country's Catholic hierarchy pointed out regularly, and insistently. Some suggested that anti-Catholicism might be rearing its head—that the Catholic Church was being singled out unfairly, that its good deeds were being ignored in favor of reporting on the scandal.

Some answers to their questions are obvious. Child sexual abuse by teachers and scoutmasters, coaches and day-care workers are serious, damaging crimes. But the betrayal of trust by a man of the cloth strikes closer to the core of a child's soul; the wounds inflicted are clearly, inevitably, deeper.

"To people, and to children in particular, a member of the clergy is a representative of God," says Mike Lew, author of *Victims No Longer*, the seminal examination of male survivors of child sexual abuse. "And if a representative of God is an agent of abuse, it's almost as if—and I'm talking about the subjective experience of the child—even God is not safe."

Less obvious is why the Catholic Church was the target of so much attention, both legal and media, to the exclusion of the many Protestant denominations or Jewish groups. Clearly, it does not maintain the religious monopoly on child sexual abusers. While there are dozens of speculations—often wild—as to the number of Catholic priests who sexually abuse children, there are simply no firm figures. By the most conservative counts, more than two hundred priests have been hauled into court on charges of molesting children. But they represent only a fraction of even those reported to Church officials. No one knows how many more there may be, since Church officials deny keeping any centralized records. But bishops in dioceses where one or two priest molesters have been sued or prosecuted speak openly about the three, four, five or six other cases they have handled in private. And they themselves know they are unaware of the many—probably the majority—which are never reported.

The best estimates on the numbers of clerical child sexual abusers in the Catholic Church suggest that 2 percent of the nation's priests act on a persistent attraction to children and another 4 percent display an occasional, or secondary, sexual interest in youth. The best comparable estimates for Protestant clergy are half those numbers—2 to 3 percent. During the unfolding of the Porter drama, five other Massachusetts clerics were accused of sexually abusing children: two Roman Catholics, one Episcopal, one Unitarian and a priest from the Polish National Catholic Church. In October 1992, one of the nation's most prominent Episcopal priests, the Reverend Wallace Frey, resigned publicly after being accused of molesting ten teenage boys. And leaders of Protestant denominations in no way denied the problem. In November 1991, Bishop Herbert W. Chilstrom, national leader of the Evangelical Lutheran Church in America, stood before the church council and announced: "While the vast majority of our lay and ordained leaders in the Evangelical Lutheran Church are persons of high integrity and strong personal morality, we are also having to deal with the very real fact that there is more abuse in the church than we may have realized."

Catholic leaders insisted that the problem looked worse in the Catholic Church only because it is the largest denomination in the country. They may well have been right. But neither the Methodists nor the Episcopalians had been forced to establish a twenty-four-hour hot line for complaints, as had the Archdiocese of Chicago. No Protestant denomination's conduct had provoked the creation of organizations like Victims of Clergy Abuse Linkup (VOCAL) or Survivors Network of Those, Who as Children, Were Abused by Priests (SNAP) to serve the victims.

Certainly, much of the attention focused on the Catholic Church because of the stark contrast between its seeming laxness in dealing with child sexual abuse by its clergy and the strict morality it imposes on its laity—and attempts to impose on the rest of society—in terms of abortion, birth control and homosexuality. "The Roman Catholic Church has been very much a dictator on sexual matters, dictating to everyone, from its celibate ivory tower, how they should behave sexually," says Dr. J. A. Loftus, a Jesuit priest and psychiatrist who directs Southdown, a treatment center for Catholic clergy near Toronto. "People were bound to pay attention when our celibate priests were revealed as molesters."

Many Catholic priests offered other candid explanations for why their Church was being singled out. "The Catholic Church is the largest denomination, but it is almost the most mysterious because of celibacy," says Father Stephen Rossetti, editor of *Slayer of the Soul*, a 1990 collection of essays about abusive priests. "I think that's the mystique and when you cast something like pedophilia over it, it shocks. Plus, we simply expect priests to be better, expect more of their moral conduct. They're sacred symbols and this mixes the despicable with the divine."

The special role of priests also guaranteed them a kind of institutional protection no Protestant cleric could enjoy. If a Presbyterian minister fondled a child, no central office could cover up the complaint and blithely transfer him to another parish. In fact, his parishioners could simply fire him. But Catholic priests don't work for their parishes; they work for their bishops. Those bishops have the power to shroud complaints in secrecy, to solve problems geographically by transferring errant priests to new parishes and to keep a priest's past from the laity he serves.

Even more shocking to devout Catholic families who came forward to offer their painful story to their church, bishops refused to believe them or retreated into legal defensiveness, insisting they were not responsible for their priests. If sued, they refused to turn over priests' personnel records or answer questions about complaints they had received, arguing that such requests intruded on the free practice of religion. This reaction—or nonreaction—by the hierarchy, almost always sparked more furor—and more public attention—than the molestation itself.

In the end, the Roman Catholic Church wound up alone on the hot seat simply because it seemed to have done such a terrible job of coping with the problem. The United Methodists and the Southern Baptists both conducted surveys to gauge the extent of the problem in their ranks; the National Conference of Catholic Bishops insisted it did not even keep records of reported cases. The Presbyterians required background checks on pastors who relocate; the Catholics transferred known abusers. The Unitarians passed out pamphlets to their members on how to make complaints against abusive clergy and the Evangelical Lutheran Church spelled out a formal disciplinary process in its constitution; most Catholic dioceses kept their policies under lock and key.

The Catholic Church simply fell into, or took refuge in, a type of denial demonstrated by few other institutions, secular or religious. Even in 1992, the head of the Church's premier treatment center for troubled priests seemed not to have grasped the seriousness of the problem. "It would be wise to avoid the exaggeration of the victimologists," wrote Father Canice Connors of St. Luke Institute in *America* magazine in May of that year, the same week that the James Porter case exploded in Massachusetts. "We are not involved with the dynamics of rape but with the far subtler dynamics of persuasion by a friend. As we speak to and about the victims we must be aware that the child sometimes retains a loving memory of the offender."

In a memo distributed in January 1993 to members of a Church-convened "Think Tank" on child sexual abuse which he co-chaired, Father Connors went even further, comparing social prejudice against molesters to social prejudice against the aging, the homeless and AIDS patients. "Is Catholic Church leadership in the United States falling into a similar cultural trap by shunning pedophile priests?" he asked.

American bishops also remained paralyzed, many argued, because they received no direction from Rome, yet feared the wrath of the pontiff should scandal erupt. Rome, meanwhile, argued that child sexual abuse was an American problem that should be handled on this side of the Atlantic. That was a stunning denial supported only by the paucity of lawsuits and other legal actions related to child sexual abuse against priests in other countries.

The fact that dozens of the priests accused of child sexual abuse in this country were on assignment from abroad—from England, Mexico, Ireland, Sri Lanka or Italy—suggests that the problem crossed all geographical boundaries. The archdioceses of Melbourne, Australia, and Wellington, New Zealand, effectively admitted to the problem by flying in American experts to help them develop policies for dealing with child sexual abuse. Events in Canada provided the clearest indication of the international dimensions of the problem of child sexual abuse by priests. In the province of Newfoundland—an island so remote that it has its own time zone—a scandal over child sexual abuse by Catholic priests forced Archbishop Alphonsus Penney to offer his resignation in July 1990. The story had unfolded like a long-drawn-out nightmare for Newfoundland's 120,000 Catholics. Over the course of two years, seven of their one hundred priests and two former priests were indicted for sexually abusing young boys. Almost all of those charged were popular and prominent men.

"How could this have happened?" asked Father Kevin Molloy, spokesman for the archdiocese. "How could it have gone undetected for so long?"

The answer catapulted the island's Catholic secrets into Canada's press: It had not gone undetected. Archbishop Penney had been informed of the accusations against Newfoundland's priests as early as 1979. "Minimal response" was the description of his behavior given by a special investigating commission convened after priests, police and social workers testified that they had lodged repeated complaints.

In province after province, Canadian priests were exposed as molesters in the early 1990s, forcing the Canadian Conference of Catholic Bishops to create yet another special commission and policy to deal with the problem.

What had kept child sexual abuse by priests from becoming a scandal in most other countries was not the absence of such behavior, but the attitudes of the different cultures toward telling and suing. But when Dutch Catholic Television dared air a special on the growing scandal of child sexual abuse by priests in the United States, more than two hundred victims from Amsterdam to Rotterdam called in with their own stories of molestation by men in collars.

Europeans, of course, do not advocate and protect children's welfare with the legal zeal of Americans. Father Rossetti believes they are also less likely to air their dirty laundry in public and more apt to be tolerant of sexual activity between children and adults. "If you're European, you probably look at us as, 'Oh, they're just a bunch of Puritans, always obsessed with rights, always anti-sexuality,' " he says.

In the end, the more relevant issue is that the way children wind up as victims of priests—and the way the Catholic Church has met such abuse with denial and disbelief—is a microcosm of a reality played out every day in secular American society. Children become vulnerable to sexual abuse in part because they are not taught to recognize that a respectable adult, approaching them with what seems like genuine caring, could harm them. Children continue to be victimized because the automatic respect they are coached to show certain adults—their teachers, their doctors, their dads—forbids them, at least in their own minds, from ever telling what those people are doing to them. And the adults who are supposed to protect them are blinded by their own disbelief and wishful thinking. They refuse to acknowledge the possibility of danger and destructive, criminal behavior in places and among people they want to believe are safe. They strive to deny a reality that confuses and terrifies them.

"People don't like to look at what seems to be questionable, perhaps perverted behavior in the images of people who are upholding what's supposed to be the best of the culture," says the Reverend Margaret Graham, an Episcopal priest who also serves as president of the National Committee for the Prevention of Child Abuse. She points out that what has happened among priests and the Catholic Church is not an isolated phenomenon —just a particularly garish and upsetting one. "Under the rubric of how you get children through those years, we gave them these lessons: 'Look before you cross the street.' 'Don't take candy from strangers.' But never was one of those lessons: 'Don't trust your parish priest.' That was one of the few safe places. So people don't want to say that. It's like saying there are no safe houses, there are no safe places, there are no safe people. And that's a terrible thing to have to say. That's a terrible thing to have to tell your children."

Most adults prefer to console themselves with the myth that a child sexual abuser is a sex-crazed pervert with stained teeth and body odor who hunkers behind bushes and snatches hapless children, that he is someone they can point to and say: "You, I know what you are." It is a comforting myth, a clear-cut case of knowing the good guys from the bad guys by glancing at their hats, appealing because it shatters no illusions. But nothing could be further from the truth.

Child sexual abusers are as likely to be well-groomed, well-paid professionals as Skid Row bums, as likely to be married with children as single and without any attachments or stability. Dr. Nicholas Groth, a psychologist who has worked with more than two thousand child molesters over the course of his career, states bluntly: "There's no way you could give me the personality characteristics of a hundred people and I could tell you which of those people molest kids. This behavior cuts across all levels."

The vast majority of molesters—85 percent by some estimates—are not strangers to their victims, but trusted grown-ups with steady access to their lives. In fact, because of their affection for kids, child sexual abusers often gravitate toward certain jobs or activities: teaching, coaching, pediatric medicine. They are often the Pied Pipers of their communities, the grown-ups whom kids adore and parents praise for their generosity, patience and, above all, unique rapport with children. In fact, modern researchers say that both Lewis Carroll, who wrote *Alice's Adventures in Wonderland*, and Sir James Barrie, who penned *Peter Pan*, were able to relate so well to the imaginations of children because they were sexually and romantically attracted to them.

Abusers are more likely to coax children into sex with attention and affection—in much the same way adults court each other—than to pin them violently to the ground. They test the waters carefully, with light touches and subtle suggestions. They know that many children will acquiesce because they don't want all the special treatment and favors to disappear. And they know that most of them won't tell because they're embarrassed and afraid mom and dad will be mad.

It is no accident that child sexual abusers are almost always discussed with masculine pronouns: The vast majority of abusers are male. Most experts estimate that more than 90 percent of the cases of child sexual abuse are perpetrated by men, although that wisdom is slowly changing. Some experts now believe that women offenders have been undercounted, in part due to cultural stereotypes. A man's sexual touch is perceived as precisely that; a woman's may be mistaken for nurturing. A man's sexual involvement with a fifteen-year-old girl is considered abuse; a woman's with a fifteen-year-old boy may be considered an initiation, even a favor.

It is important to note that not all child sexual abusers are alike, and researchers have often tried to separate them into a few neat categories based on the reasons they seek children out for sex. Two principal groups emerge. One consists of adults who seem to be primarily attracted to their peers but occasionally, in spontaneous moments, reach for children. It may happen when they're experiencing unusual stress, agonizing loneliness or intense anger, or when drugs or alcohol blur their judgment and the boundaries of acceptable behavior.

The other group consists of adults whose primary attraction is for children. They don't choose to be aroused by children. They don't sit down, weigh their options and decide children are more exciting. They are simply drawn to blond ten-year-old boys or girls the way other adults are drawn to svelte brunettes in their thirties or muscle-bound surfers just out of college. Knowing that their desires are condemned and criminal, some manage to satisfy themselves with kiddie porn or films, and quick encounters, sometimes bought. But others pursue steady romantic relationships, inevitably doomed as the child partner grows up. They nurture. In their own way, they love. And the sexual attraction they feel —in many cases, an actual pathology—is as powerful as any other, and as difficult to change.

"They're feeling emotions you and I would normally consider terrific," says Dr. Fred Berlin, a professor at the Johns Hopkins University School of Medicine and perhaps the nation's leading expert on sexual disorders. "There's affection, companionship, a desire to express love through sexual intimacy. Here are all these wonderful feelings—only they're attached to a child."

They don't intend to inflict harm and are often unaware that they do. Some experts say that's because they are so narcissistic, so self-absorbed, that they cannot appreciate the effects their actions have on others. Others say these abusers, because they are fundamentally decent people, create elaborate justifications for their predations as a way of preserving self-esteem. They convince themselves that children want sex or need to be tutored in it. They convince themselves that children are their equals. "We often get angry at pedophiles because of the problems they're causing in the lives of others," Berlin explains. "But often it's like getting mad at the blind man for not seeing."

The word *pedophile* applies accurately only to some of the abusers with a primary sexual interest in children. Technically, pedophilia is a psychiatric disorder signaled by an adult's persistent attraction to children who have not yet reached adolescence —children usually under the age of thirteen. Most experts consider it manageable but essentially incurable: A pedophile can learn not to act on his desires but he cannot exorcise what basically amounts to a sexual orientation.

Many of the abusers in this book, however, experienced an attraction to adolescents, ages thirteen to fifteen, and experts have yet to reach any consensus on whether these desires and actions represent an aberrant sexual orientation all its own—which has been dubbed *ephebophilia*—or an immature and inappropriate partner choice. Nonetheless, these men committed child sexual abuse: They exploited their positions as adults to engage in potentially destructive sexual relations with youths under the age of consent, which varies from state to state. Because the phrases "child sexual abuse" or "child molestation" encompass the widest variety of situations and types of offenders, and because they avoid classifications of abusers that are still being debated, they are the phrases used most frequently in this book.

The scientific inquiry into the motivations and behaviors of child molesters is still so new that more questions than answers attend any honest discussion of child sexual abuse. Are abusers —whether pedophiles, ephebophiles or adults with only sporadic sexual encounters with children—excited by the power they have over them? Or are their impulses more purely sexual? What is the cause of pedophilia, or of ephebophilia? Some experts believe abusers are born, that a genetic flaw or a physiological imbalance inclines them to an attraction now branded both criminal and immoral. Other experts believe abusers are made; they cite questionable estimates that more than half of all molesters were themselves sexually abused and are now trying to re-create or avenge what happened. And a few experts even believe these abusers validate Sigmund Freud's suggestion that without a prevailing morality, people can become sexually attracted to just about anything. Abusers, then, are people who somehow resist cultural conditioning, lose sight of taboos or feel exempt from society's rules. They become sexually fixated on children at some point, and that orientation follows them through their lives.

Experts offer other possibilities as well. Perhaps the sexual development of these abusers was thwarted by a premature introduction to sex. Perhaps—the opposite—they grew up in environments where sexuality was overzealously repressed. Perhaps, whatever the reason, they are simply so immature that they are stuck, sexually, where they started at the age of twelve or fourteen, and, as adults, are seeking out the same partners that they would have had then, when they themselves were children.

Another mystery that nags researchers is why different types of child sexual abusers seem to target one gender of child over the other. When it comes to abusers whose primary attraction is to adults and who only occasionally initiate sex with children, the victims are most often female. But when it comes to abusers whose primary attraction is to children, the victims are more often male. Nonetheless, men in this second group of so-called fixated abusers are more likely—if they have any secondary, or adult, sexual attachments—to be heterosexual than homosexual. And some men in this group abuse both girls and boys; the age of their victims means more to them than the gender.

There are few hard truths. One is that victims of child sexual abuse are far more common than society has ever really acknowledged. In the most definitive survey to date, a *Los Angeles Times* telephone poll of 2,626 adults nationwide, 27 percent of the women interviewed and 16 percent of the men said they had been sexually abused as children.

The other is that adults who molest once almost invariably molest again—even dozens of times. That is the lesson the Catholic Church has had the most difficulty learning. Church leaders dedicated to the gospel of forgiveness have taken comfort in priests' pleas for a second chance, for the opportunity to use God's grace to overcome temptation. They have assumed that prayer could erase pathology. In ignoring one of the few certainties experts can offer them, they have left thousands of Catholic children open to victimization—and the Church to what is fast becoming the most serious crisis its American branch has ever faced.

Chapter 3

GENESIS

THE TALE OF WIDESPREAD SEXUAL ABUSE
of children by Roman Catholic priests riv-
eted people's attention not just because it demonstrated that abusers in general could appear
in benign guises, but because it contradicted
every expectation that people had about Catholic priests in particular. These men, more than
any other clergy in our society, were held up
as personifications of virtue and selflessness,
the ideal toward which everyone else could
only strive. They were reputed to be above and
beyond carnal desires. Moreover, they served
a church that was supposed to be a house of
refuge and solace, the calm eye in the storm of
everyday life. And yet, as many Americans
learned in 1992, hundreds of priests—perhaps
even thousands of them—had molested children. On the surface, at least, it seemed impossible. It seemed incredible.

In fact, it was inevitable.

The child sexual abuse crisis in the Catholic Church was bound to happen. The very structure of the Church—the kind of men attracted to its priesthood, the pressures placed on them, the status granted them and the hierarchy in which they were tucked away—virtually guaranteed there would be trouble, and the trouble was quite likely to involve sex. The trouble was also likely to involve exploitation of the vulnerable and the voiceless, and those adjectives apply to no class of citizens in this country better than to children.

The Catholic Church doesn't talk so much about men choosing the priesthood as the priesthood choosing them. According to Catholic theology, God calls these men to the task. So their ordination into the priesthood is less a career path than a spiritual destiny. Priests are not made; they are born.

But human motivation is infinitely complex, human perception infinitely flawed, and it stands to reason that other, more worldly forces shape the priesthood as well. Some men turn their backs on a calling because the practical realities of a priest's life daunt them. Others hear a calling because those same realities appeal to them. As is the case with any profession, the composition of the priesthood to some degree reflects the requirements of the job.

The conditions of the priesthood are forbidding, especially in a modern society that finds less and less logic and virtue in the kind of life-style a priest is expected to adopt. A man entering the priesthood must, for the most part, forsake wealth. He must be willing to stand removed from society, living in a monastery or isolated rectory, often by himself or with just one or two other men. Perhaps most off-putting of all, he must pledge himself to celibacy, to never experiencing sexual intimacy with another person, never marrying, never creating his own family.

Most men who enter the priesthood accept these terms because they find an importance in the priesthood that transcends or renders insignificant any of its limitations. But some become priests, often unconsciously, because the specific sacrifices that deter others don't seem so burdensome at all to them.

The condition of mandatory celibacy, which is perhaps the most distinctive feature of the Catholic priesthood, is a perfect example. Celibacy was not mandated by Jesus Christ or the apostles, but by Catholic leaders in the twelfth century. They decided that men of the cloth should liberate themselves from the pleasures of the flesh and harness those energies to the service of God and the salvation of humankind. But despite that exalted rationale, celibacy is a tough sell. Catholic dioceses across this country—and around the globe—are crowded with former priests who abandoned their vocations to marry, with seminarians who stopped short of ordination because they could not reconcile themselves to celibacy, with devoutly Catholic men who early on in life pushed aside aspirations to the priesthood because this demand, among all the others, seemed too great.

Who, then, are the takers? Certainly, many are men who perceive a validity and relevance in celibacy as defined by the Church leaders who instituted it. But others find celibacy attractive in and of itself. They are running away from sex. Reared in a conservative, strict Catholic ethic that portrays unbridled sexual urges as the basest and most venal of human desires, they equate flesh with weakness. And in some cases, they feel sexual stirrings—such as a desire for children—that have been branded aberrant, sinful, even evil.

True pedophiles usually begin to feel this attraction at an early age—more than half before they turn eighteen, according to one study. Despite popular portrayals of such people as depraved perverts without any semblance of conscience, many are actually ashamed of, and frightened by, what they feel. Some repress it far below conscious awareness. Others knowingly struggle to buck their impulses.

If a man with these feelings is Catholic, and religious, entering the celibate culture of the priesthood seems like a perfect defense—a commitment to holiness that promises to keep the demons at bay. As Dr. John Money, one of the world's foremost authorities on human sexual orientation, wrote in 1987: "These future priests become seminarians partly in the belief that they will, through religion, gain control over the very sexual desires that they resist or fight against."

About fifty-five priests who waged and lost the battle to sublimate their sexual desire for children have been treated at the

Menninger Clinic in Topeka, Kansas, one of the nation's premier psychiatric treatment facilities. Its director, Dr. Glen Gabbard, says: "The most striking thing is the number of them who went into the profession as a way of dealing with those very impulses. The impulses to molest children, the sexual feelings to molest children, don't emerge *de novo* after they enter the priesthood. They are there consciously, subconsciously, or preconsciously. They're present when one makes a vocational choice.

"They have the feeling that these impulses are overwhelming and hard to control, so they think that maybe the structure of the Church and the code of celibacy will somehow help them avoid acting on them. These are people who are basically ethical and are trying to control their impulses so they don't act unethically."

Gabbard's observations are so widely shared by the nation's top experts on sexual abusers of children that even some Catholic leaders have begun to acknowledge the theory's logic and plausibility. "It could well be that a person with this kind of a hidden psychosexual problem could escape to the seminary and the like, thinking in some way that this would be a way of sublimating this problem," says Archbishop Daniel Sheehan of Omaha, Nebraska. "I suppose it would be a problem that a person would think they could hide in the celibate priesthood." Bishop Kenneth Untener of Saginaw, Michigan, is even blunter: "Because you are being drawn to a life that has a strange sexual peg to it, probably a greater number of people with sexual aberrations would show up at the door."

For such a man, mandatory celibacy is also less of a sacrifice than it is for a man with sexual yearnings for peers. That man can easily envision a life outside the priesthood in which he fulfills his desires while finding respect. He would clearly be turning his back on something attainable and acceptable to become a priest. Never marrying, never fathering a child—these are the phrases most often used to define the price of celibacy. But the man who fantasizes about children doesn't expect to be able to fulfill his desires while living a tranquil and open life. If he is fully or partly aware of his predicament, celibacy affords him a way to live a life without sex and have no questions asked. If he's suppressed his desires to the point of no longer consciously experiencing them, pledging celibacy seems like a formality. He's not much interested in sex, anyway. This way, he gets honored for his abstinence.

Honor and respect, in fact, are often special goals for people who fear they don't deserve them. The man who lusts after children and perceives his desire as immoral seeks the very affirmation of his righteousness that entrance into the priesthood provides. "Ordination as shame reduction" is what Mark Laaser, a former United Church of Christ minister who counsels clergy with sexual compulsions or disorders, calls it. "I think a lot of this may be unconscious," Laaser is quick to point out. "But I think there's this myth that if you achieve the status of clergy, you'll be a wonderful person and act that way. I think that a lot of people go into ministry thinking they'll get respect and they'll be liked and they'll like themselves because they're giving to others."

Laaser says some men and women feel that the mere act of ordination would trigger a mystical transformation that would lift their desires. One female Protestant minister lived a life of compulsive sexual promiscuity before her ordination. After entering the clergy, she expected her sexual obsessions to end. But they continued and even worsened over time. She began to cruise sex clubs in Manhattan where she and other leather-clad patrons sated their appetites for sadism and masochism. When she finally entered therapy with Laaser, she said that what she really needed was to be ordained again. The first time, she told him, "it didn't take."

But the Catholic priesthood can turn out to be a dangerous place even for some men who are neither disordered nor especially troubled when they first take their vows. Until the past two decades, men who became priests frequently entered seminary in high school, at ages as young as twelve. Even those who entered in college or later usually came from strict Catholic schools. Tracked early for the priesthood—and celibacy—they stopped dating as teenagers, if they ever dated at all. Few went through the same paces of psychosexual development as other men. So later on in life, if their unmet sexual needs compelled them to break their pledge of celibacy, they sought involvements with those they felt were their emotional peers. Those partners were teenagers.

After all, the seminary experience didn't encourage sexual maturity. The goal was to prepare men to take their oath of celibacy, and to steer them clear of any involvement that might derail them from that track. Superiors portrayed women as perfume-scented, sweet-talking temptresses with nothing but trouble in mind—an army of Eves in the Garden of Eden. Seminarians were often forbidden to ride in cars with women other than their mothers and sisters. Private time between two men was suspect, too. Although the word *homosexuality* was seldom if ever mentioned, the possibility of such behavior was clearly recognized in the regulations at some seminaries. If two seminarians were seen walking or talking alone together too often, they were reprimanded. If a seminarian had someone in his private room, the door had to be open.

That extreme vigilance waned considerably over the past two decades. During the same period, candidates for the priesthood began entering seminaries at older ages. Only a tiny fraction now begin in high school; most start after college. Even so, an atmosphere of staunch sexual prohibition and lurking sexual danger still exists in many seminaries and in many of the Catholic high schools and colleges that feed them. And it is accompanied by a sexual ethic that discourages any healthy understanding of physical intimacy between two adults. The Catholic Church still espouses the view that the primary purpose of sex is procreation, and that sexual feelings experienced outside the covenant of matrimony are only invitations to disgrace. Psychotherapist and ex-priest Richard Sipe likes to tell the story of a seminary instructor—now a bishop—whose students once asked why masturbation was a mortal sin. The instructor's response: If it wasn't, men wouldn't get married and father children.

Seminaries taught an ethic of denial and repression. Discussions of sexuality were marked by reticence, embarrassment and even disdain. Seminarians pushed their sexual feelings to the back of some high shelf in the mind and sealed them tight in a box—forbidden and strange and threatening. Amid the Church reform of the 1960s based on the Second Vatican Council—loosely called

Vatican II—many seminaries converted lessons on most of the Ten Commandments into English. But Latin remained the language of instruction for the two commandments that concerned sex: Thou shalt not commit adultery and Thou shalt not covet thy neighbor's wife. In the past decade, many seminary directors have tried to institute candid sexual education, operating on the premise that it is healthier for would-be priests to examine their sexual feelings so they might understand what they are renouncing. Some of those pioneers have been beaten back, censured, ostracized. The prevailing advice to priests wondering how they will manage inevitable sexual impulses mirrors Nancy Reagan's approach to the drug problem: Just Say No.

Priests are also likely to lack maturity in ways other than sexual. In a landmark 1971 study of the personality characteristics of American priests, psychologist Eugene Kennedy, one of the country's most prominent Catholic scholars, noted that 57 percent of the 218 priests in his sample had not passed through all the stages of growth leading to mature behavior and were somehow arrested in their psychological development. He noted that their lack of maturity involved not just sexual feelings but a poor sense of personal identity and command of interpersonal relationships. Although the study is two decades old, Kennedy is confident that it would yield similar results today. He says that in many ways, priests are overprotected from many of life's harsh realities, cut off from the kind of intense intimate commitments, such as marriage, that demand personal compromise. Once ordained, they have virtual job security for life. A rectory housekeeper or church volunteer prepares their meals and does the laundry. By virtue of the collars that priests wear, they are guaranteed a respect and affection not contingent on their deeds.

These men live with peculiar handicaps, under peculiar stresses, that might foster child sexual abuse. Their celibate commitment and domestic isolation, for example, can place them so far out of touch with their sexual feelings—in extreme cases, they don't even realize they have them—that those impulses sneak up on them. A perfectly well adjusted adult might see an attractive fourteen- or fifteen-year-old and feel a vague sexual stirring. But that adult, knowing the feeling and knowing that there are more appropriate objects for it, will quickly shove it away. A priest with a poor sense of his sexual self, or with a sense that he has purged sexual desires from his life, may not recognize what he's feeling, say many therapists who have evaluated or treated priest molesters. He may not see that the hugs he's giving to teenagers are more than platonic. He may not be watchful of the boundary between acceptable and unacceptable behavior or cognizant of when he's crossed it. "They don't know their sexual insides," says Sipe, who adds that the Church's message to priests is that "you can't have a desire, because if you have it, you'll act on it. That's terribly primitive. What you have is some priests who think masturbation or any orgasmic feeling is a mortal sin. So what happens is the water gets so high over the dam and then the sexual instinct is uncontrollable."

A priest is also rendered vulnerable by his loneliness. Although his life is crowded with masses, funerals, baptisms and weddings, a priest stands at a remove from all of these ceremonies, a presider rather than a participant. He has no real domestic life. He is not allowed any real, full-bodied, open intimacy with another person. And at the end of the day, when a priest slips into bed, there's no one there to share his joy, no one to salve his sorrow, no one to hold. He's all alone. In some priests, the need for closeness becomes overwhelming, and the longing easily turns sexual.

"I ache for my fellow clergy in the Roman Church, because I think they are very lonely," says the Reverend Margaret Graham, the Episcopal priest who heads the National Committee for the Prevention of Child Abuse. "Despite the vestments, despite the collar, despite the cross, these are people who are also God's creatures, and they are subject to loneliness. Their vows make them very much isolated. Do they not reach out in ways that are inappropriate because of this?"

Vincent Bilotta, a Massachusetts psychologist who has treated priests who molest, says: "Too many men—with the best of intentions—have been ordained and then sent off to the slaughter. Many have come through seminaries that were repressive and sexually dysfunctional; they find that the ongoing formation they were promised is nonexistent; they live an itinerant life, going from parish to parish, living with men with whom they may have nothing in common. They live with extraordinary stress and, as is true of anyone in stress, their bodies ache to be relieved. And here are these young kids, who look up to the priest with great esteem and admiration, who offer direct access to emotional contact."

That some priests turn to these children for sex is a reflection of their own stunted development. If Kennedy is right, they're still children themselves. Their most recent memories of courtship and romance may date to their teenage years, before they set their sights on the priesthood. So in turning to a fourteen-year-old, a priest is often choosing a kind of sexual peer with whom he feels the most comfort. "This young boy or girl probably represents sexual awakening—unfinished business," says Dr. Nicholas Groth, one of the country's foremost experts on child sexual abuse.

Teenagers are also often the safest and most available sexual companions. If a priest makes sexual advances toward an adult, the adult is more likely to tell, less likely to be swayed by the priest's exhortation to silence. If a priest begins spending vast amounts of private time with a single adult, parishioners may well wonder if Father is being tempted into a sexual liaison. But if Father takes a young teenager under wing, particularly a male teenager, he is simply playing surrogate parent and spiritual teacher, simply playing out his role as mentor to the young.

Teenagers are also low-risk because they are not in a position to make too many demands, or exert too much control. An adult partner might suddenly want a sexual relationship to turn formal and public. A teenager will hardly request that. Dr. Judith Becker, an Arizona psychologist who has evaluated several priest abusers, says, "They knew on some level that having a relationship with a teenager, they were not going to live with the teenager, it was not going to be a cause to leave the priesthood. It was not a threat to their priesthood in a sense."

All of these situational factors, coupled with the celibate culture's power as a magnet for people fleeing unwanted sexual impulses, guarantee that a significant fraction of the nation's 53,000

Roman Catholic priests will become child sexual abusers. But how significant? Sipe is the only person who has really attempted to answer that question. Based on a sort of sexual inventory of 2,700 priests he conducted from 1960 to 1992, he estimates that 2 percent of the nation's priests—or roughly 1,050—are true pedophiles. He further estimates that 4 percent—or roughly 2,100 —are men who might be called situational abusers: At some point in their adult lives, they have had sexual contact with children or teenagers under the legal age of consent. There's no way to know how these percentages stack up against those of the adult population at large, or against those of another professional class. Child sexual abuse experts have no idea how many abusers there are.

In any case, such comparisons distract from more compelling concerns. Regardless of whether the percentages are in synch with the rest of the society, priest abusers have a unique and tragic opportunity to do damage. Their position of trust gives them special access to, and influence over, children and their families. Catholics go to priests in their moments of greatest vulnerability and emotional nakedness—when they confess their sins. They bare their souls to Father because out of all the mortals on Earth, he can be counted on to understand and forgive them. And he is bound by Church law to guard their secrets. He is safe.

So a priest can pass countless hours in the company of children. Little second graders take lessons from him for their first Communion. Older seventh graders take lessons from him for their confirmation. Adolescent boys listen and bow to Father as he guides them through all they need to learn to become altar boys who will come to the church early to set up for Mass, then stand and kneel beside him during the service.

A priest also forges more personal relationships with children in his parish, counseling them when they are troubled. He becomes part of the fabric of their families' lives. He goes over at night to sit at the family's dinner table, sharing pot roast and discussions about the kids' report cards. He says grace. After the meal, he goes upstairs to tuck the kids in. Mom and Dad smile. Father will lead the children in their good-night prayers.

In dozens of the cases where priests sexually abused children, they were able to do so largely because parents entrusted their children to them in situations where they would not so easily have trusted any other adult, perhaps even a blood relative. They let their child spend hour after hour in Father's bedroom in the rectory beside the church, never thinking a place so near the altar at which they worshipped could be a scene of danger. They let their child accompany Father on long day trips, or on overnight camping expeditions.

Trust provides an abusive priest almost unparalleled opportunity. But it is his power and influence that enable him to exploit that opportunity so well, seducing his victims into sexual acts and enlisting their silence. Since most children are not forced but cajoled by adults into sexual acts, their perception of an adult's integrity and authority significantly influences their vulnerability to that adult.

Many Catholics perceive priests as their conduits to God, men who walk with one foot on earth, one in heaven. In Latin, the phrase by which priests are known is Alter Christi—other Christ. Minneapolis psychologist Gary Schoener, who has met or counseled many victims of molestation by priests, says it's not unusual for them to describe their child's-eye view of the men as ethereal, almost otherworldly. One victim told him she was taught that if she encountered both a priest and an angel on the street, she should walk toward the priest, because he is closer to God.

A priest speaks the direct message of God—in the form of the Gospel—from the altar during Mass. But even when he steps down from that high perch, he is considered a moral arbiter of what is right and what is wrong. His words carry special weight —so when a priest makes sexual advances to a child and assures that child, as abusers inevitably do, that what he is proposing is acceptable and normal, he is bound to be more convincing than a school teacher, or a soccer coach, or a Boy Scout troop leader.

"The higher the level of trust and authority, the more vulnerable a child will be," says Gail Ryan, a therapist at the Kempe Center in Denver, Colorado, which specializes in sexual abuse counseling. "And if you're talking about clergy, you're talking about very high levels of authority. They can invoke God being on their side. You don't get much more coercion than that. That's just as powerful in terms of mental coercion as a gun is in terms of physical coercion."

Just as children are particularly vulnerable to priests, they aren't likely to tell on them, either. Children often keep silent if they have affection for their abuser, if he is someone who can cloak his actions in genuine or professed caring; and a priest, like a parent, is such a person. Children are often silent if their abuser is a person held in high esteem because they are more likely to feel that they—not their abuser—are at fault. And children often remain silent if they sense that their abuser is so revered by the adults around them that no one will believe the truth—a worry children would certainly have if their abuser is a priest.

"If everybody says this person is wonderful, it's like the emperor's new clothes," says Mike Lew, author of *Victims No Longer*, one of the definitive books on sexually abused boys. "It makes you question your very interpretation of reality." Some children, he says, may have been reprimanded, even punished, on other occasions when they showed disrespect for religion or the family priest. "I don't think a kid needs to hear that too many times to know that he should keep his mouth shut," Lew says.

These are truths that apply not just to priests but to any clergy member who sexually abuses children. In a self-help book for such clergy, a Protestant minister imprisoned for child sexual abuse chillingly describes the power and unquestioned respect that enabled his abusive behavior. "I used my power and trust to counsel boys, find out their secrets, and fed my deviance off of what I learned," he writes. "No one would ever suspect or even want to think that their pastor who they love is a child molester. My foster son, one of my victims for three years, desperately tried to reveal the things I had done, but no one believed him, in or out of the parish. That's how powerful I'd become in the ministry. The community and my parish overlooked his accusations, believing me, rather than him."

Finally, priests who abuse children belong to a culture and institution that are uniquely unable to confront the problem in an open and decisive manner, and to make sure that the priests don't molest again. The relationship of parishioners to the institution is not one that encourages them to demand accountability. The relationship of the institution to its priests is not one that encourages and allows it to act harshly toward them. And the very character of the Catholic Church and the men who lead it are antithetical to a public and swift response to a problem like sexual abuse by clergy.

The Catholic Church and the culture that has evolved around it teach laity deference and obedience. While leaders of the laity in other faiths actually convene every few years to formulate new church policy, Catholics have no say. While most Protestant congregations hire and fire their pastors, Catholic congregations simply accept whichever priest the local diocese assigns to them. If they suspect that their priest is an abuser, or are unhappy with him for any reason, they can inform the bishop of the diocese, but they cannot trigger the priest's removal themselves. If a bishop decides to recycle an abusive priest to a new parish, the people of that parish have no way of knowing it. They cannot demand the priest's career history, and in fact would be unlikely even to ask for it. They've been too well trained.

Parishioners unhappy with the way the institution is being run have little power to reform it. And although Catholics can choose on private terms to affirm certain pronouncements and reject others, those who want to hold on to their religion seldom feel that they can leave the Church. Unlike most branches of Protestantism, unlike Judaism, Catholicism embraces and espouses the belief that it is the one and only true faith. It's a monopoly, not subject to any kind of public regulation.

So as more and more cases of priest abusers came to light over the past decade, it fell to local bishops—lords of their individual dioceses and answerable only to the pope—to take the matter in hand. They were not the right men for the job. The problem straddled two worlds in which they felt particularly uncomfortable—sex and psychology. When told that Father had fondled a twelve-year-old boy or girl, most bishops had to battle disbelief and squeamishness. As men of prayer, not science, they were ill prepared to comprehend the gravity of the behavior, seeing it instead as a moral lapse. If a priest confessed and repented, and took a short spiritual retreat to reflect and meditate, a bishop often assumed that he would not transgress again. He gave the priest a second chance, heeding his faith's twin tenets of the possibility of redemption for all sinners and of forgiveness.

That course of action also reflected the paternal relationship bishops have with their priests. Most bishops believe their duty is not to accept or reject them but to nurture and protect them. They respect the sacrifices made by men who become priests and are loath to turn their backs on them.

And underlying the bishops' decisions is their fierce loyalty to their institution whose image must never be sullied, whose authority must never be compromised, whose faithful followers must never be given reason to disbelieve. They accomplish this by avoiding scandal. So when bishops were confronted with allegations that priests in their dioceses had sexually abused children, the alarms went off and the defenses went up. They talked to the victims privately, if at all. They confronted the priests in closed quarters, never seeking or drawing the attention of law enforcement authorities. In so doing, they protected these priests from public exposure and punishment and allowed them to continue working. "Priests can do anything they damn please to lay people and feel pretty confident that they can get away with it," fumes Father Andrew Greeley, noted Catholic novelist, sociologist and frequent critic of the institutional Church.

If bishops fail to act, change cannot occur. That is the way things work in a hierarchy, where all power is concentrated near the top and flows down only. The Catholic Church is a classic example of a rigidly hierarchical institution, which is its overriding and perhaps biggest problem. It creates a class system— bishop above priest, priest above common man, man above woman, adult above child—that bestows privilege and respect in accordance with a person's role rather than merit, garb rather than deed. Those on the lower rungs learn fealty to those above them. Those on the higher rungs nurse a sense of entitlement over those below them. The whole system presents a potent dynamic for abuse, and an awesome barrier to any redress of grievances.

"They would have a hard time creating a situation more disposed to child sexual abuse than they have," says a Minneapolis psychologist who, like Schoener, has evaluated abusive priests and their victims in the Twin Cities area. "It would be hard to improve on it."

Richard Sipe renders the same message to Church leaders in more colorful language. "Someone has to tell them," he says, "that they have booked passage on the sexual *Titanic*."

PART II

If we speak we are afraid

that our words will be used against us

And if we do not speak

we are still afraid.

—Audre Lorde

Chapter 4

SUFFER THE CHILDREN

ROSE MARTINEZ'S FAMILY MET FATHER
Jason Sigler when they rushed from Albuquerque to the northern New Mexico town
of Las Vegas where Rose's mother lay dying.
As they hovered over the critically ill woman,
a fair-skinned priest appeared at her bedside,
dabbed his fingers with holy oil, traced the sign
of the cross on her forehead and forgave her
sins.

The next day, the Martinez clan huddled in
the front pew of the small town's Gothic
church as it filled to capacity for the funeral
Mass. Father Jay rose to the pulpit and reached
out to them with God's Gospel. His thick
glasses and receding hairline lent him a gentle,
avuncular air. He talked of God's grace and
eternal life. He eased the Martinez family's
sorrow.

In gratitude, they opened the door to their

home—and to their hearts. Over the following months and years, Father Jason Sigler would drive several hours down to Albuquerque to trade hours of solace for plates of Rose Martinez's homemade beans. The Martinez family would return the visits, and at Sunday Mass in Father Jay's small-town parish, Rose and her husband, Louis, would glow when Father Jay singled out their family from the pulpit for praise. Their son Tim would stand beside him in his own miniature cassock, invited to serve the priest as his altar boy.

Rose slipped the good padre ten dollars whenever she had a little extra in her wallet. She cut his hair and adjusted his back. She liked being close to him. "He was clean and neat," she says. "He smelled clean. He even smelled holy."

Father Jay, in turn, never missed a birthday or a family event. Flowers for Rose. Cards for Tim. The priest seemed especially fond of the young boy. Whenever Tim walked into the room, the priest's eyes lit up. Wherever Tim went, the priest's gaze followed. It pleased Tim's parents to see this. Maybe the boy was special. Maybe he would grow up to become a priest.

In the spring of 1977, Father Jay invited the thirteen-year-old boy to spend a week's vacation with him. His parents were flattered at the invitation; their son had indeed been chosen. And in rural New Mexico in the 1970s, sending your son to spend time with a priest seemed as safe as sending him into God's hands.

The two drove together through the sparsely populated mountains of northern New Mexico as Father Jay stopped by the parish churches he had once served and dropped in on parishioners whose weddings he had performed, whose children he had baptized. One afternoon, as the priest and the boy wound along the narrow roads cut into the sides of steep canyons, Father Jay slipped his hand onto Tim's knee. Then onto his thigh. Then onto his groin.

Tim froze. He couldn't believe what was happening. A priest wasn't supposed to do something like this. After a few moments, Father Jay withdrew his hand. Tim breathed a sigh of relief, and decided to pretend nothing had happened.

A few weeks later, Tim went to spend a week with his grandfather in Las Vegas. The old man was lonely; it had been almost a year since his wife's death. Tim arrived to discover that Father Jay had arranged for him to sleep in the guest room in the rectory.

The first night, as Tim lay sleeping, Father Jay allegedly padded quietly down the long upstairs hall of the rectory, careful not to disturb the other priest sleeping downstairs. He entered Tim's room. The boy awoke to the curious sensation of the priest's mouth caressing his penis. He was too taken aback to speak. He lay there, feigning sleep, until Father Jay was finished and retreated to his own room.

Over the months that followed, Father Jay would slip down to Albuquerque during the week to spend time with Tim, to continue their sexual encounters. The priest followed Rose and Louis's work schedules carefully. He always knew when he could find the boy home alone.

Tim said nothing about that first night in the rectory—or about any of the priest's secret visits during the six years he and Father Jay were sexual partners. He said nothing when Father Jay took him into the bathroom at his parents' house and asked him to perform oral sex. He said nothing about the kisses he and the priest shared during his visits to Las Vegas.

Father Jay told the boy: "This is between you and me. This is something special. God would approve." And Tim believed him.

"Not once was this ever forcible," he says now. "He made me feel proud. He never forgot my birthday. Anyway, you just can't go around saying a priest did something wrong in a community where priests almost walk on water."

It's a familiar story. In case after case across the nation, families placed their deepest trust in men of the cloth, who turned that trust into opportunity.

Victims of child sexual abuse are not selected randomly from the thousands of young people priests bless in church on occasional Sundays or run into at weddings and baptisms and funerals. They almost inevitably wear the crisp uniforms of parochial school students and the cassocks of altar boys practicing for the priesthood. They answer the rectory phones on Saturdays, organize Catholic Youth Organization meetings and, in many cases, dream of taking religious vows when they reach adulthood.

Most are children of cautious, often overprotective parents

who impose early curfews and strict controls yet send their sons to sleep in rectories and on trips across the country with their confessors. They come from families who avoid psychologists but confidently send their children for private counseling with the parish priest. They are heirs to a belief—too often naive—that the Fathers of the Church are holy men who offer only safety and comfort.

The abused are children of parish council members and master catechists, Eucharistic ministers and volunteers at the dozens of church carnivals and socials that build parishes into communities. Priests are welcome, honored guests at these families' dinner tables. And they are treated as full-fledged members of these families, trusted with parents' most intimate secrets, and with their most precious possessions—their children.

The victims are the sons of the very men and women who make the American Catholic Church a vibrant institution. And they are the daughters. No myth persists more endurably—or more harmfully—than that most molesters are gay, most victims young boys. Pedophilia, after all, is a proclivity independent of a homosexual or heterosexual adult orientation. And the best available estimates for child sexual abuse in the general population reveal that 71 percent of the victims of male perpetrators are female. "Child sexual abuse has as much to do with homosexuality as rape has to do with heterosexuality," says Richard Sipe, the Baltimore psychotherapist and former priest.

Clearly the proportions change with victims of sexual abuse by priests, because priests have much readier access to boys than to girls. Girls, after all, are still barred from serving with priests on the altar. In fact, the records of criminal and civil cases filed against priests make it appear that females, for the most part, have been saved from victimization.

But those figures are deceiving, says Gary Schoener, a Minneapolis psychologist who evaluates both priests and their victims for the Archdiocese of St. Paul-Minneapolis. Schoener says that, in private, he has seen more female victims than male, but that their abuse is less likely to become public. "Young men's families cry harder for blood," he says, noting that the notion of a boy being raped seems even more monstrous because it leaves the child with the taint of homosexuality in a culture where homosexuality is defined as sinful. Furthermore, he says, while abused girls tend to internalize the damage—punishing themselves physically and psychologically—boys are more likely to act out their trauma violently and aggressively against others. The damage is clearer, more public. The tendency to sue that much greater.

Schoener also believes that boys are more likely to have the type of civil cases that lawyers believe they can win. Male abusers of boys tend to be less monogamous—and thus have more victims whose testimony can be marshaled. Finally, Schoener points out, "Nobody accuses young boys of being seductive. It's a piece of sexism. It's a piece of bullshit." But the assumption that girls might "ask for" or provoke their own abuse is so widespread that their cases are more difficult to win in court.

The myth of the molester as homosexual predator is a dangerous one. Even parents who may be alert to the possibility of Father's interest in their sons don't think twice when they send their daughters off to parochial school or to the parish church for a youth carnival.

ANTHONY FONTANA ALMOST LEARNED THIS LESSON THE HARD way. An attorney in Lafayette, Louisiana, Fontana had lost his innocence about the purity of priests when the first child victims of Father Gilbert Gauthe appeared on his television screen, and then in his office, in 1985. As he prepared to file suit against Gauthe and the local diocese, Fontana immersed himself in the research about child sexual abuse. A former altar boy himself, and an active Catholic, Fontana felt sickened as he watched the sordid details of the Church's protection of Gauthe unfold.

But no alarm bells rang when his wife came home from his daughter Renee's art class and announced: "Father John says Renee has real talent."

Fontana beamed with parental pride although he thought the eight-year-old's drawings looked like classic kid's scrawlings. Then again, what did he know about art?

"Father John says Renee has such an angelic look, such rosy cheeks," Fontana's wife reported a few evenings later. Again, Fontana beamed with parental pride. This time, after all, he agreed.

"Father John wants to paint Renee," his wife said next. Fontana beamed—yet again.

"He was playing on what parents want to hear," Fontana now says. "I knew more than almost anyone else about pedophilia and I'm a cynical person by nature and I didn't see it. I didn't see him setting up my daughter."

He only saw it when a stranger showed up in his office with the nightmarish story of Bonnie Butaud Bonin, a Chitimacha Indian from Cypremort Point, a remote community in the coastal marshes of Louisiana where hurricanes sweep the earth with merciless regularity. It was Hurricane Audrey's turn in 1957 and the house that Bonnie's father had built splintered into matchsticks. The family took refuge in the rectory at St. Helen's in Louisa. Their savior: Father John. Father John Engbers.

The Dutch priest, ordained in Louisiana in 1949, was attractive and seemed sophisticated to the twenty-five families he served on Cypremort Point. It was a backwater community and Father John, a painter and photographer who played classical music in his rectory, was like an exotic missionary. "We didn't see him as a man," Bonnie says, "but as an extension of God our Father."

Bonnie's mother, Martha, was no exception. Every day, she sent one of her eleven children to the rectory after school to help Father with his chores. Every evening, she trekked over to the church with an infant in her arms to lay out his vestments before Mass. Every night, she cooked him dinner.

When Bonnie was eight years old, Father John hoisted her onto his lap to tell her about a problem he was having. He sometimes had to advise parishioners about sex, but didn't know much about it himself. He didn't know how it felt to be touched in special places, he told the girl as he slipped his hand inside her panties. She had been chosen by God to help him learn the ways of human flesh, he said as he fondled her vagina.

"He explained that God demanded this be our secret," Bonnie recalls. "I was terrified and ashamed at being chosen for such an ugly destiny. But I accepted my fate without question."

She didn't argue with Father John. But she appealed to God. She sat up straight and proper in the front pew of the church and prayed: "Watch me, God. You've made a mistake here. I'm a good girl."

Twice a week, Bonnie trudged over to the rectory to take her turn at helping out Father John. As dusk fell, she alleges, her chores always ended the same way: on Father John's lap or in his bed. When her breasts developed, the priest found something new to explore. Bonnie doesn't remember how old she was when Father John began to expose himself to her. But she recalls exactly when he first asked her to rub up and down on his penis. She had just turned twelve.

Two years later, alarmed at the menstrual blood staining her panties, Bonnie turned to her twelve-year-old sister in the bed they shared.

"Father John is hurting me," she confessed to Lois.

"Me too," Lois responded.

The two sisters went to their mother, the president of the Ladies' Altar Society, who had been decorated by the bishop for service to the church. She exploded in fury, screaming, "All I'm raising is a bunch of whores." She never asked for the details. She never confronted the priest. She was terrified that her daughters would tell her husband, a notorious drunk with a rotten temper. If he found out, he might hurt Father John. Martha Butaud simply repeated what she had taught her daughters all their lives: Women are born to suffer. She continued to send her children to Father John and his church.

When lawyer Fontana heard this story years later, he felt a pang of fear. He immediately pulled his daughter Renee out of Engber's art class and vowed to see Father John removed from the priesthood. And when he met with Bonnie, he asked a question she had never considered: "What about your other sisters?"

Bonnie's answer was instantaneous: "No way, just Lois and me."

But just to be sure, she rushed home and called the baby of the family, Chantelle. "I have a simple question for you," she said. "Just answer yes or no. Did Father John touch you?"

"Yes," Chantelle replied.

"At what age?"

"It began when I was three."

Bonnie asked her sister Shirleen next. The answer was the same. Shirleen still won't say exactly what Father John did to her. All she says is that they played a little game in which she was Pinocchio and he was Gepetto, carving her body.

Bonnie asked her sister Marguerite last because she didn't want to upset her pregnancy. But she was frantic: Marguerite planned to name her baby after Father John. The day after the newborn boy's birth, Bonnie rushed to the hospital. "Did he touch you too?" Bonnie asked. Marguerite said yes. And she said that she, like her sisters, had thought she was the only one. She named her son Jeremy.

Bonnie has been trying to heal the scars of her abuse for most of her life. She left home at the age of eighteen, marrying the first man who would get her away from the marshes—and Father John. She had one, simple goal: "I said to God, 'I'm going to prove to you that I'm good for something other than being a whore.' Engbers never used the word *whore* for me. But when I grew up, I knew what I'd been. I've spent twenty-five years trying to prove to God that I'm better than that."

JENNIFER KRASKOUSKAS KNOWS SHE'S NOT A WHORE, BUT SHE'S still not sure what she is. Raised a Catholic and taught that "you're either a virgin until you're married or you're a whore," she was caught in limbo before she was old enough to don her first bra.

Now nineteen, she can't console herself that she was abused in the name of God or God's plans. Unlike many other victims, she can't tell herself that she had no choice because her abuser threatened her, or her family, with physical harm. And unlike many other victims, she was never told the devil would get her if she didn't cooperate.

Father Robert Kelley used his collar to gain entrée to her family. But he didn't seduce her with religion or threats. He did it with an E.T. doll.

In 1983, Father Kelley was the new priest in Gardner, Massachusetts, a dynamic man who could pull contributions out of a hat. He brought dozens of helium-filled balloons to his parish welcome party. When he took parish kids to Chinese restaurants, he'd break into gibberish, pretending to speak Chinese. When he took them to Wendy's, he'd put salt in the sugar bowl and fill the suggestion box with notes like "Your food gives me gas." He raced around town in a light blue Datsun sports car.

He might have been forty years old but he fit right in with nine-year-old Jennifer. He'd drive ninety minutes to show up in Providence, Rhode Island, at her swim meets and race to Cape Cod after Sunday Mass to spend the day with her family.

He was a pain in the parental neck, always appearing at the Kraskouskas house just in time for dinner, inviting himself to birthday parties and somehow winding up with the family on their vacations. Once he managed to tag along on a trip to Prince Edward Island, insisting he was going on to New Brunswick to see friends. He never left the Kraskouskases' rented cabin. Out of respect, Jennifer's parents ceded him their bed and slept on the fold-out couch.

They never complained, of course. "We were brought up to respect priests, so we considered it an honor to have a priest in the house," Jackie Kraskouskas says. In fact, her husband, Tony, adds: "We wondered if we were holy enough to be with this person."

Jennifer was too young to be worried about holiness. Her major concern was stuffed animals. She never had as many as she wanted. Father Kelley took care of that. He gave her a stuffed dragon and a stuffed monkey, a dark brown teddy bear and a cinnamon-colored one. After every swim meet there was another furry soul to add to the menagerie that lived on Jennifer's bed.

And then there was E.T. He was Jennifer's favorite, her special friend who protected her from the world. She'd carry him everywhere and speak through him in her special E.T. voice. Then, one day, he was kidnapped. Father Kelley ran to the rescue, posting reward signs around Jennifer's school. But when E.T. was rescued—from a bathtub in a neighboring house—his prognosis was poor. Her dad tried to save the water-logged alien with the blue marble eyes by placing him on the glowing hearth. He wound up cremated instead.

Father Kelley rushed out for a replacement. Gardner's toy

stores were bare. He finally drove all the way up to Maine to spare young Jennie disappointment. Father Kelley would strap E.T. to a kite and parachute him off the roof of the house. He'd bring over raisins—which he called "marinated deer droppings" —and feed them to the extraterrestrial. Jennifer and the priest played at E.T., talking their own secret alien language. "It was like a symbol, maybe of the secret we were keeping," Jennifer says now.

Late at night, when Jennifer went off to bed, Father Kelley would sneak into her room and abuse her. "First he began touching me where little girls didn't need to be touched," Jennifer says. "He would claim he did this because I was his favorite. After a short while, he had me touch him, as he touched me." The priest said all the right things. "Sex is okay," he told the girl. "This is the way God would have it."

Jennifer didn't believe him. Even he didn't seem convinced. "He'd look at me and say, 'Your eyes, you can see right through me, and you know the truth,' " Jennifer says. She did. She knew God hadn't chosen her. "I knew I'd be in trouble eventually with God," she says.

Jennifer didn't really know how to resist. Kelley was her friend, her companion. Like many molesters, he was a trusted and caring figure in her life. Like many victims, she was too young— and too close to him emotionally—to put limits on their relationship. Some nights she would try by leaving the light on when she went to sleep, thinking he "wouldn't do it" to her in the glare. But he'd enter her room and turn it off with soft words: "If you don't see me, it'll be easier." Other nights she'd snuggle under her covers and carefully arrange her stuffed animals all around her, literally burying herself in fake fur. But Father Kelley would pluck them off, promising to replace each one carefully when he was done.

Sometimes, she didn't resist at all. "What he did hurt at times, but it also felt good too," she says now, with a mixture of shame and befuddlement common to victims of this type of abuse. Father Kelley approached her tenderly, lovingly, not the way she imagined a molester would touch a victim. "It felt good. It was confusing."

While her friends gossiped about which boy in school was French-kissing which girl and while her dad raised funds for the parish school, Jennifer worried that she might be pregnant with a priest's child. She had not yet begun to menstruate. She was too young to understand the relevance.

At moments, Jennifer thrived on the attention Father Kelley showered on her. "I liked the feeling of being the favorite," she admits. But at others, Father Kelley was a simple pest. "I felt there was nowhere I could go to escape this man," she says. "No matter where I went, my parents would tell him where I was."

Tony and Jackie Kraskouskas never wondered why Father Kelley was always looking for Jennifer. When he walked upstairs in their house late in the evening, they figured he was sneaking cigarettes—theirs was a nonsmoking household. They knew him as nothing other than a moral man, notorious for tirades against the local convenience store for carrying pornography. So they never objected when he took Jennifer and her sister to art shows or on nature walks.

Although Father Kelley later pleaded guilty to the abuse and was sent to prison, Jennifer is still tormented by the tenderness of what happened between her and the priest. Like many young victims who were seduced rather than forcibly violated, she still has some trouble thinking of herself as the victim of a sexual assault. "That's not how he approached me," she says. "He was tender, not harsh."

FATHER TERRENCE PINKOWSKI WAS NEITHER TENDER NOR HARSH with fourteen-year-old Ed Morris. He was firm with his charge, like a good spiritual director.

Like many young Catholics, Morris was taught to turn to priests in moments of profound confusion and trouble, moments of rawness, moments of vulnerability. So when his brother was killed by a drunk driver in July 1976, it was natural for Morris to seek out a priest. Before the tragedy, Morris was a good—but hardly perfect—Catholic boy. He'd get up early every morning, grab his bike and pedal over to Mass. "I always wanted to be good," he says. "I always wanted to be devout." But after his

brother's death, he approached the Church and religion with a
new fervor. He needed protection. He needed consolation. He
looked for both in the company of Father Terrence.

Soon, Father Terrence was driving the boy home from prayer
group meetings and working his way into Ed's large Irish clan in
Northeast Philadelphia. He baptized Ed's younger brothers and
sisters. He ate dinner at their house five nights a week. He joined
them on family vacations. He became such an integral part of
their lives that years later, when Ed tried to purge him from the
family photo album, he found that he couldn't without erasing
the record of dozens of family events.

Ed's abuse began as a condition of absolution. The youth confessed to impure thoughts and to the sin of pride. Father Terrence
directed him to learn self-control. The lesson was simple, Ed alleges: the priest would masturbate Morris, or lie on top of him
rubbing their groins together, but would stop just shy of Ed's
ejaculation. "Desensitization," Father Terrence called this penance. "No matter how you go to the altar, as a priest or to marry,
this will help you," Ed remembers Father Terrence telling him.
"You are special. You are pleasing to God. But you have a cor-
ruptible side you must learn to control."

Ed threw himself into his salvation. He attended charismatic
prayer meetings and conventions. He wrote out a contract with
Father Terrence in which he pledged he would die rather than
commit a mortal sin. He "confessed" and did "penance" with
Father Terrence every single day. "I was going for heroic sanctity," he now says.

Ed pursued heroic sanctity for five years: in the chapel at Archbishop Ryan High School and the cell of the friary where Father
Terrence lived, in the confessional and in cars, at a rented bun-
galow in Ocean City, New Jersey, and even at the Green Bay,
Wisconsin, headquarters of Father Terrence's Franciscan province. "By the time I was nineteen, I knew every good parking spot
in the city—but was still a virgin," he says.

Like other abusers who use their authority to manipulate
children—or even adults—for their own desires, Father Terrence
maintained careful control over his young charge. If Ed went out
on a date, Father Terrence followed. If he started spending too

much time with a girl, the priest grew hysterical, insisting that he confess, and would then teach him all over again about self-control. "He would straddle me, lay on top of me and rub against me, tickling me at the same time," he says. "When I said I couldn't take it anymore, he'd say it was just my Irish pride and keep going."

One night while they were parked in the priest's car in the dark lot behind the Sisters of the Blessed Sacrament Convent, six police cars pulled up with flashing red lights. One officer plucked Father Terrence out of the car while Morris struggled to put his pants back on.

"Are you okay, son?" the officer asked Ed.

"Sure," he responded. "This is just a quiet place we come to for him to hear my confession."

The officer looked skeptical, but drove away.

Ed's father, a Philadelphia police officer, was equally trusting. Father Terrence would stay at their house until 11 P.M., then sit in his car with Ed for another three hours.

Ed finally stopped seeing the priest when he was seventeen. By then, Father Terrence's authority had been eroded by Ed's growing up. By then, Ed was old enough to understand that what they had been doing together had ruined his chance for heroic sanctity. But he went on a quest for the soul that he felt Father Terrence stole. He tried the seminary, but was too filled with bitterness to feel any comfort in the company of priests. He tried prayer, but was too estranged from his faith to feel any peace.

"I feel like I had an illicit affair with the devil," he says, "and can no longer be intimate with God."

Chapter 5

FALSE IDOLS

FATHER NED BEGAN TIMIDLY, SLYLY GRAB-bing a twelve-year-old boy's crotch during a play wrestling match, pretending to bump up accidentally against a thirteen-year-old altar boy's rear end as they cleaned up after Mass. He hoped the boys didn't realize his touches were intentional, and tried to push any concern over the incidents out of his mind. Then, at night, he would get into bed and relive the brief encounters, masturbating to the memories before he drifted off to sleep.

He soon grew bolder. And as he befriended more families during his first year as a priest, he drew ever closer to children. The opportunities expanded. A couple who liked him especially well and frequently invited him to dinner had a boy who was the perfect age for Father Ned—thirteen years old. He wrestled with the boy; he brushed against him. And once, at bedtime, he went upstairs to tuck him in, rubbing the boy's belly and then moving his hand several inches, until it wriggled between the boy's legs.

His fantasies became more elaborate, more intense. In his favorite one, he imagined that he stumbled upon a pair or trio of boys self-consciously fumbling with each other's genitals, experimenting with sex. "No," he told them. "You're doing it all wrong." He made them his pupils. He taught one how to perform oral sex on him. He instructed another to bend over so he could sodomize him.

One of Father Ned's altar boys was a thirteen-year-old whose father drank too much and constantly picked on him. The boy was needy. Father Ned talked to him, took him biking and let him hang around the rectory. The boy came to love him and, as Father Ned remembers it, even initiated many of their sexual encounters. They had sex in the rectory and even at the boy's home, where Father Ned once climbed on top of him and rubbed against his leg as the boy lay on a cot on the family's porch. Mom and Dad were inside the house.

Many years later, Father Ned began reading the morning newspaper in a different way. As soon as he got it, he turned to the obituaries, searching for the boy's name and praying that he wouldn't see it. He had just heard that the boy, now a young man, had AIDS. And he was wracked with guilt and with questions: Was it because the boy turned promiscuous, and was that promiscuity one of the scars of the abuse? Is it my fault? How will I ever be able to make up for what I've done?

By this point Father Ned had been in jail, serving six months for his crimes. He had spent hundreds of hours in therapy, sorting through his actions and motivations and trying to wring some sense out of it all. He had apologized to the families of his victims, forced to do so only by his own conscience. And he had wept, less for himself and the desires that had gripped him like a vise than for the boys and the families whose pain he could never erase.

Now, Father Ned does everything he can to atone for what he did. Prison was harsh, but it was not enough. He is not sure anything will ever be enough. He talks openly to bishops and other priests about the psychology of abusers, calling on his own experience. He addresses small gatherings of church leaders and mental health professionals, even though he has sacrificed most of his privacy among fellow clergy in his local diocese by doing so. His only condition for sharing his story in this book was that his real name and certain dates and biographical details be omitted. But he is willing to recount everything he did, no matter how embarrassing it feels or how awful it sounds, because it may help others to understand abusers and to combat abuse.

He says they need to understand that a man can be openly devoted to good, can be essentially caring—can even be a priest —and still not be able to beat back the compulsions that lead him to sexually abuse children. "I was the charming priest," he says. "I was the hero. I looked great on the outside, but I was a very sick man. I had a psychic disease, and it can be so powerfully compelling that it overrides rational thought, it overrides moral resolve. I violated my own code. I violated everything I stand for and everything I could preach about. I shit on my own parade."

When he was publicly exposed and forced to confront his actions and their consequences more honestly and painfully than ever before, Father Ned almost collapsed from shame. "Nobody could have hated me as much as I hated myself. When they sentenced me, if they had said they were going to put me out on a red ant hill, I would have said, 'Okay. Do it. Until they eat me alive.' "

IT'S EASY FOR MOST PEOPLE TO UNDERSTAND THE VULNERABILITY of children who are victimized by priests, and how children can be seduced and silenced by men of immense moral authority. But it's impossible for most people to understand how those men can stand tall in their pulpits as representatives of God and cause such damage and pain. Sure, there are child sexual abusers in every corner of society, among every profession. But priests? How can they wear the collar, yet commit the crime? How can they bless the symbolic body of Christ, then violate the body and spirit of a boy or girl?

They can because their sexual disorders exert a power far

greater than any sense of right and wrong. Because their needs eclipse their consciences. Because their denial runs deeper than their shame. And in the case of many of these abusers, the priesthood is part of the problem. Many are hardly aware of their sexuality and the stresses those needs place on them. Their loneliness and estrangement from intimacy set them up for immature and destructive sexual behavior.

Father Martin, who consented to an interview for this book on the condition that his real name not be used, was convinced he didn't have any sexual feelings at all. The idea of sex embarrassed him, as did any word or image that reminded him of it. At Mass, when he paid homage to the Virgin Mary in a common and beloved prayer, he blushed and cringed at reciting, "Blessed is the fruit of thy womb, Jesus." "The word *womb* upset me," he says. "I wondered how you could reconcile putting that word in prayer."

He has not figured out the precise origin of that embarrassment but traces it to his childhood in Ireland, where he grew up in a large, conservative, devout middle-class family. His two most vivid memories of any sexual awareness or arousal as a child are laced with fear. He remembers going to the doctor at the age of six because he was still wetting his bed. When the doctor held his penis and pushed back the foreskin, he was seized by shame. Then, one summer when he was fifteen, he got an erection while listening to friends talk about sex. His mother saw the bulge in his shorts and, not recognizing what it was, grabbed it as she said, "What's that you have in your pocket?" When she realized her mistake, she hurried away without saying a word. "I wished the ground would open up and swallow me," Father Martin recalls.

He doesn't remember having any sexual thoughts when he was an older teenager. So when he went on a Catholic spiritual retreat just before his high school graduation and felt moved by a Jesuit's pep talk about the priesthood, Father Martin didn't give a moment's thought to whether he could abide a celibate life. That was already his reality. It seemed to be his fate. He entered the seminary the following year.

The priests there warned young seminarians about the temptations of the flesh. He listened and nodded. The young men rarely discussed sex, but when they did, their longings confused him. A friend once said: "It must be comforting to have a wife to hold and love." "Comforting?" Father Martin thought. "Sex is just about humping."

After his ordination, he was assigned to a parish in the United States. The priesthood seemed to suit him as well as anything else had—he didn't really feel passionate about anything. He did his job, kept to himself. After a few years, he put in for an assignment in South America, just for a change of scenery.

He arrived there in the late 1960s and the first seven years passed uneventfully, until he found himself in a parish that operated a day-care center with more than a dozen young children, all under age ten. The women who ran it told him many of the children didn't have fathers at home and that it would be nice if he stopped by. Whenever he did, the kids rushed to him, pulling at his arm, climbing into his lap. He loved the attention and warmth. He wasn't any good at making adult friends and felt so physically self-conscious that handshakes made him nervous. With the children, he felt uninhibited. He began stopping by to see them every day.

He liked one eight-year-old boy especially and held him tight in his lap. One day, as they hugged, Father Martin took the boy's hand and guided it to his penis. The boy seemed neither uncomfortable nor upset. So Father Martin did it again on other days. He also put his own hand down the boy's pants. Somehow, he thought of the touching as affectionate, not sexual. He didn't consider that what he was doing might be wrong.

Father Martin had always guarded himself around women because he knew that priests sometimes were tempted by them. He also knew that some priests were tempted by other men. But the possibility that a child's touch could be physically arousing had never occurred to him. And he was so utterly alienated from any sense of sexuality in himself that as he patted and stroked and hugged the children, he couldn't see where it was leading. "It didn't dawn on me," he says. "It just didn't connect. I crossed the line without being aware of it. It went from being affectionate to being sexual, and I didn't see it."

Soon he did, because he found himself craving and initiating these encounters with children. He had unleashed something inside himself that he couldn't control. He fondled nine-year-old boys. Ten-year-old boys. Eleven-year-old boys. Over the course of a decade, he fondled about fifty boys in all, spanning the ages from seven to seventeen. He even had oral sex with a few of them and anal sex with one. He tried to fondle girls, but they seemed less receptive. Father Martin's psychiatrist believes girls' bodies also seemed more foreign to the shy and sexually naive priest and that touching a girl somehow seemed more overtly and embarrassingly sexual to him than touching a boy.

Sometimes Father Martin prayed for help and resolved that he would stop. But he never succeeded. More often, he just shoved all thoughts of what he was doing from his mind. It was easy, because the man who thrilled to these sexual encounters seemed like a total stranger, an uninvited visitor to the rest of Father Martin's life. During the weeks and often months that passed between encounters, Father Martin forgot that man—who could always sneak up on him because Father Martin wasn't looking.

Then, in the 1980s, a boy told Father Martin's supervising priest what had been going on. When the supervisor confronted Father Martin, he confessed. The supervisor's mouth fell open. "I'm shocked," he said in a tone of utter horror. And at that moment, it hit Father Martin as it had never hit him before: "What I've done is shocking."

Father Martin was sent back to his diocese in the United States and never faced prosecution for his crimes. He has been in therapy for years. His bishop did not ask him to leave the priesthood but told him he could never again do parish work and gave him an assignment as a hospital chaplain. A few of the people with whom he works have been instructed to monitor his behavior, and he watches himself. He still hasn't learned to explore his sexual feelings or needs, and worries that they could catch him unaware again. He still feels acutely embarrassed by sex. He says the only truly candid discussions he has had about it have been during therapy and during interviews for this book. "What I'm going to say right now," he says, "I've never said to another human being. 'I feel horny.' I'm not saying I feel that way now. I don't. I'm saying I've never said those words to another person. I never felt they could be said—that they could ever be said and discussed."

While Father Martin's level of repression is extraordinary, it is not unique among priests. Therapists who have treated priest sexual abusers say that many entered the Catholic clergy with no sexual experience and little sex education. They believed their pledge of celibacy meant an end to any sexual need.

Dr. James Pedigo, a Philadelphia psychiatrist, says one priest was so convinced of this that he never interpreted anything in his behavior as sexual. About twice a month, when the priest went to urinate, he noticed that a different kind of fluid emerged. He didn't connect it to sex. "He had a special term for it, kind of like a bowel movement," Pedigo says. "He didn't know in advance that this was going to happen. He is so unaware, consciously, of what goes on inside him sexually. He just knew this process was different from urination—it came out in spurts. He didn't notice until I asked if he had an erection."

According to Pedigo, the priest's bishop received so many complaints about his behavior with young boys that he moved the priest from one parish to another four times. With each accusation, the priest offered a genuine rebuttal. When he was accused of masturbating his nephew as the adolescent boy showered, he answered that he had reason to believe the boy was being sexually abused by someone else and was checking his testicles for damage. When he was accused of shepherding three adolescent boys into the rectory and making them drop their pants, he answered that he had reason to believe the boys were injecting heroin and wanted to check their penises for hidden track marks.

While some priest abusers suffer a destructive sexual repression, others harbor a profound sexual immaturity that is never challenged in the celibate priesthood, which basically sends the message: Stop developing right where you are. If you're not very far, that message is dangerous, because you're still at a point of intense sexual curiosity and poor sexual self-control.

That was certainly the case with Father Mark Lehman, a Phoenix, Arizona, priest who pleaded guilty to the fondling of three girls in his wealthy parish and was sentenced in 1992 to ten years in prison. He was just thirty years old at the time.

When Father Mark arrived at St. Thomas the Apostle Church

at the age of twenty-six, he cut a dashing figure. He was so boyishly handsome, in fact, that prosecutors saw it as a potential
obstacle to winning a jury trial against him. Younger women in
the jury would want to date him, they feared. Older women
would want to claim him as a son and feed him dinner. As it was,
secretaries from the prosecutors' office sometimes showed up in
the courtroom during his trial because they thought he had such
a cute, trim body. Who was going to believe that such a man
would turn to little girls for sex?

Some parents at the parish, though, began to wonder about
Father Mark soon after he arrived. With adults, he kept his dis-
tance, coming across as quiet and restrained. Around children, his
reserve vanished. He frolicked with them on the playground of
the parish school, tickling them and picking them up under the
arms to swing them. At school dances, he took to the floor with
the twelve- and thirteen-year-old girls. They felt so comfortable
with him that one of them once handed him a condom as a joke.
Father Mark took it into the bathroom, then came back out a
few seconds later and said: "It's not long enough."

Father Mark was a little boy, and he had a little boy's self-
consciousness about sex. In a risk assessment done by psychologists during his criminal proceedings, he admitted to being so shy
about his level of sexual experience—he had never had
intercourse—that he sometimes made up lies about it. He worried
that other people would think he was abnormal. He worried that
other adults wouldn't like him. He worried that his penis was too
small.

So even though he felt attracted to adult women as well as to
young girls, the girls became the objects of his abrupt, furtive
sexual advances. He ran into a sleeping girl's bedroom, lifted her
bedcovers, touched her bare bottom and bolted. Under the guise
of tickling, he felt girls' bottoms and their breasts. He also had
fetishes. Once, he sifted through the clothing at a church rummage
sale, found a pair of panties which he used as a prop to get excited, masturbated, and then returned them to the pile.

Father Mark's psychological assessment suggested he had
never developed a healthy, adult attitude toward sex—a problem
exacerbated by his decision to become a priest. "Obviously, this

young man's current problems may well have been avoided had there been more discreet education and training experiences during his seminary years," his evaluators wrote. "He has very little comprehension or appreciation of the process of psychosexual development in the junior high and teenage periods."

Another pitfall of the celibate priesthood that may render priests especially vulnerable to child sexual abuse is the loneliness it can create. Living by themselves, forbidden to form romantic partnerships, priests miss out on much of the intimacy that other men experience. A sense of isolation may swell over the years until it overwhelms some priests and blinds their judgment. They reach out to the most available and gullible people around them, and sometimes those people are children.

Father Charles, which is not his real name, felt alienated from the men and women in his parish. They had families, they had busy lives, and when they did take time to talk with him, they had requests and demands. He was always doing for others, while nobody seemed to be doing for him. The only parishioners who had the freedom and time simply to hang around the parish and chat were children.

One day, a fifteen-year-old boy to whom Father Charles had paid special attention came up to him, hugged him and said: "Father, I really love you." The priest felt a rush of warmth unlike anything he had ever felt before. "Nobody had ever put their arms around me like that and told me they loved me," he says, adding that his parents had been formal, distant. "That was an awesome experience in my life. And I had to be thirty years old at the time. Can you believe that?"

Father Charles does not believe the experience triggered a previously nonexistent attraction to boys. He suspects the attraction was always within him and suddenly found voice and expression because there was no other intimacy in his life. "I sought that feeling out after that. I began to look for and depend on affection from younger persons. I don't know exactly when the sex came in, but it did."

He began fondling and performing oral sex on some of the fourteen- and fifteen-year-old boys he befriended. He knew it was wrong, but was so transfixed by need that he couldn't stop himself. At the same time, he was consumed by rage over the demands and sacrifices of living as a priest. "There had been so many needs that had been unmet and so many disappointments and so many pains and so many rejections that it didn't matter," he says. "After twenty years of parish life, I guess I felt that nobody gave a damn about me."

Eventually, he was caught and served several years in prison. His bishop came to visit him there and gave him a choice: Resign the priesthood and I'll pay you a stipend for the next two years, or fight me as I force you out and I won't make it pleasant. Father Charles left. He is now attending graduate school in a new state, and, at the age of fifty-seven, trying to forge a new life. He cannot see through his own pain to the damage he inflicted on others. He rails at the Catholic Church for not picking him up when he was down. He blames the priesthood for his fall. He says his psychiatrist once told him: "I feel very sad for you. You're a man who has broken your neck for the Church."

Other priest abusers divine ways to rationalize that what they are doing when they touch children is not harmful, not sinful. Child sexual abusers are adept at playing such mind games with themselves, and clergy members are no different. In fact, priest abusers often invoke religious ideals and symbols to convince themselves that what they are doing is spiritual, holy. Some of them insist on developing a definition of celibacy much different from anything the Church intended, saying that only sex with a woman violates their promise, or that only sex with another adult does. They press their religion into the service of their pathology.

Father Robert Kirsch had a whole theology worked out for what was happening between him and Susan Sandoval, a New Mexico girl who alleged in a lawsuit that the priest sexually abused her from the time she was fourteen years old to the time she was eighteen. Susan says they had sexual intercourse. Father Bob says they had something else entirely.

"I may have had a reserved embrace," he admitted in a deposition in 1992, more than fifteen years after the alleged abuse ended. Father Bob then went on to explain what he meant. Sexual intercourse, he said, doesn't occur unless a man clutches a woman in passion and ejaculates into her. Yes, he had lain atop Susan.

Yes, he had put his penis into her vagina. But there was "no passion, no kissing, no nothing," he said. And he had not ejaculated.

"I don't think that is sexual intercourse," Father Bob said. "Reserved embrace, yes, that's what we call it. . . . This is a very calm embrace. It's not a real sex act, as you would think of one." It's also not a violation of celibacy, he said, because celibacy simply means not marrying. And while the Catholic Church condemns sex outside marriage as sinful, Father Bob didn't see any sin here. "Sex would be . . . reserved embrace would be something other than that," he said. "I wouldn't consider it a sin, no. And I have to decide that, not you, because the definition is mine."

Sister Georgene Stuppy similarly wrapped her allegedly abusive behavior in religious justifications. Although Sister Georgene, who denies any wrongdoing, seems to be the only Catholic nun in the United States ever legally accused of molesting a child, some experts believe sexual abuse by nuns may be underreported—as is sexual abuse by women in secular society—and unrecognized even by those children who are its victims. In fact, Kenneth Lanning, the FBI's expert on child sexual abuse, who attended Catholic schools as a child, wonders if some nuns' notorious penchant for physical discipline may betray a degree of sexual sadism. "When somebody takes a ruler and bends you over the desk and whacks you with the ruler, is it discipline?" Lanning asks. "Is it physical abuse? Or is it sexual abuse? My opinion is it could be any of the three."

Sister Georgene's actions came to light in a 1990 civil suit filed by a Minnesota woman who says that in the late 1970s, when she was in the eighth grade, Sister Georgene began to fondle and suck her breasts regularly. It went on for several years.

Sister Georgene, in a 1991 deposition, admitted the fondling. She admitted the sucking. But she professed total and seemingly genuine confusion as to why the lawyers questioning her insisted on describing these gestures as sexual. "It really hurts when you say sexual contact," Sister Georgene said, "but I know that's what we have to say." The nun explained that she and the girl were simply spiritual companions on a "shared journey." Through each other, the two were discovering God's divine love.

Sister Georgene's letters to the girl—gushing proclamations of caring punctuated with heart-shaped drawings—alternately suggested that the girl was a direct gift and communication from God, or that the girl was the mother of God, or that the girl was the personification of Jesus Christ. In one missive, the nun described a dream in which she experienced God through the girl: "You took my hand gently, turned it over, extended my arm so I was reaching out to touch His face and then somehow His face was your face. I can right now feel in my fingers the warmth and softness of your face. At first your face is dry and then I feel literally running through my fingers oceans and oceans of tears."

The nun wrote that the girl was her "dearest wounded healer" and explained that the two of them, both besieged by pain in the world, were coming to know the suffering of Jesus Christ. Spiritual appeals and religious allusions crowded nearly every page of Sister Georgene's voluminous correspondence to the girl. Even when the nun left God out of it, her sentiments toward the girl remained worshipful. After the girl left a class that Sister Georgene taught, the nun wrote: "When I moved your desk to the side, I found myself bowing and kissing it."

Some abusers' pathology is so profound that there is just no way for them to construct a theological or intellectual defense of their behavior, so they sink into a total denial of their problem, which only allows it to gather steam and force. That certainly seems to have been the case with Father James Porter, the most destructive child sexual abuser unveiled in the Catholic Church so far.

The stories told by his victims—at least 125 boys and girls in at least four states—portray an abuser with insatiable appetites and a relentless compulsion. Nothing stopped him. Not the many times he was allegedly reported to his superiors and transferred to a new parish or new state. Not the many times he received psychiatric treatment. Not even thirteen months of electroshock therapy. And nothing daunted him. He allegedly would grope a child whose parents sat unknowing in a nearby room. He allegedly would rub against a child while another priest knocked on the door to ask about the cries coming from the room.

But when he wasn't chasing or straddling children, he maintained a tranquil facade. Some acquaintances fondly recall Father Porter leading neighborhood children in orderly games of stickball. Others remember him as witty, spirited and kind. He seemed unburdened by his crimes, unaware of the pain he was causing, sunny in his outlook even when confronting his actions.

"I am feeling much better and doing very well, positively," he wrote his bishop in 1964 after he was reported for molesting children and ordered to take a leave. "There have been many temptations as you can imagine, but thank God, with His grace, I have handled them well." The next day, Father Porter molested two more children, according to criminal charges filed in early 1992.

When Frank Fitzpatrick, the Rhode Island private detective who says he was abused by Father Porter in the 1960s, called him in Minnesota in the spring of 1991, the now ex-priest seemed to be in an even better mood. "That's all been taken care of years ago," he said to Fitzpatrick about his sexual problems, adding that once he left the priesthood, got married and started a family, he stopped molesting children. "It's funny how things worked out. . . . It's been marvelous, how I've had no difficulty whatsoever. . . . Right now, it is absolutely marvelous for me and the family." A year later, he was convicted in Minnesota of molesting a teenage girl who baby-sat with his children in 1987.

Father Porter, however, must be seen as an anomaly. Most child sexual abusers claim fewer victims. Most approach them affectionately, and many feel genuine caring for these children, who they don't really intend to hurt. Many also feel deep, even crippling remorse.

When Father Paul Henry Leech was reported in 1984 for molesting a teenage boy in a Rhode Island parish, he suddenly came to terms with what he had done and at least one of the forces that had driven him to it: he had been molested himself as a teenage boy. Filled with guilt, he took it upon himself to visit the parents of his victims so they would know their sons had been abused and might need help. One of those parents, a woman whom he had counseled after her husband's sudden death, told police interviewers that in confessing his actions to her, Father

Paul also begged to know if he had been of any help to her, if he had done any good deeds to balance the bad. He seemed desperate to believe that he had.

At least three priests accused of child sexual abuse have committed suicide. One, a Benedictine monk who was about to go on trial for molesting a twelve-year-old altar boy, went out for his regular morning stroll at St. Bernard Abbey in Cullman, Alabama, and shot himself in the head. He left this handwritten note near his body: "My friends, the presumed guilty are an embarrassment, the dead soon forgotten. So I take the liberty of being a dead memory rather than a living symbol and disgrace to the Church, to my brothers. I suffer from no lack of faith. For indeed, I have faith that He will have mercy on me for being presumptuous that now is the time He is calling me home."

Monsignor William Reinecke did not leave a note. In fact, no one can be sure why he took his life. But two days before, on August 9, 1992, a man from his past came to see him. Joseph McDonald, executive director of the Mental Health Association of Northern Virginia, says he told Reinecke that he remembered being abused by the priest when he was an altar boy more than twenty years earlier. He says he also told Reinecke he didn't think the priest—who had become chancellor of the diocese of Arlington, Virginia—should work with children. Reinecke apologized and asked if they could talk again when he got back from a retreat scheduled to begin the next day. McDonald handed Reinecke his business card.

Reinecke never came back from the retreat. His body was found on August 11 in the fields of Berryville, Virginia, near the Holy Cross Monastery. He had shot himself in the head. Since his death, another man has come forward publicly to charge that Reinecke also molested him when he was a boy. Other men with similar stories have talked privately with victim support groups and law enforcement authorities.

Father Ned, the priest who reads the obituaries every day, thought about killing himself. When he was exposed to Church authorities as a child molester, he figured his priesthood was finished, his life over. And he felt suffocated by pain and guilt. Over and over he asked himself: Why? Why hadn't he been stronger? Why hadn't God saved him and his victims? Why had he always felt this burning desire for boys?

The desire had been with him since childhood. When he was thirteen years old, he played around sexually with other thirteen-year-olds. When he was sixteen, he still played around with thirteen-year-olds. By the time he was nineteen, he had stopped, but only because he realized that what he was doing was considered sinful and aberrant. He still had the desire. His most intense sexual fantasies revolved around young boys.

He was flooded with shame. He wonders now if that shame is part of what attracted him to the priesthood. "The two forces were so strong—the shame and self-hatred on one hand, and the enormous desire to be a priest on the other," he says. "There was this awful secret, but then there was this great goal. It seems like I felt so good when I was doing priestly things. It was like . . . this person is judged worthy."

During his graduate seminary years, he helped a parish priest with youth groups and activities. He took kids camping. He rough-housed with them during sports activities. The images he carried back to his dormitory room fueled the fantasies to which he masturbated. He consoled himself with the thought that at least he wasn't trying to make the fantasies real.

The day of his ordination was the most joyful in his life. Several dozen of his relatives and close friends attended, some of them flying as many as three hours to be there. They sat among hundreds of reverent spectators in the endless pews of the splendid cathedral, its walls encrusted with shimmering gold leaf. They gazed at him with what seemed a newfound admiration. For that brief moment in his life, he saw himself as one of the luckiest men alive. He felt blessed.

Just a few weeks into his first parish assignment, his pastor became seriously ill and left Father Ned alone. Church officials offered to send someone in to help, but said they felt confident he could handle the parish by himself. Father Ned gave it a shot, working ten-hour and twelve-hour and fourteen-hour days. Parishioners were wowed, and told him so. "It felt fabulous," he says. "It felt heroic."

But it put enormous stress on him, which is why, he believes, his desires caught him so off guard. Horsing around with a parish youngster, he slipped his hand onto the boy's groin. Praising an altar boy for a Mass well done, he patted him on the rear. He found himself grateful for the loose, billowing robe he wore to say Mass. It hid the erection he sometimes got when tussling with altar boys in the sacristy after Mass.

The more he touched them, the harder it became to control his gestures. "It opened up a hunger," he says. "Now fantasy was not enough. It's like—how does a person go back to masturbation when he's had intercourse?"

No one seemed to notice his closeness with the boys. If they did, they didn't question it. Who would think such a thing about a strapping, ruggedly handsome six-foot priest whose star was rising quickly and brilliantly? "There was a halo around me that I think blinded everybody," he says. But Father Ned could see. And sometimes, when a parishioner came up to him to praise his work, he thought: If only you knew. If only you knew that I was putting my hands down your kids' pants and fantasizing about them when I masturbate.

It haunted him. Once, as he stood on the pulpit to say Mass, he looked down at the sweet face of an altar boy who was quietly praying and thought: Here's this beautiful, trusting little boy who's looking up to me because I preside over the sacraments in this religious ritual. I want him to look at me with respect and not be using him for my desires. I have to remember who he is, and what I am.

He would resolve to stop and pray to God for help. He would break his resolve. He would feel worthless and sink into depression. Then he would seek quick relief from his pain in his favorite drug: touching and fantasizing about boys. And the cycle would repeat itself, again and again.

Most of his touching was superficial and veiled as play. He fondled just two boys, and that too was furtive, in quick gestures. But there was one boy with whom he went further. They met frequently to talk about the boy's problems at home. They took walks together. They kissed. They masturbated each other. And they performed oral sex on each other.

After five years in the parish, Father Ned and the diocese decided he should continue his education. He was being groomed for future leadership in the Church. His parishioners got a keg of beer and a bunch of bratwurst and threw him a going-away cookout on the parish lawn. But then, just a few weeks before he was scheduled to leave, he was summoned to see the vicar general.

When he walked into his office, Father Ned saw that the chancellor for the diocese was there too. His stomach tightened. The vicar general handed Father Ned a letter that the boy with whom he had been most intensely involved had written the priest. The boy's parents had found it before it was sent. As Father Ned read the words, he struggled for breath. The boy wrote of how much he was going to miss Father Ned, and of the physical pleasure they had shared.

"Is it true?" the vicar general asked Father Ned.

Father Ned's mind raced. The boy was troubled and might not seem credible. Maybe Father Ned could get out of this somehow. Then he realized he didn't want to. He couldn't keep this secret any longer. It was tearing him apart.

"Yes," he said. "It's true." He wept.

He was charged with the crime, pleaded guilty, and served his jail time. His sentencing made local newspapers and TV. So when he got to the jail, the inmates were expecting him. "Father baby rapist!" they shouted at him. They made jokes about other inmates' kids who were in Catholic schools and whether those kids were safe. Father Ned skipped meals just to stay away from them. He read the Bible, dwelling on passages that spoke of God's forgiveness of sinners. Could God forgive him?

After his release, his diocese decided he could remain a priest, so long as he took an administrative post and stayed away from parish work. He could live in a rectory, but couldn't say Mass. So on Sundays, he would take a seat on the couch in his room, place his chalice and several communion wafers on the coffee table in front of him, and celebrate the Eucharist by himself. "This is the body of Christ," he intoned, holding up a wafer. There was no one to say, "Amen."

He went regularly to therapy, at first expecting to be told precisely how he could fix his problem. He discovered instead that he would never be cured, that he is a true pedophile. His desire would never leave him. It was like alcoholism, he learned: the disease didn't disappear, but could be controlled. He taught himself to look away from attractive adolescent boys he saw on the street and to bring friends from his support group with him whenever he had to go places where there were likely to be many young boys. He learned not to be ashamed of what he felt, but to take responsibility for what he did with it.

He tried to make amends. He wrote to the couples whose sons he had hurt to tell them he was sorry. He offered to let his victims confront him if it would help in their healing. In his letter to the couple who had been such good friends, he wrote: "I would come back from the ends of the earth if there is any way I could undo the damage I've done." The couple never wrote back, but he ran into the woman a few years later. "I'm sorry," he told her. With an expression of kindness, she answered: "I'm sorry, too, that we never felt we could talk to you."

Impressed by his remorse, Church officials found a place for him to celebrate the Eucharist with others again—at a local convent. The nuns there were having trouble finding priests to say their daily Mass and the sister in charge agreed to accept Father Ned. During his first service, Father Ned's heart hammered in his chest. He fumbled several lines in the liturgy, and his hands trembled as he held up the symbolic body of Christ, which suddenly felt fragile and breakable, like an egg. But he was filled with joy. "There was a deep level of my soul, my gut, that was saying, 'Yes! This is what's important!' "

Other than the nun in charge, none of the sisters at the convent had been told about Father Ned's past. After he had performed Mass several times, he gathered them together to tell his story. When he had finished, they all agreed that they still wanted him as their priest. One nun walked quietly up to him and whispered: "Father, there are all sorts of other stories in this room. Yours is not the only story of struggle and pain and a fall from grace."

Bit by bit, Father Ned put his life back together and began to respect himself again. He told almost everyone in his life—friends, work associates, the housekeeper at the rectory—about what he had done and about the desires that led him to it. He wanted to own up to it in every way possible. He didn't want to get in the habit of keeping secrets ever again.

His resolve and his reform impressed even those officials in his diocese who initially had been appalled by his actions and angry over the embarrassment and pain he had caused the Church. "What he did was horrible," says the vicar general of the diocese. "But that's not the whole of the man. He has not tried to run away from what he's done, or pretend that he did not do some serious harm to people. That comes from his gut. In his willingness to submit to all that happened to him, I see that God is working through him. I see God's grace in him."

After several years of therapy, Father Ned felt he knew enough about his sexual disorder to help others understand it. He gave his first speech to a group of psychiatrists and psychologists. He gave his second to a group of religious leaders, many of them Catholic, trying to educate themselves about clergy members who abuse.

He shared the podium with a man who had been sexually abused as a teenage boy. That man went first. When Father Ned got up to speak, he wasn't sure how he would be received. He felt as if he were wearing a scarlet letter on his chest. But he did his best to explain how his compulsions overwhelmed his conscience, how he never really meant to hurt. He gave voice to his remorse and pain.

His words so moved several Catholic Church leaders that they asked aloud if men like him had to be treated so harshly—locked behind bars and forever denied parish work. Yes, Father Ned told them. "Don't spare the perpetrator," he said, explaining that everything he lost and every price he paid was integral to his sense of justice replacing the injustices he'd created.

After Father Ned finished, the victim who had spoken before he did walked over and looked him in the eye. "We're much more alike than we are different," the man said as he wrapped Father Ned in an embrace. "We're two people who are wounded."

Chapter 6

THE SILENCING OF THE LAMBS

CHILDREN WHO ARE MOLESTED RARELY
run home to their mothers and blurt it
out. There are countless reasons why. They're
in shock. They're embarrassed. They're afraid
—of both the pain they'll cause their parents
and the wrath of their assailants, who may
have threatened them with punishment. And,
in many cases, therapists say, they're confused:
How come some of the touching felt so good?
Is it my fault that it happened?

Experts say children are most likely to talk
about what happened if the abuser is a
stranger, someone unconnected to their lives.
But if the abuser is a loved one—a parent, an
uncle, a priest—they seem to know instinctively that the cost of telling may be exorbitant: Will mommy start crying and scream at
me and daddy? Will my cousins still come over
to play? Will we still be able to go to church?
Will God still love me?

If the abuser is someone as honored and respected as a priest, kids have added reasons to remain silent. Father's word and example carry so much weight that children suddenly begin to question if what happened was really bad. Their shame is deeper, their fears more profound. "He's such a holy man; I must really be a whore," victims reason. "God will never forgive me; I'm damned forever." Sometimes they are intimidated by open threats. One priest in California made his eight-year-old victim a hostage to the terrorism of silence with the chilling warning: "Be quiet or the devil will get you."

Other victims seem to sense instinctively that no one will believe Father could do this, anyway. And there's no mortal more powerful than Father to tell. He's more powerful than mommy and daddy, more powerful than anyone but God. "Consider, if you will, the impact on a child who is sexually abused during the week, and on Sundays witnesses his parents bowing, kneeling, genuflecting, praying and receiving sacraments and graciously thanking the priest for his involvement in their lives," wrote five Lafayette, Louisiana, psychologists after interviewing fifteen children who were sexually abused by a priest. "Such events make him believe that such sexual activities have been sanctioned by his parents. The even more astonishing act of molesting the child while in the confessional, followed by granting of absolution of the child, would be expected to inculcate very, very strong feelings of guilt."

All of those forces kept Calvin Mire, a victim of that same Louisiana priest, silent. But what initially drew the nine-year-old boy to Father Gilbert Gauthe was something more simple. Father Gauthe was just about the coolest priest on the face of the earth in the eyes of his young parishioners. He drove a dirt bike through the marshes of coastal Louisiana, zoomed around in a black Camaro Z28 with a CB radio and shot ducks off the roof of his rectory.

In tiny hamlets like Esther and Louisa, where most of the priests had been doddering, serious old men, Father Gauthe was like a rock star. Calvin would stand at the marina pumping gas on Saturdays and watch the priest and the gang of boys who hung out in his cabin in the marshes drive up in a boat and throw dozens of ducks onto the docks. "I would have done anything to be with them," Calvin says. "It was every kid's dream. He had me so wound up to go there."

Calvin became extra-attentive when he served as Father Gauthe's altar boy on weekends. He kept his white robe clean and was careful to straighten the altar after Mass. The other kids told him that would not be enough for a ticket to Father Gauthe's paradise; he'd have to have a physical.

"No sweat," Calvin answered quickly. "I'll have my mom take me to the doctor."

"No way," they responded. "He has to give it to you."

One morning after 8 A.M. Mass, Calvin's big chance came. He'd snuffed out the candles and removed the Eucharist from the altar. Father Gauthe took him into the back room and told him he seemed trustworthy enough to join the gang at the camp. Then the priest led him into a confessional and performed a "physical," alternately reminding the boy to trust him and threatening to hurt his family if Calvin talked.

Calvin Mire did not rush home and confide to his mother that he'd been molested by the parish priest. He did not pick up the phone and dial 911. For years, he told no one about how Father Gauthe would feel up the altar boys under the guise of adjusting their cassocks and red tassels. He said nothing about the group sex Father Gauthe orchestrated as part of their initiation into the Knights of Columbus.

Calvin joined dozens of boys in the rural bayous of Cajun Louisiana for whom Father Gilbert Gauthe's sex lessons—"Messing around with girls is bad, messing around with boys is good"—became a secret they didn't dare discuss, even among themselves. "He literally brainwashed us, preaching and preaching and preaching to us all the time about what was right and what was wrong," Mire says. "I was so confused I didn't know what was right. I had my first experience with a girl when I was ten, and he came down on me, telling me I had to repent."

There were many other reasons Calvin didn't tell. Father Gauthe had threatened to hurt him or his family if he did. And in the macho world of rural Louisiana, a boy just couldn't go around admitting that he let some guy have sex with him, even if he was ten and the other guy was in his thirties, even if he was an altar boy and the other guy was a priest. It simply wasn't the manly thing to do. That's precisely what Calvin's older brother said when the secret finally came out. "If it had been me, I would have kicked him in the ass."

But above all, Calvin was silenced by the simple fact that there was no one he could turn to. After all, as a priest, Father Gauthe was the ultimate human authority figure in Calvin's hierarchy. "You've got God," he explains. "You've got priests. Then you've got your parents. Then yourself. I couldn't turn to my mother because Father Gauthe was above her."

Calvin probably would never have told anyone if an Abbeville lawyer hadn't appeared on his parents' doorstep one afternoon just as the first young men were coming forward with their tales of Father Gauthe's lurid exploits. Using old altar boy rosters, attorneys and their investigators were looking for other victims.

"I think your son's been molested," lawyer Anthony Fontana said to Mrs. Mire. She'd been watching the Father Gauthe case on television but remained skeptical. Calvin's such a big mouth, she thought. He would have told me. But just to be sure, she confronted her son, then eighteen, the minute he came home. And Calvin finally broke his silence, admitting that he too had been abused.

Most of the other victims who filed suit were quickly offered generous settlements by the diocese of Lafayette. Calvin, however, was forced into court. The diocese felt he had a weaker case than the others because he didn't seem as damaged. Now he had to tell total strangers the secret he had guarded so carefully for so many years. It was precisely the type of scenario he had tried to avoid by staying silent ever since his first "physical" in Father Gauthe's confessional.

"Imagine a young girl, a twelve-year-old girl, in a crowd of people with a white skirt on and she starts her period," he says in describing how he felt in court. "That's embarrassment. That's total embarrassment. And that's how I felt. Everybody was staring at me. I cried. I cried my eyes out. And I had to use words like penis and anus. I'm not used to using these kinds of words. I wasn't raised that way."

IT IS HARD TO OVERSTATE THE AWE THE CATHOLIC CHURCH IN-spires in children who kneel before the crucifix on God's altar amidst candlelight and incense. It is equally difficult to overstate the submissiveness that awe inspires in them. They learn of the wrath God brings to bear on those who are sinful. Their teacher is the parish priest who admonishes them against evil and demands penance for their sins. In rural Hispanic communities, where Catholicism is woven into the cloth of tradition, where respect for elders is a sacred concept, priests are, in the literal sense of the Latin, the Other Christ.

If all priests in that world possess awesome powers, Father Robert Kirsch's powers appeared supernatural in the eyes of young Susan Sandoval. One day, in a rage at the order of his superior, the priest stomped out of his rectory and began ranting and screaming: "Screw the Church, screw the Church." Susan froze. She knew Father Bob was bordering on heresy.

"Screw the Church," he yelled again as he threw a cross on the ground and stomped on it. Susan waited for the skies to open. "Nothing happened," she says quietly. "He wasn't struck down. I knew then he was bigger than God."

Susan knew, also, that there was no way she could ever tell anyone she and Father Bob were having sex. Father Bob was all-powerful. She was just fifteen years old.

Susan had been raised to silence in any case, in the peek-and-plumb town of Abiquiu—"You peek at it and you're plumb out of town," she explains. Three hundred Hispanic families lived in a community so Catholic that no one thought it odd when Susan's mother refused to attend her own son's wedding because his bride-to-be had been married once before.

Father Bob arrived in Abiquiu when Susan was twelve. He piloted his own plane—people called him the Flying Priest. He insisted on speaking Spanish (although he mutilated it with his Brooklyn accent) because he said it was the language of love. He rode around the hills in his pickup truck, using its bed as an altar for baptisms. He flew around the state—and the country—organizing Christian leadership missions and raising money for poor mountain parishes.

Father Bob began to court Susan when she was fourteen, sending her love letters, poems and small gifts. She still has boxes of his correspondence. They allegedly began to have sex when she was fifteen. And when she turned seventeen, he gave her a ring, "a gold and garnet, I'll-love-you-forever ring," she calls it. At age thirty-four, she still wears it on a chain around her neck. "I wear it like a horsehair shirt to remind myself of how stupid I was."

Father Bob cultivated her silence both overtly and subtly. He exalted their union by comparing it to the relationship of Saint Francis and Saint Claire, the archetypal platonic soul mates in Catholic lore.

He kept reminding her that they had something special that would be destroyed if revealed. "Our magic bubble would break," he'd tell her.

Father Bob was a workaholic, always pale and exhausted. He'd forget to eat, to change his clothes. "He was an accident waiting to happen," Susan remembers. Constantly complaining that he had to take care of everyone else—"if I were a woman my tits would be down to my knees," was his phrase. He begged her to take care of him, to keep him going. Susan understood: "If I let this priest down, I'll let down the whole community. He needs to be there for them."

He wrote her long letters, telling her she must love him forever, setting her up to feel guilty if she left him. In one of his endless epistles, he said: "I am now more certain than ever before that we are lover friends, one to the other, for much time after the other people we know in our lives have also come and gone. St. Paul tells us that 'el amor nunca se muera.' [Love never dies.] A woman told me that she 'used to' love her husband. Well, para mi, either she STILL does or she never did. . . . Don't you agree? I think that you do, Darling Susan!"

Susan could neither escape Father Bob nor reveal their secret. "He became God, the giver of life who made all things possible," she says. "He nurtured me in his own twisted way. I had no faith. He was it."

When Susan fell in love with the man she would later marry, she told the priest the sex had to stop. She never imagined he would mind. They were essentially soul mates, after all. She was wrong. It was the end of their relationship.

Now, as she reflects on what made her a victim and what kept her silent for all those years, Susan is chilled by the depth of the cultural collusion in her abuse. "We are sheep waiting to be taken to the slaughter," she says. "Our strong sense of privacy, our strong sense of respect for elders, our loyalty to the Church make us incredibly vulnerable. If I want to teach my daughter how not to become a victim, I have to teach her to be a little less Hispanic."

SOMETIMES VICTIMS STAY SILENT BECAUSE THEY SIMPLY DON'T remember what happened. Their minds have blocked it out. This phenomenon is called *repressed memory*, and it occurs when the brain veils a horror that the psyche cannot absorb. The process isn't a conscious decision but an automatic self-defense against an event that is so jarring or terrifying it threatens to unhinge a person.

Children who witness the mutilation and death of their classmates in a school bus accident simply forget the details. The Central Park jogger, who was raped and pummeled by a roving gang of teenagers in 1989, cannot recall the attack. The subconscious seems to decide: "If I don't remember, then it never happened," explains Mike Lew, a psychologist who has witnessed the phenomenon of repressed memory time and again in victims of child sexual abuse. "If it never happened, then I don't have to deal with it."

For those victims, repressed memory is most common when the abuser is an especially trusted figure, such as a priest. Blocking allows victims to continue going to church, to avoid any challenge to their faith. It lets them maintain the familiar stability that telling would inevitably disrupt.

Blocking worked perfectly for David Clohessy of St. Louis for nearly twenty years. His memories of childhood chronicled an uneventful era with no more trauma or pain than any kid endures.

But that all changed one evening in 1988 when he and his fiancée went to see the movie *Nuts*. Before the movie, Clohessy says, "If somebody had been taking a survey on the sidewalk in front of the theater asking, 'Have you ever known anybody who was sexually abused?' I would have said categorically, absolutely, no." After the movie, Clohessy would never again be able to give such an answer.

As he sat in the theater, watching Barbra Streisand play the part of a prostitute who was molested as a child, he began to feel strangely upset and fidgeted in his seat. When he and his fiancée later went to grab a bite to eat at a pancake house, he still felt nervous and couldn't stay focused on their conversation.

That night, he was too agitated to sleep. His fiancée, who lay beside him, held him tight and struggled to stay awake with him. At 2 A.M, he broke down in tears as a series of fragmented images flitted through his mind. He remembered lying in the back of a van parked in a wilderness area beside a lake. He remembered telling the man who had taken him there that his stomach hurt. And he remembered the voice of that man—Father John Whiteley, his parish priest and a close family friend—saying, "Maybe this will make it feel better," as he rubbed David's stomach and then, tentatively, his genitals.

David turned to his fiancée and said: "What happened to that little girl in *Nuts* happened to me."

Over subsequent weeks and months, more memories surfaced. He remembered various outings and vacations with the priest: skiing in Colorado, camping in Arkansas. And he remembered the fondling and sodomy that allegedly occurred on many of those trips. He never knew when a new recollection would hit him, triggering tears and a deep depression, and felt ambushed by this new uncertainty in his life. He sought the help of a therapist in digging out the buried pain, confronting and overcoming it. He sifted through postcards he had sent to his parents while on his vacations with the priest and forced himself to remember: Did something happen here? Did Father John hurt me that time?

To date, he has recalled about a dozen occasions when Father John allegedly abused him from the time he was twelve years old to the time he was fifteen. He believes that's the whole of it but is cautious about saying so. "I don't ever want to say something that's unqualified," he explains. "I don't want to get blown out of the water some night by a new memory."

Even after David's memories emerged, it wasn't easy to speak out about his abuse. He knew that if and when he did, it would send shock waves through his world and, particularly, that of his family. His parents were devout Roman Catholics who had frequently set a place for Father John at the family dinner table while David was growing up. His brother had become a priest in the Diocese of Jefferson City, Missouri, where the family had lived and where Father John still worked.

For more than a year, David didn't tell any of them what was going on. Then, one Friday night after work, he drove six hours from St. Louis to Indiana, where his parents had moved. His heart hammered in his chest the whole way there. "I was nervous as hell," he recalls. "I even made sure I had gassed up the car before I got to the house so if they didn't react well, I could just get right back into the car and drive all the way to St. Louis."

By noon on Saturday, he was ready. "I've got to call it what it was," he kept reminding himself. Fighting back tears, he sat before his folks and announced, "Father John sexually molested me." His mother's face turned ashen. She kept one hand over her heart. David started backpedaling as swiftly as he could. "I'm okay now, so don't worry," he reassured his parents. "I'm in therapy. I know there's no way you could have known. I don't want you to feel guilty. This was a thousand years ago and nobody knew about kids being molested." His father stood up and went out into the yard to shovel dog shit—to clean up the only mess he could.

That was just the beginning of his subsequent estrangement from his family, and that was just the first test of David's courage in making his abuse known. When he filed a lawsuit against the Diocese of Jefferson City in August 1991, several voices in the local news media criticized the fact that he had done so anonymously, saying it was unfair for the priest's name to be published while his accuser's was concealed. David felt forced to identify himself to the world. His parents, who had not wanted him to sue or go public, grew reticent and distant. His brother Kevin, the priest, told him: "From this point on, we probably shouldn't talk."

Since then, David has been absent from family Thanksgiving and Christmas celebrations. His parents rarely call him. "I think they're in shock," he says. "I think they're ashamed. And I think they feel very guilty. And compounding all of that, they don't approve of how I'm dealing with this."

David, now thirty-seven, sees his story as an example of all the forces and obstacles that keep victims of sexual abuse silent. Victims have to remember. They have to decide that it's important to talk. They have to be willing to risk the discomfort of family members and friends. And they have to be prepared to identify themselves publicly as abuse victims, no matter how much of their privacy is sacrificed by doing so.

David remembers that after his name began to appear in newspapers, he worried occasionally that parents in his neighborhood would begin to look at him with suspicion. After all, he was always reading in the newspapers and hearing on television that most abusers had themselves been abused as children, that being molested as a kid might somehow predispose a person to committing those same crimes.

But he does not regret the decisions he made once his memories emerged. "I'm convinced," he says, "that abuse thrives in secrecy."

CRISTINE CLARK ALWAYS REMEMBERED FATHER ED STEFANICH. She could hardly forget him. He baptized her father as a Catholic and remarried her parents. He taught her first catechism, served her first Communion, listened to her first confession—and gave her her first kiss. The latter—bestowed when she was fourteen years old—must have been her own fault, the Joliet, Illinois, seventh grader reasoned. Priests just don't do things like that on their own.

So she didn't tell because she feared that she had been the seductress. She didn't tell because she liked it. She had a crush on Father Ed, like she did on rock singer Huey Lewis. When Father

Ed came to dinner at her parents' house, she mooned over the tall priest with the bright blue eyes and broad shoulders.

In the beginning, of course, Father Ed was just a fantasy. So when he stopped her in the corridor of St. Scholastica after religion class and whispered, "I love you," Cristine ran away. She raced to the drinking fountain and splashed water on her face. Calm down, she told herself. It doesn't mean anything. Priests are always talking about love.

When he smacked her on her bottom with a textbook, she bolted to the bathroom in embarrassment. This is weird, she thought. Weird but neat.

When he made eye contact with her in religion class or blew kisses at her as he drove by on the street, she felt an occasional twinge of guilt. But mostly, the shy little girl with glasses was flattered. "I felt special," she says. "Singled out."

She was on cloud nine when Father Ed gave her a job in the rectory. She and Father Ed were alone together. It was like getting paid to be a groupie. And suddenly she had money to buy herself a real cashmere sweater. Suddenly there was always someone there taking time to talk to her, to rub her back.

One Thursday, Cristine sat in the rectory office preparing the Sunday church bulletin and listening to the sounds of the annual parish carnival going on outside when Father Ed walked in dressed casually in slacks and a shirt with no Roman collar. His eyes seemed to bore into her.

"Come over here and sit on my lap," he said. Cristine felt uncomfortable there, but the priest calmed her down by telling her what a good job she was doing, how much it meant to him. As she tried to squirm away, he started whispering about how much he cared for her. He held her tight, kissed her on the lips and moved his fingertips to her small breasts.

Father Ed started picking Cristine up for school every morning. He took her on picnics at Morton Arboretum, to the ballet or to Maximilian's in suburban Chicago for shrimp. Three afternoons a week, she went to his rectory—to work, her mother thought. They lay half-naked in each other's arms. He explored her body and taught her to masturbate him.

Father Ed planned their future in full detail. He'd ask for permission to marry her when she turned eighteen. He'd leave the priesthood and sell real estate and insurance. He'd buy a house. He wrote a marriage agreement for them both to sign. In the eyes of God, he said, they were already man and wife.

He tried to have intercourse with her, but said she was too small. He asked her to defecate and urinate on him. It was the only request she denied him.

He bought her lacy lingerie, diamond-and-ruby earrings and a diamond ring. He opened a bank account in her name and deposited $620. He even bought her a red Pontiac Fiero that they kept at the rectory. She was too young to drive, after all.

When Cristine worried that she would go to hell for what they were doing, the priest assured her he knew what God's will was, that God would stop them if He were displeased. But it was not Father Ed's religious declarations that deterred Cristine from running home and telling. Love did. When he told Cristine that her mother wouldn't understand their relationship, that she would be jealous because she wanted him for herself, the sheltered fourteen-year-old believed him—and kept distant from her mom.

"I wasn't confused," she says. "I was fourteen, fifteen, and I thought I was in love. He manipulated me perfectly so I thought it was all right."

It almost came to an end when one of Cristine's schoolmates saw her kissing Father Ed in his car and told a psychologist who was also a church deacon. He reported the matter to the bishop, who asked Father Ed about it. When the priest passed it off as an absurd rumor, the bishop dropped the subject.

Then, several months later, Father Ed asked Cristine's parents for permission to marry her as soon as she turned sixteen. Her mother got hysterical. Her father barred Father Ed from the house. Cristine and the priest were left with furtive phone calls and stolen kisses at the local 7-Eleven.

In any case, the romance was wearing off, at least for Cristine. She found herself looking at boys in school and fantasizing about dating them. She started thinking about the proms she was missing. When her thoughts began to stray from Father Ed, she felt guilty. "I thought something was wrong with me if I couldn't stick to one person," she says shyly.

Finally, Cristine's mother found the diaries her daughter had been hiding. In them, Cristine alluded to what she and Father Ed had been doing all those afternoons at the rectory. Her mother called the Diocese of Joliet and was told Father Ed would be taken care of. They referred her to a psychologist, the same man who had reported Father Ed to the bishop months earlier. Realizing the Church had not removed the priest from contact with the young girl, he called the police.

A few days later, uniformed officers knocked on Cristine's door just after she returned home from school. She panicked and ran sobbing out of the house. She tried to hide at a neighbor's. She was certain she was going to jail.

The police found her. When she got to the station, Detective Jim Grady took her in his arms, hugged her and let her cry. "It wasn't your fault, it wasn't your fault," he kept repeating. As if to drive the point home, he told her about Father Ed's last teenage girlfriend, whom he had also showered with rings and promises of marriage and seduced into sex. It sounded too much like her own story to be a lie. Cristine collapsed. "I felt betrayal, total betrayal," she says. "And I can still feel it."

Cristine Clark broke her silence long enough to ensure that Father Ed was arrested and charged, convicted and jailed. She dropped out of school and locked herself away in her room. All that kept her going was the belief that the Church would have simply transferred Father Ed if she hadn't put him away.

There were moments when the police seemed skeptical of certain aspects of her story, especially when she told them Father Ed was so paranoid that he always carried a gun in each pocket and another behind his coat. She could see it on their faces: "Maybe this kid is making this all up." Then they got to his rectory and found his arsenal: pistols and shotguns and semiautomatic weapons—sixteen in all—along with an ax and a bludgeon that was hidden in his piano bench. Any lingering doubts about Cristine's veracity were finally erased when she told police the precise location of the only surgical scar on Father Ed's body: underneath his pubic hair.

During his plea bargaining sessions, Father Ed tried desperately to avoid jail time. Cristine insisted he be put behind bars.

When he finally agreed to serve six months, she added one condition: that he leave the priesthood.

To ward off a lawsuit for willful negligence, the Diocese of Joliet offered Cristine Clark and her family $450,000. The price of the settlement: a secrecy pledge. Cristine promised never to comment on her case to the news media and never to disclose the price the Church paid for her silence. She signed it on April 15, 1988.

At the age of sixteen, Cristine dedicated her life to forgetting. She found the fastest possible crowd to run with, the wildest possible boyfriend to date. She moved out to California with him and spent virtually all her settlement money on his drugs and debts.

She still believed that everything that happened with Father Ed was her fault, her sin. She felt guilty that her mother had stopped going to church, that her father became enraged at the mere sight of a man in a priestly collar. She was haunted by the memory that she had been too scared to enjoy her first kiss.

Eventually, she left her boyfriend, and in 1989 met Don. Less than a year later, she blew the last $17,000 of her settlement money on their wedding in San Diego's Balboa Park. In 1990, her daughter Kristen was born. Two years later, her son Brandon followed.

As she healed, Cristine realized that shame is erased only when silence is broken. She decided to join the growing number of victims from all across the country who had concluded that their silence was tacit collaboration with the Church, that by not speaking out they were allowing yet another generation of parochial school children to be abused. In the fall of 1992, despite her legal agreement with the Diocese of Joliet, Cristine Clark volunteered to tell her story, to warn other Catholics, especially Catholic parents, about the vulnerability of children to men of the cloth. Her message is quietly eloquent:

"I was always taught to respect priests, to obey them. That attitude means they get their pickings of whoever they want. After all, everyone thinks a sexual abuser is some kind of weird hunchback you can recognize. I would never have believed my priest could have done this. Yet anyone's priest can do this. Teach your kids to trust no one, not even a priest."

Chapter 7

CASTING
OUT LEPERS

IF STAYING SILENT CREATES A PRIVATE NIGHT-mare, telling often unleashes a public one. Children summon forth their courage, swallow their shame and speak out—only to find they have strayed into a minefield. This is particularly true if the person they accuse is someone as respected and beloved as a priest, and if the institution from which they are demanding accountability is as defensive, secretive and image-conscious as the Catholic Church.

In case after case of child sexual abuse by a priest, victims and their families have learned that no one wants to hear about their pain. Not fellow parishioners, who perceive any challenge to a priest's virtue as an assault on their faith and refuse to believe it. Not Church leaders, who fear costly and embarrassing lawsuits and retreat into silence and stonewalling. So they are left twisting in the wind—aban-

doned by, and alienated from, the very faith community they expected to anchor them in a time of crisis.

That's certainly what happened to the families who dared to
level accusations of child sexual abuse against a Phoenix, Arizona,
priest named Father Mark Lehman. The criminal case, which
erupted in May 1990 and played out over the next two years, left
almost everyone who brushed up against it in tears or in tatters
—from the families at its center, to the friends who saw them
ostracized, to the law enforcement officials who struggled mightily
to make justice happen. "I've only had four cases that made me
cry," said Susan Lindley, an investigator from the Maricopa
County District Attorney's office who worked the case. "This was
one of them."

Father Mark attracted attention from the moment he arrived
at St. Thomas the Apostle Church in July 1988. Just twenty-six
years old, he was boyishly handsome and youthfully exuberant,
a vivid contrast to the older, more subdued priests around town.
Parishioners often talked about the way his kind eyes and full
beard evoked the image of Christ. Many took an immediate shine
to him.

So nearly two years later they were shocked when word began
to trickle out that several seventh-grade girls at the parish school
had complained about Father Mark. Two of them—Amy Hanson
and Dawn Barton, both thirteen years old—had brought their
concerns to the school youth director. (Both girls have been given
pseudonyms, as have other members of the Hanson family and
the girl identified below as Anna Ramos.)

Amy said that Father Mark frequently hugged her tightly and
occasionally touched her, through her clothing, on her breast.
Dawn said that when she and other girls went with Father Mark
on an outing to Sunsplash, a local water park, he had reached
around her back and felt her breast. The youth director talked to
child welfare authorities and to parents of several other girls who
had been on the Sunsplash trip. One of those parents called the
police, who began an investigation. The Catholic Diocese of Phoenix immediately suspended Father Mark.

What church officials didn't do, however, was help parishioners sort through their confusion over the unfolding events, which

had yet to become public in any way. As a result, many of the faithful at St. Thomas decided to dismiss the unpleasantness as a misunderstanding, or a downright lie. These were mostly well-to-do, conservative Catholics—many members of the Charles Keating family, of savings and loan scandal fame, worshipped there—who didn't like any mess in their gilded lives. The grounds around the Moorish-looking St. Thomas were immaculately tended, with shrubbery so well trimmed it almost looked sculpted. At Mass, parishioners didn't drop quarters into the collection basket, but $5 and $10 and $20 bills. A priest giving a homily about grace under pressure invoked examples of golf and tennis stars—Jack Nicklaus, Andre Agassi and Monica Seles.

Parishioners tittered about the girls who had gone on the Sunsplash trip, suggesting they had provoked the handsome Father Mark by parading around in their swimsuits and wading too close to him in the pool. Dawn, they snickered, was a little loose, staying out too late for a girl her age and befriending too many boys. And Amy? She was just the malleable pawn of her mother, who had planted a lie in her daughter's head just to hurt parish officials. The word around the parish was that Patty had grown too big for her britches, wanted more control over the place than anyone would give her and left in a huff, bent on revenge.

For seventeen years, Patty had directed the church music program, first as a volunteer and then as a paid employee. Her small Christian band—a keyboardist, a bassist, and Patty on vocals—grew in fame over the years and went on to cut several albums. Whenever a prominent Catholic in the Phoenix area got married or had a death in the family, Patty was the first choice to perform at the ceremony. Many St. Thomas parishioners had joined the parish because it was the only place she sang full-time.

She had suddenly quit her job there in December 1989. Now, just six months later, her oldest child was telling stories to the police. Patty had said she left work because she needed more time at home. But maybe, parishioners reasoned, she'd walked out in bitterness. She was always so showy, so loud. Maybe she had started making demands, then got bent out of shape when they weren't met. When parishioners started hearing rumors that Patty's second child, Maureen, eleven, was also talking to police about Father Mark, it only gave them more reason to doubt. Two kids in one family? Wasn't that a little odd?

Even without all the talk, Patty and her husband were in enough pain. Father Mark had betrayed them. They had frequently invited him to their house because he loved to go into their recording studio and hear himself sing and play guitar. They had taught all four of their children to respect him because he wore the collar of a Catholic priest. Now Amy and Maureen were saying that they had spent much of the past year frightened of Father Mark and the way he was always getting so close to them and touching them. He had never taken off their clothes or gone beyond groping and hugging. But his gropings still had disturbed the girls enough that they were starting to have nightmares.

On top of it all, the girls were being ostracized. Friends from the parish weren't spending as much time with them, saying their parents had warned them away from the trouble-making Hanson family. Amy even heard the school principal talking behind her back. Patty felt compelled to put the children in public school. She knew what the kids were up against. Her friends weren't calling her either, and her musical gigs in area churches were drying up.

Parish officials could have defused the situation. They could have told the people of St. Thomas that the Hanson and Barton families weren't alone in their accusations, that police were interviewing children from other families as well, that there were compelling reasons to believe Father Mark had claimed many victims. Instead, they stressed that Father Mark was only the victim of an accusation. To some ears, it sounded like parish officials themselves didn't believe it. At Mass one weekend they made a perfunctory offer to provide counseling to anyone troubled by the events. But they did not gather parents together to ask them how their children were dealing with Father Mark's removal. They did not launch any kind of vigorous search for victims of the priest who were perhaps too scared to come forward.

Elizabeth Evarts, whose nine-year-old daughter, Laura, had been in a class of second graders that Father Mark prepared for first Communion, grew so frustrated by the paucity of official information that she approached the pastor, Father Robert Skagen, after Mass one day. "Is this true?" she asked him, referring to the rumors she was hearing about a widening police investigation. "I can't talk about this," he said. "The bishop has asked us not to talk about it."

Elizabeth had other, more immediate problems to worry about. For the past year, her daughter, Laura, had sunk into a deep depression. Elizabeth, a single parent of comfortable means, had adopted Laura just two years earlier from the Philippines, where the little girl's parents had died in a typhoon. Elizabeth had fought to get Laura—the government of the Philippines wasn't letting single parents adopt. But Elizabeth knew that children like Laura, from poor countries, seldom got a real shot at a good life, and she wanted to give Laura a chance.

At first the girl had adjusted well to her new surroundings. But during her second grade year at St. Thomas, she started changing. She began stealing pencils and erasers from other children. She constantly told lies. Then, one summer day when she was swimming over at the Franciscan Renewal Center, she defecated in the pool. When Elizabeth asked her why she hadn't used the bathroom, Laura said: "Well, there were two priests standing there. I didn't want to go by them."

After the first reports of Father Mark's removal, Elizabeth had asked Laura if he had ever touched her in a bad way. Laura insisted he had not. Elizabeth let it go. She moved her daughter to a new school where the girl could get more attention. But still she worried. She had taken enough psychology courses and read enough articles to know that children often kept sexual abuse a secret. Was that what was haunting her little girl?

In January 1991, Father Mark was formally charged with the attempted sexual abuse of Amy Hanson and pleaded no contest. His sentencing date was scheduled for the following month, then postponed several times. In March, Elizabeth received a strange and alarming phone call from another mother with children at St. Thomas. The woman told Elizabeth that parish administrators and police believed Father Mark had molested many of the children in Laura's Communion class. The caller urged Elizabeth: "Talk to Laura again. Tell her she's not alone."

Laura happened to be sitting right beside Elizabeth as she

talked on the phone. Now the girl blurted it all out: Father Mark had often asked her to sit on his lap and, at least once, massaged one of her breasts and then moved his hand down toward her vagina. She had been too scared of Father Mark to say anything before, but now that he had been charged with a crime and she had changed schools she felt safer.

Elizabeth called the school's principal, Sister Mary Louise Ante. Sister Mary Louise confirmed that police were interviewing other children from Laura's class, but said she didn't see any need for Laura to be included. "Laura's not here at the school anymore," Sister Mary Louise said. "Let's not add her to the indictments. You can let this go." Flabbergasted and outraged, Elizabeth hung up and called the police.

As Elizabeth reeled from Laura's confession, the Hansons confronted new horrors. The entire family had gone into counseling, and during one session, nine-year-old Kevin Hanson said that Father Mark had sexually abused him, too. Kevin's accusations were far more chilling than his sisters'. He said that Father Mark, who would come into his classroom to play guitar for the kids, always asked him to help carry the guitar back to the rectory. Along the way, Father Mark would make detours to molest him, Kevin said.

Kevin said the priest had sucked on his penis and his bottom. He said the priest had put his own penis in his bottom. Once, the boy said, Father Mark had molested him in the stall of a bathroom, making him stand on the toilet so only one set of feet would be visible to anyone who entered the room. The boy remembered worrying that his feet would slip and he would fall into the toilet water. He said the priest had promised that terrible things would happen to the Hanson family if Kevin told. The boy had believed it then, and believed it even more as time passed. After all, his sisters had told on Father Mark, and now everybody was being mean to his family and his mommy and daddy were fighting all the time.

In May, a grand jury indicted Father Mark Lehman on a dozen additional charges covering the sexual abuse of Kevin Hanson, Maureen Hanson, Laura Evarts, Dawn Barton and Anna Ramos, another girl the same age as Dawn Barton and Amy Hanson who said Father Mark frequently grabbed and tickled her private parts. With the avalanche of new charges against him, Father Mark withdrew his no-contest plea. The stakes were higher now. He pleaded innocent.

The victims and their families went into court in June 1991, for a bail hearing for Father Mark, who had been free for most of the time since his initial arrest. When they walked in, they saw that about twenty people had showed up to support the priest. Some were from the parish. One was the head pastor, Father Skagen, who had already written to the judge saying he was "morally certain" Father Mark would never offend again.

The victims and their families received icy stares from Father Mark's supporters. Occasionally, they overheard them mutter angry words: "travesty," "outrage," "lies." A counselor from the prosecutor's office tried to calm and distract Kevin Hanson, who was nervous and upset, by asking him to draw pictures for her and by whispering inane jokes. When the boy giggled, one of Father Mark's supporters snarled at the nine-year-old: "I don't think this is very funny at all!" The counselor was shocked by the venom in the woman's voice and by the air of tension and hostility in the courtroom. She had never witnessed anything like it before.

Patty Hanson took the stand to beg that Father Mark be kept in jail, saying her children were terrified of him. Elizabeth Evarts took the stand to say that her daughter, Laura, was scared, too. Elizabeth explained that Father Mark was regularly visiting a parish family who lived just one house away from her to say Mass for a group of loyal parish supporters. He was visible through the neighbor's bay window, Elizabeth said. Little Laura had seen him there.

That neighbor, Ann Malone, was sitting with Father Mark's supporters in the courtroom and immediately stood to speak. "I live around the corner from Mrs. Evarts," she told the judge. "I don't know if it was me she is speaking of but Father Mark is a close personal friend of ours. If it pleases the Court, we will not see him at our home, but I am in no way afraid of him coming to my home with my four children."

Father Mark's defense attorney asked everyone who had come in support of Father Mark to stand. The victims and their families watched in disbelief and crushing pain as their pastor, Father Ska-gen, rose. Father Mark was granted a reasonable bail but on several conditions, including that he not go within one mile of the Evarts' home. After the hearing, as Patty Hanson huddled with her children and a counselor, a woman who had come into court to support Father Mark charged toward her, fury etched on her face. "It's just an outrage, it's just an outrage," she sputtered. Patty shot back: "You leave me and my family alone!" Her son, Kevin, clutched her leg and cowered behind her. A bailiff came rushing out of the courtroom to see what all the shouting was about.

The Hanson family was unraveling. Patty and her husband were divorcing. Crippled by their hurt, they didn't know what to say to each other, and they didn't know how to love each other anymore. Early in the case, counselors and prosecutors had warned them that marriages seldom survive such an ordeal. "We laughed," Patty says. "Our marriage was so strong. But then the walls just went up and they wouldn't come down. When you touch someone you love, all of a sudden that touch doesn't mean the same thing. It means something vile. It means something that happened to your child."

The family filed a lawsuit against the Diocese of Phoenix. It only made matters worse. They got nasty letters saying they were ruthless liars peddling trumped-up accusations and exaggerated suffering for a little limelight and a lot of cash. They got harassing phone calls at 3 A.M. and anonymous death threats.

Private investigators followed Patty—to try to dig up dirt on her for the Church's defense against the lawsuit, she assumed. The spare tire that hung on the back of her Jeep-style truck was slashed. As she got more depressed and more hysterical, people said it only proved that she had been crazy from the start. When she ran into St. Thomas parishioners around town, some snapped at her: "Blasphemous bitch." Despite the hostility, she brought Amy to the eighth grade graduation at St. Thomas so the girl could see some of the classmates she had felt forced to leave behind. The two were received coldly. A teacher asked Patty to leave, saying her presence was upsetting the others. A parent told Patty: "You don't belong here."

At one point, the Hanson children sent letters to the judge in Father Mark's case to tell him about their isolation and pain. Amy wrote: "I would do almost anything to be back with my friends, but I know that really isn't possible. I want Mark to know what it feels like to lose your best friends and to feel like the whole world has come to an end." Maureen wrote: "I lay awake at night trying to figure out which way is up. I hear my little brother and sister crying themselves to sleep at night and then my mom cries because they are crying. I think the reason people are so mad at my family is we pressed charges against a 'holy man.' "

Elizabeth Evarts endured similar travails. She too received death threats by mail and phone. She too had her tires slashed— on the same day it happened to Patty Hanson. And she too watched as old friends suddenly disappeared from her life. She didn't understand it. When news of Laura's abuse became public, she had expected dozens of calls of support. She received exactly five. She had expected a call from the bishop, or at least one of the parish administrators, asking her what the Church could do for Laura. That call never came. She stopped going to services at St. Thomas, but then, after a long absence, went back in 1991 with Laura's two siblings for a special Christmas Mass. She quickly regretted it. A woman she had known for twenty-five years sat several rows ahead of her. The woman did not greet her, but turned around repeatedly to stare at Elizabeth with a look of contempt. Elizabeth's oldest child, Jennifer, twenty-three, started crying and asked her mother if they could leave. No, Elizabeth said. They would not cave in under this.

Why, Elizabeth wondered, were these people so ready to blindly assume that a priest must be innocent and that his accusers must be liars? Apparently none of them had bothered to talk to police or prosecutors, or to find out that, in interviews with psychologists after his arrest, Father Mark had admitted fondling little girls. They seemed to Elizabeth like obedient members of a tribe that protected its leaders at all costs. One night, when Elizabeth couldn't sleep, she took out a sheet of purple paper, grabbed a blue pen and tried to put her disillusionment into words. "I am irritable, angry, exhausted and disillusioned," she wrote. "Most of all, I am sick to death of the Catholicity of it all. I'm surrounded by a Catholic environment, neighborhood, city and, worst of all, mentality. I am afraid of being defeated by the ugliness and constant reminders that surround me in this squalid mess."

The people who kept the Evarts and Hanson families going were a trio of fiercely committed women from the Maricopa County Attorney's office. Paula Anderson, the victim advocate, Susan Lindley, the investigator, and Laura Reckart, the prosecutor, had worked together on dozens of child sexual abuse cases. They knew how treacherous the waters could be, especially when the accused was someone as prominent and beloved as a Catholic priest. A few years before the Lehman case, another priest in Phoenix, Father George Bredemann, had been convicted of child sexual abuse. Although Paula, Susan and Laura hadn't worked that case, they remembered it well.

Father George had molested three boys out at a ramshackle desert retreat he had built and named "The Castle." One of the families who pursued prosecution faced regular intimidation by Father George's loyal followers and other faithful Catholics in the area. The aunt and uncle went on a local radio talk show, only to have listeners phone in and call them liars. The mother drove past a neighborhood intersection one day to find a white cross bearing her name planted in the grass, as if to say "Rest in Peace." When all three went into court, they did so under guard.

Now Paula, Susan and Laura were watching the same kind of terrorism visited upon Father Mark's victims. Paula, whose job was to help and support families bringing cases into court, had never seen people as besieged as the Hansons, or community members as hostile as the Catholics around Phoenix. She grew so concerned about the family that she broke one of her cardinal rules about not getting too involved with her job. She gave the Hanson family her home phone number.

So many forces—Church officials, parish employees, area Catholics—seemed to be aligned against the Hanson and Evarts families that it spooked Paula, who is a devout Catholic herself. Was God taking sides, too? During the case, she was visited by a string of bad luck unlike any she had ever known. In one five-week period, she and her husband lost all their tax records; the pipes in their house burst; her grandfather died; and her car was stolen from its parking place just outside a church in which she and her daughter were praying. "God is punishing me!" she wept to Susan and Laura one day at the office. She was only half kidding.

Susan and Laura were more outraged than depressed. The more they delved into the case against Father Mark, the more convinced they became that parish administrators had ignored clear warning signs about him. Susan and Laura learned that a year before Father Mark's arrest, a group of boys and girls at the school had begun to refer to Father Mark as "Chester the Molester." The taunts had gotten back to the principal, Sister Mary Louise. Her response was to call some of the children in and threaten them with suspension if they didn't stop.

Susan and Laura also felt parish administrators were stonewalling them, protecting the priest at the expense of the children he had already victimized and the children he still might victimize if he beat the charges against him. The worst was Sister Mary Louise. She went on the attack against the victims and witnesses. She said Patty Hanson was power hungry. She said Maureen Hanson was strangely bookish and withdrawn. She said Kevin Hanson had an overactive imagination. If that were true about Kevin, asked Susan and Laura, how come another boy had verified Kevin's claim that Father Mark frequently took Kevin out of class? Sister Mary Louise said the boy was a little liar.

"It was nothing less than witness bashing and victim bashing," Laura says. "It was a cover-your-ass mentality. I've never felt more in a case that it was going to be an uphill battle. All lips were sealed. There's a saying that goes, 'Justice needs to be tempered by mercy.' Their philosophy seemed to be that justice needs to be hidden by faith." Laura and Susan felt certain that Father Skagen and Sister Mary Louise were hiding information and wondered if there might be some way to go after the parish officials for failure to report Father Mark or for obstruction of justice. They felt certain there were more victims out there who had somehow been scared or cajoled into silence. Some parish parents wouldn't even come to the phone when Laura and Susan called. But Laura and Susan had their hands full with the case as it was.

They had to stay focused on simply putting Father Mark behind bars.

A few of the St. Thomas parishioners who had remained friendly with the families in the case and were familiar with the evidence also grew sickened by the way the Church was acting. "God can only judge what went on in their heads, but for me, it was clearly a case of protecting their finances, protecting their reputation," says Dennis Desmond, a past president of the parish school board. "This was the kind of time when you should put your arms around people and say, 'Where do you hurt and how can we help?' Not when you put your hand in your back pocket to check your wallet. The Church seemed to say, 'I'm taking care of myself first, and you're on your own.' They turned their backs on the victims; they treated them like they were lying and there was some conspiracy against St. Thomas. It's very disillusioning. I'm forty-four years old, and I still want heroes."

Father Mark ultimately made a deal. He pleaded guilty to just three victims—Amy Hanson, Anna Ramos and Laura Evarts— for a prison sentence of ten years with no chance of early parole. Prosecutors felt he deserved more, but feared that a trial would heighten the passions among Father Mark's supporters and other disbelievers. It might push victims and their families over the edge.

But even after Father Mark had entered his plea, the madness didn't end. A group of parishioners decided to throw him a last supper, a potluck farewell event. Ann Malone hosted it. She believed that Elizabeth Evarts had taken up residence in a new house in the suburbs and that Father Mark wouldn't be violating his one-mile prohibition. But Elizabeth was only in the process of moving and still occupied her home near the Malones. When she caught wind of the party, she called the prosecutor's office.

Laura Reckart and Susan Lindley got scared. Why was the farewell dinner being held a full week before Father Mark's sentencing? Was he headed for what the women jokingly called Club Fled? Laura sent the police out to the Malones, but the gathering had dispersed. She and Susan then sped to the suburban apartment where Mark was staying to make sure he was still around. He was. But the women from the prosecutor's office weren't taking any chances. Over the next week, until the priest was finally taken into custody to begin serving his sentence, Laura, Susan and Paula took turns driving by Father Mark's place to make sure he hadn't vanished. "We felt sort of like the Keystone Kops," Susan says.

Only then did Elizabeth Evarts get her call from Bishop Thomas O'Brien. It was too late, and turned out to be too little. He mispronounced her name so that it sounded like "E-farts." He said that Father Mark's going to prison must be a nice way for "Laurie" to end the eighth grade. Elizabeth pointed out that Laura was only in the fifth. The call didn't last five minutes.

In June 1992, Elizabeth filed suit against Father Mark and the Church that she believes harbored and protected him. In October, Father Mark Lehman's lawyers slapped both Elizabeth and her daughter with a legal document naming them as potentially liable for damages to his reputation. The document, a countersuit of sorts, claims that Elizabeth and her daughter "churned and manipulated" allegations that led to a "vindictive and malicious prosecution." Elizabeth is more amused than outraged. "Wouldn't it be awful if Mark Lehman and Father Skagen ended up sitting in a chateau with my inheritance?" she jests. "I mean . . . sued by a molester! What are they thinking? What are they thinking?"

THEY ARE UNDOUBTEDLY THINKING ABOUT WINNING. WHENEVER defending itself against lawsuits, the Church has proven itself willing to exploit any tactic—no matter how unkind, no matter how uncharitable. That became evident the very first time the Church battled a civil suit concerning child sexual abuse in court.

Glenn and Faye Gastal were poor farmers who operated a feed store in the southwestern Louisiana town of Abbeville. As devout Catholics, they felt proud when their seven-year-old son, Scott, became an altar boy and began spending long hours with Father Gilbert Gauthe. Father Gilbert seemed to be such a thoughtful, caring man. When Scott was put in the hospital for a few days, the priest came to visit and brought him a toy car. Scott was being treated for an unexplained case of rectal bleeding.

In July 1983, a year after Scott began serving Mass with Father Gilbert, the priest suddenly left the parish. The Gastals, like almost everyone else, had no idea why. The Gastals also had no explanation for some strange changes in Scott's behavior. He seemed scared all the time. He didn't want to take Communion. And he didn't like to pray anymore. "I couldn't get him on his knees," his mother later said.

Then, six months after Father Gilbert's disappearance, a family friend told the Gastals about rumors that the priest had molested children. They brought Scott to a counselor, and the boy began sharing a horror story about all the sex acts the priest had regularly performed on him for more than a year. The Gastals were shocked. They were even more shocked when they went to see a lawyer who told them he had just handled nine similar complaints about Father Gauthe. The Church had paid an average of $450,000 to each family. But there were two conditions. The Church would not admit liability and the cases would be sealed, guaranteeing no publicity. An entire community, including the Gastals, had been kept in the dark about Father Gilbert.

The Gastals wanted the secret out, and their conviction only deepened when they learned that Father Gilbert's history of sexually abusing children dated back many years, to many parishes. Whenever someone had complained, Church officials had simply hushed it up and given Father Gilbert a new assignment. It had to stop, the Gastals decided. Other parents had to know that their children, too, might be suffering in silence. The Gastals searched for a lawyer who was willing to bring their case into open court, with full news media coverage. They found J. Minos Simon, a brilliant if bombastic attorney with the physique of a fireplug and the oratorical genius of a preacher.

Even before the civil trial, the Church admitted liability. The only fight was over how high a price the Church should pay. Simon went for the jugular, demanding $10 million. His argument: That the Gastals, now alienated from the Catholic Church, felt they could no longer hope for eternal salvation. The Church, he argued, should compensate them for the loss of their souls.

Bob Wright, the Church lawyer, had to mount some kind of defense. But he picked a particularly cruel strategy. He put the

Gastals on trial, insinuating that they had caused their own child as much damage as Father Gilbert had and were therefore equally at fault. In his opening argument, he pointed out that Glenn Gastal was on his second marriage, and that little Scott Gastal had been held back a year in school. On cross-examination, he questioned the Gastals' parenting, blaming them for decisions and actions that were in no way unusual for devout Catholics in a rural area. How thoroughly had they checked out Father Gilbert before letting their son spend the night in the rectory? How come they didn't put their son in therapy immediately after noticing changes in his behavior?

Wright suggested that if the Gastals truly cared about their child, they would not have come into court. They would have kept silent. "The actions of going public and subjecting this young man to the embarrassment and, if you will, possible ridicule among his friends and others in the community has greatly increased the damages that this young man has sustained," he said.

Jury members didn't see it that way. After deliberating just two hours, they awarded the Gastals $1.25 million. But not everyone in the community was sympathetic. Before, during and after the trial, the Gastals encountered occasional hostility from other Catholics in the area. Business at Glenn Gastal's feed store dropped off so sharply that he had to close it. And at one point, someone wrote to J. Minos Simon to make this observation about young Scott: "If the boy is old enough to go on the stand, he was old enough two years ago not to let Father Gauthe do that."

The Gastals weren't the only ones whose pursuit of justice in the Gauthe case provoked the wrath of fellow Catholics. The sister of Raul Bencomo, a New Orleans attorney who represented other Gauthe victims, went to a wedding where a priest, upon hearing her last name, handed her a piece of paper with a biblical verse on it. The verse was a passage about traitors.

The Gastals' victory in court served some sense of justice, but it could not erase their disillusionment and bitterness. "For six months when I first found out my child was involved in this I used to look down the driveway and think one of the authorities of my Church—of the people that made me believe what is good in the world—would drive up here and make all this better," Glenn Gastal said at one point. "Now we're two years down the road. It hasn't happened yet."

VICTIMS AND THEIR FAMILIES AREN'T THE ONLY ONES WHO WIND up on the firing line. The Church seems willing to shoot any messenger who dares attack its good name. In New Mexico, they also appeared willing to use any ammunition necessary to do so.

Money-grubbing Jew, priest-hater, and Catholic-basher are just a few of the epithets hurled by attorneys, investigators and priests of the Archdiocese of Santa Fe against Bruce Pasternack, the Albuquerque lawyer who has forced the faithful of New Mexico to confront the reality of child sexual abuse by priests in their poor, rural state.

In early 1991, Pasternack began insisting that New Mexico had a unique problem. "Just as New Mexico is the nuclear waste dumping ground of the United States," he said, "it is the ecclesiastical dumping ground of the Catholic Church." The statement smacked of hyperbole, but in dozens of lawsuits, Pasternack has mounted the evidence to support it.

The first suit was on behalf of Susan Sandoval, alleging her abuse by Father Robert Kirsch in the early 1970s. Pasternack showed that Kirsch had arrived in New Mexico as a patient at the Servants of the Paraclete, a religious center in Jemez Springs dedicated to the healing of men of the cloth—alcoholics, bulemics, depressives and child molesters. Kirsch belonged in the last category. When he finished treatment, he was accepted as a priest in the local archdiocese.

Next came Father Jason Sigler, sent to the Servants of the Paraclete by the bishop of Winnipeg for alcoholism and child molestation. After treatment, he too was accepted as a priest in the Archdiocese of Santa Fe. Although he was sent back into treatment two more times for fondling children, he was allowed to continue working in the diocese. Finally, in 1982, he was arrested for abusing boys under the age of thirteen. Pasternack initially sued him on behalf of a single victim. But when the news got out, sixteen others came forward.

Then, in the summer of 1991, as the scandal of James Porter was erupting in Massachusetts, Pasternack realized that his state, too, might have Porter victims. Porter had been in treatment with the Servants of the Paraclete in the 1960s. While there, the priest had spent weekends saying Mass in rural communities. Pasternack's investigator began combing the hills for victims. When he was done, three boys from Truth or Consequences and another from Albuquerque had filed suit.

After Pasternack detailed what he calls the "pervert pipeline" that funneled child sexual abusers into New Mexico through the Paraclete Center, Church officials went on the attack. Who was this Jew daring to sully their good name? He has a clear agenda, one attorney for the archdiocese told the media: "Animosity to the Catholic Church."

Pasternack knows he's an outsider in a world where rules of reverence and respect are woven into Hispanic culture and tradition. Although born in Albuquerque, his folks were New Yorkers who fled the East Coast in 1949. But it's not that Pasternack doesn't know the rules. He just refuses to abide by them. "I'm too abrupt for New Mexico, too high strung," he says with uncharacteristic understatement. He sits in his office talking at the speed of a true Brooklynite. He looks the part of any rising Manhattan attorney. Only the cowboy boots give him away.

"I've sued surgeons and psychologists and drug rehabilitation counselors," he says. "I'd sue a Buddhist monk, a Protestant minister or a rabbi. I don't have any animosity toward the Catholic Church. I just have animosity for people who rape children. This isn't about the religion of the offender. It's about the commission of the offense. If Jesus were to come back to Earth today, whose side do you think he'd be on?"

When the attacks on Pasternack began, the attorney tried to suggest politely to Archbishop Robert Sanchez that anti-Semitic slurs were inappropriate. He reminded Sanchez of the Hebrew inscription carved above the entrance to St. Francis Cathedral in Santa Fe. "Do you know why it's there?" he asked. "When the Catholics ran out of money to finish the cathedral, the Jewish merchants of Santa Fe raised the money to finish it."

Pasternack thought he had made his point. He was wrong. As soon as the next case broke, the name-calling resumed.

In October 1992, Pasternack filed suit against the pastor of Albuquerque's largest and wealthiest church. Father Arthur Perrault was a member of Sanchez's inner circle, the editor of the diocesan newspaper, a priest clearly on his way to becoming bishop. He was also a child sexual abuser—and a known one to boot, Pasternack insisted in lawsuits on behalf of seven clients.

Sanchez was forced to admit it. In a stunning performance designed to win the forgiveness of his flock, the archbishop took to the airwaves on Albuquerque's WKOB-TV to confess his misjudgment. He explained that when accusations were made against Perrault in the early 1980s, the Church regularly gave priest child sexual abusers second, even third chances. The Church believed in forgiveness, he said, and its psychologists misled them about the risk that these priests would abuse again.

"If your father has a heart attack and the doctor says he can go back to work, you have to believe him," Sanchez said. He acknowledged that eight current or former priests in a diocese of ninety-seven had been accused of molesting children. It was an odd statement. Civil lawsuits and criminal indictments had already been filed against ten.

Sanchez fought back tears as he offered to step down if the pope requested his resignation. But while the bishop was confessing, his minions were launching new offensives against Pasternack. Chancellor Ron Wolf accused him of grandstanding: "The barrage he uses has the effect of publicly trying these clerics in the press." Karen Kennedy, an archdiocesan attorney, accused him of greed: "A number of sources have told me Mr. Pasternack indicated publicly that he intends to retire on earnings from suing the Church." Priests on the pulpit accused him of priest-bashing. And one archdiocesan investigator who tried to convince a victim to withdraw his lawsuit called the attorney "a Jew bastard."

Pasternack refused to rise to the bait. "They want me to lose my cool and I'm not going to do that," he says. "These cases aren't about me. They're about priests who molest children."

While Church officials insisted that the crimes he was citing were isolated, or fictitious, Pasternack went nearly deaf fielding phone calls. Accusers from across the state and men and women who had left New Mexico for Hawaii and Colorado asked for representation in child sexual abuse suits against the Church. His name and face had been splashed across newspapers nationwide as the New Mexico attorney willing to take on the Church.

Pasternack became a walking file cabinet on the sexual proclivities of New Mexico's clergy, fed by an odd collection of informants calling with disturbing information about priests and their bishops. His investigator, Jerry Mazon, worked seven days a week weeding out the crackpots. Pasternack, who hates to lose, was picky about the cases he took on. "Our motto around here is corroboration and penetration," he explained.

If anything, the attacks on Pasternack's character have made him even more relentless, more cunning in his legal maneuverings against the Church. During his deposition of Sanchez in one case, Pasternack refused to let the bishop get by with transparently evasive answers.

"Do you remember discussions with Father Clarence Galli about allegations against Sigler?" Pasternack asked the bishop.

"I do not recall," the bishop said.

"Do you remember discussing allegations against Sigler with Father Ted Hunt?"

"I do not recall."

Pasternack pressed the bishop, asking how he could have so little recollection of such serious matters. Sanchez explained that he had been hit in the head by a falling backstop during a softball game.

Pasternack asked the court to order a full neuropsychological examination of the bishop.

But while Pasternack took the Church's attacks and stonewalling in stride, his clients felt wounded. Every time Church leaders impugned his integrity, they disparaged his clients' credibility. "Bruce has been there for me when the Church has done nothing but spit in my face," says Susan Sandoval, Pasternack's first client in his suits against the archdiocese. "It's my feeling that the archdiocese would do anything—anything—to silence anyone."

As Pasternack filed a mounting number of lawsuits—thirty-nine by January 1993—even he began to wonder if Sandoval might not be right. Several weeks before the details of Archbishop Robert Sanchez's own sexual activities forced his resignation, the wife of Pasternack's private investigator received an anonymous phone call informing her that her husband, Jerry, was having an affair. Jerry Mazon denied the accusation and, suspicious of the caller, warned Pasternack that he too might become the target of such attacks. Pasternack, in turn, warned his wife, a prominent Albuquerque attorney. Hours later, she too received an anonymous phone call informing her that her husband was having an affair.

"With a woman?" she asked her caller.

"Yes," the unidentified man replied.

"Thank God," she responded. "The last time it was with an animal."

Chapter 8

THE
CRUCIFIXION
OF INNOCENCE

HE WAS ALWAYS AFRAID, ALWAYS ON guard. Life, as he saw it, held more danger than hope. Trust no one. Need no one. Turn your back for a moment and you're vulnerable again.

So he never turned his. He seldom spent more than forty-five minutes in a crowded room. When he went to the movies, he headed for the back row. In a large group, he clung to the edges, never daring to test its center. Sometimes he didn't even sit down; he felt more comfortable standing, poised for flight.

He refused to let anyone get close. He couldn't bear to let anyone cut his hair, choosing instead to do it himself. He learned to move his three-hundred-pound marble tabletop on his own. Solitude was his only safe harbor, so he lived with an almost desperate loneliness that he blotted out with Scotch and pot and LSD. He was rarely sober long enough to feel the pain.

Even his dreams tormented him. They trapped him in the murkiness of surreal landscapes. He painted his terror on canvas with a palette of grays and blacks, dark browns and muddy purples. He rendered faces vague and indistinct. He shattered images into fragments, like broken china.

He moved constantly. From his home in North Attleboro, Massachusetts, to Iowa, from Omaha to Washington, D.C. He drove cross-country from Maine and wound up in Puerto Rico. New Hampshire. Martha's Vineyard. Connecticut. Baltimore. Nowhere was far enough away.

There was just no safe living in Dennis Gaboury's world, no way to make sense of it all. The rules and assumptions didn't work. The people who were supposed to console you might prey on you. The institutions that were supposed to guide you might betray you. You could count only on yourself—and you might be evil.

He had learned that lesson at the age of ten, inside St. Mary's Church. He had just finished serving Mass as the altar boy for Father James Porter, and the priest offered him a glass of milk and butter cookies. Then the priest invited the fourth grader into his office. "It felt like it was a privilege," he says. "It meant I was special."

There, Porter put him down on the fading Oriental carpet like a rag doll, pulled down his pants and flung himself on top of the ninety-pound child. Two hours later, the rectory housekeeper tapped on the door: "Father Porter, Mr. Gaboury is waiting for his son." The priest dismounted Dennis without a word. The boy pulled on his tan chinos, let his long-sleeved yellow button-down shirt hang out loose, and went out to meet his dad.

"Where the hell have you been?" he asked, impatient after searching for him for more than a hour.

"Father Porter invited me in for milk and cookies," Dennis replied in a tiny voice.

He locked his secret deep inside a wall of solitude, the only haven he could imagine in a world now fraught with danger. In the schoolyard, he stood alone, hugging the trees on the sidelines, hoping not to be noticed. Sometimes he'd head over to where the

girls played, knowing he could lose himself in that crowd. He
retreated into a world inside his head where he could be safe, a
world split off from reality by the shock and terror of two hours
with Porter.

Dennis had learned that priests were good, but "the nuns
taught me I was nothing but a big black vat of sin," he says. At
his first confession, he had spilled out the thousands of bad
thoughts and unkindnesses he had committed. He was only seven.

So Dennis knew that what had happened behind the closed
doors of the rectory office could not be the fault of the man who
transformed Communion wafers into the body of Christ. Dennis
himself must be bad. Sinful. Evil.

Porter had ripped the soul out of Dennis's small body. Desperate to get it back, he struggled for perfection. He began to
dress meticulously. He smeared Vaseline petroleum jelly through
his hair to keep each strand in place. He threw himself into his
faith with the obsessiveness of the damned. At night, alone in his
room, he would see visions of the Blessed Virgin Mary at the foot
of his bed. By the time he was thirteen, he was convinced his only
salvation lay in the priesthood. He entered a high school seminary. It didn't work.

"This is not something you can wash off with water," he says
now. "So you start taking a spiritual shower. And you shower
and shower until you're sick and tired of scrubbing. But it still
doesn't work. Finally you resign yourself to being sinful."

Dennis exiled himself from home at the age of eighteen. Filled
with shame and self-loathing, he tried to shed his skin. He tried
out new names: Gabe, Hap, anything but Dennis. He tried out
new personae: the Big Man on Campus, the drugged-out hippie
living in a shed called Motley in the backwoods of New Hampshire, the artsy bohemian painting murals in town, hand-carving
wooden coatracks and sketching in graveyards. But there was no
adventure. There was only loneliness and flight. "I was trying
desperately to keep one step ahead of a tidal wave of crap," he
says.

And then there was the void where Dennis's soul had been.
He searched frantically to understand why he was rotting inside.
He turned to homeopathy and bubble-gum psychology, psychic

readings and crystals. He turned to a pastoral counselor who gave him a pitifully simplistic solution: Just learn to be average. For years, Dennis ached to be average; he didn't know how. But by the age of thirty, the only solace Dennis had found was drugs and alcohol.

In the fall of 1980, he hit a bird with his car, a terrifying omen of death in his French-Canadian family. He cried for two weeks straight. He was in danger and needed to escape it. He ran from drugs and alcohol and impending self-destruction to California and Washington, D.C., and Puerto Rico, where he would hide in piles of leaves for days. He ran from nightmares into rum, from rum into nightmares. Finally, Dennis tried sobriety. "I remember that first day walking down the corridor of the rehabilitation center feeling like I was a dry, brittle, hot brown paper bag," he says. "There was a pinhole at the end, a tiny pinhole just big enough to let in a little light, a little hope. At that time, hope was my God."

Gradually, in his dreams, that hope displaced despair. One morning in 1984, he awoke almost breathless from the images. He had sunk into an underwater cave and followed a dirt path along a stream encrusted with jewels. He wound up in a magic grove alive with trees where he met his father, who had died fifteen years earlier. "I'm just here to show you where to go," he told his son. Dennis followed his directions to a boulder among the olive trees. Christ sat atop it.

Jesus' mere presence was enough. Dennis knew he was worthy of salvation.

But he couldn't finish the healing until he resurrected the demon that still pursued him. Father Porter had not been mentioned in the six volumes of diaries Dennis had kept, off and on, for the eighteen years since his abuse. But as he wrestled with his agony, the nightmare began to surface in fleeting images. He needed more. He revisited St. Mary's, listened to the creaking of the wooden steps, explored the darkness of the sacristy and sifted through the drawers where the priest had kept his vestments. He fell apart when he entered the office, so unchanged. With all the vulnerability of the ten-year-old boy he still was, Dennis went home and told his mother what had happened in the rectory. But still the memories weren't complete. That same weekend, he picked a private detective out of the Boston phone book and hired him to find the priest. The search proved fruitless.

The only answers were on the inside. Dennis began to put his life together like a jigsaw puzzle, turning each piece over and fitting it into the whole with agonizing slowness. He forced himself out of the comfortable solitude that imprisoned him in a house in the center of Baltimore. He edged his way out of the margins of society into an M.B.A. and a profession.

In April 1992, Dennis flew to North Attleboro for a Mass at St. Mary's commemorating his uncle's death. As his mother walked down the aisle after taking Communion, a flashback hit. "The priest suddenly seemed huge," he says. "The altar boys became tiny." Dennis burst into tears, pushed his mother aside and ran out of the church.

The flashbacks came like lightning. Father Porter in his cassock crossing the lawn heading toward him. Father Porter pressing his genitals against his face. Suddenly, Dennis remembered the priest in vivid and excruciating detail.

Two weeks later, the phone rang. "They've found Porter," his sister announced. Frank Fitzpatrick had just appeared on Boston television station WBZ with eight other victims and his audiotape of James Porter admitting the abuse. The next day, Dennis flew to Massachusetts. He manned the phones in Fitzpatrick's office as Porter victims started calling. Familiar voices from his childhood came on the line: old classmates, the bullies in the schoolyard, the guys from the in-crowd who had tormented his youth with cries of "Holy Boy." They too had hidden wounds inflicted by the priest.

"These were not forty-year-old men calling," Dennis says. "It was as if we were ten years old and calling each other from home. Suddenly, for the first time ever, I had something in common with these guys. We were talking to each other."

After a decade of sobriety and a long struggle out of the pit into which he'd been pushed at the age of ten, Dennis was liberated by a voice playing in his head: "It's not a secret anymore.

It's not a secret anymore." Dennis broadcast his long-held secret to the world on radio talk shows, on national television programs and in newspaper interviews.

"Do you forgive James Porter?" he was asked by an interviewer for CNN.

The Baltimore executive who weaves words with startling eloquence was speechless. "Forgiveness?" he says now, having reflected on the answer. "When I went to confession, you said three Hail Marys, three Our Fathers and it was gone. This won't be gone with three Hail Marys and three Our Fathers. Forgiveness is not the issue. Forgiveness means it's over. And it's not over."

Dennis has traded New Testament concern with forgiveness for Old Testament demand for justice. As he discovered how many complaints there had been against Porter, and how many times the Church had protected him, Dennis also discovered righteous indignation. Its target is not James Porter. "The Church is the real sodomist," he says. "It's as if they were standing behind Porter cheering him on with every thrust."

In October 1992, Dennis wrote to his hometown newspaper: "With their coverup, collusion, finger-pointing and minimization, the Church hierarchy have declared nuclear war on their faithful's souls."

Dennis Gaboury never goes to church. "I find it meaningless," he says flatly. "It has nothing to do with my spirituality." His older brother, Vic, a priest in Chicago, struggles to find peace with his brother's trauma. But even he finds little solace in the institution that has been his home for thirty-five years. His fellow priests stare blankly when he tries to talk about it. "They freeze me out," he says. "They would like to deny this. They don't want to face the reality that the Church is not facing up to this situation."

Dennis's mother is caught between the agony inflicted on her son and the Church that has grounded her for eighty-one years. She replays Dennis's youth in her mind trying to understand how she missed the pain. She remembers how he would take to the woods alone and refuse to answer her calls. She is haunted by his earliest paintings. "So dark, so much black," she says. "And the faces, so strange, so weird."

Since the Porter scandal erupted, she simply hasn't been able to walk into a church. She prays every night, offering up her pain, and her children, to God. But she cannot go to Mass. "Every time I go, if the priest touches the altar boy, I want to yell, get your hands off of him, get your hands off him," she says. "I'm still so angry. I don't believe anything they say during the sermon. I can't believe anything they say anymore. I've only been to church six times since this all came out," she says, sobbing. "It's gone. It's just gone, and I miss it so."

On September 23, 1992, Dennis made the eight-hour trip from Baltimore to Fall River, Massachusetts, in six hours in his silver taupe Toyota Camry. He waited with forty other Porter victims for the man who had always seemed so much larger, so much more powerful, to be arraigned. Suddenly—out of nowhere, it seemed to Dennis—Porter appeared in handcuffs. Older. Heavier. Looking worn out, Dennis says, like the faded Oriental carpet in his rectory office.

Two months later, just before he received a settlement check signed with a cross by the bishop of Fall River, Dennis awoke at 2 A.M. smiling. In his dream, he'd run an obstacle course through the halls of a school. He'd passed through a huge hollow medallion studded with swords poised to skewer him and over tiles in the floor that collapsed into a bottomless pit. When he crossed the final hurdle, he walked down a long ramp—just like the ramps at St. Mary's School—and out the glass double doors.

"The school building was me and I finally learned how to get through all the obstacles set up when I was ten years old," he says. "I could finally grow up. It was finally safe. After thirty years, the broken boy who left Porter's office had become the child who walked in."

CHILD SEXUAL ABUSE LEAVES NO VISIBLE SCARS ON ITS VICTIMS. Unlike a beating, it leaves no bruises. Unlike a knifing, no oozing wound. As adults, survivors cannot open their shirts and declare: Here, see the marks. But they only appear unblemished. They are damaged by a violation of trust more profound than any violation of the body. They are scarred by a premature loss of childhood innocence that prevents them from becoming healthy adults.

Small children revert to infantile acts. They wet their beds. They refuse to sleep alone. Older ones retreat from family and friends, hiding in their rooms or turning their terror into terrorism, lashing out at others. If they fail to break the silence imposed by self-blame and shame, they grow to adulthood imprisoned by the rickety shelters they create to build some semblance of safety in a dangerous world. Without help, they become unmoored— from their bodies, from their families, from any possibility of intimacy.

Survivors tell familiar stories of years of depression, anxiety, self-loathing and fear of others. They organize their lives around their wounds. Many hate their bodies, which betrayed them by attracting the abuse. They eat too much or too little, suffer from bulimia or anorexia. Others can't sleep, besieged by nightmares. Some find sex so dirty that they cannot bear to touch; others fall into promiscuity. Plagued with fears and self-doubts, they shut down emotionally, sometimes with the help of drugs and alcohol. They destroy their marriages. Sometimes, they destroy themselves.

When the abuser wears a priest's collar, the wounds are deeper, and closer to the core. "I believe these children were damaged more than any other children I have seen in the past twenty-five years," says Alexander Zaphiris, a therapist who evaluated more than a dozen victims of Father Gilbert Gauthe. "I've seen kids abused by a YMCA leader. I've seen kids abused by Boy Scout leaders. This is different. These victims were much more vulnerable and much more traumatized. They didn't respect their parents. They didn't respect their Church. They didn't respect anyone. They were completely empty. I saw bodies, empty bodies. That's something I had not seen before in my work."

Mic Hunter, a St. Paul psychologist who has treated two dozen victims of priests, offers an explanation for why abuse by a priest causes such severe devastation: "They have a sense that they must be real shit if a messenger of God would do this to them."

Fearing God has abandoned them—or singled them out for a

terrible fate—they are faced with the ultimate test of faith: to turn to the church of their abusers or face the world without the only spiritual home they have known. It's a Hobson's choice for most, who find the Church less a house of solace than a wall of denial.

Few are able to seek comfort in another house of worship. "If a Methodist is abused by a minister, he can simply become a Presbyterian," says Marie Fortune, a United Church of Christ minister who works to heal parishes devastated by the sexual misdeed of their clergy. "Catholics don't have that choice. They've been taught that theirs is the only true Church." They are left, then, physically violated, emotionally raw, psychologically damaged—and spiritually abandoned.

The pain was so overwhelming for Christopher Schultz that he could find no way to escape it. At the age of twelve, he couldn't erase the memories of Brother Edmund Coakeley, a Franciscan teacher and scoutmaster, locking the doors of the school gym and demanding that the boy whip him with a cat-o'-nine-tails. He couldn't forget being dressed in flimsy underwear and acting out the Stations of the Cross in the nude.

For seven months, the boy's life became a nightmare of hospitalizations and therapists' sessions. Chris hallucinated that Coakeley was in his house, trying to get him. He tried to slash his wrists. His family went on suicide watch, keeping sharp objects out of reach, listening for his footsteps as he wandered their spacious house in the New Jersey suburbs of New York City.

On May 28, 1979, the sixth grader sat watching television in his bedroom with his mother. He got up and went into the bathroom, opened the medicine cabinet and drank a full bottle of oil of wintergreen. He began to hyperventilate. Fluid filled his lungs. He fell into a coma. The next day he was dead.

Chris Schultz's devastation was extreme, but not unique. The victim of one Florida priest hanged himself in his parents' backyard in the late 1980s. Before he died, the young man asked his brother to contact his abuser: "Tell him I forgive him."

Not all survivors turn the destruction inward. One of two brothers allegedly abused by Father Francis Luddy, a Pennsylvania priest, has been jailed for armed robbery, assault of a gay man and theft. He's spent time in prison and mental institutions. One of Porter's victims is serving time in the Barnstable, Massachusetts, prison for reenacting his own abuse by raping a child.

Gregory Riedle went after the source of his pain. The St. Paul man set out to murder his alleged abuser with a butcher knife and a club. His girlfriend called the police before he could carry out his plan. They found him in a bar emboldening himself with swigs of alcohol. In his car lay a simple note: "He has to die. Unfortunately, with his death, comes mine."

A Seattle victim cannot resist attacking Roman Catholic churches. Every year during Holy Week, which was the week of his abuse, he tries to burn one down, although the police have never been able to catch him. Most years, he only manages to char their interiors. But one year he succeeded in leveling an entire structure, and admitted the crime to his psychotherapist. The diocese has now arranged for him to be hospitalized from Palm Sunday to Easter.

But the worst damage is often less dramatic. It is the subtle insinuation of fear and shame into the most intimate corners of victims' lives.

Even at thirty, one California victim still feels like she is a tramp, no matter how often she reminds herself that she was thirteen and her abuser was sixty-two, that she wore the green plaid uniform and knee socks of a parochial school girl and he wore a collar. The San Diego woman has spent most of her adult life reinforcing that conclusion. She prefers to have sex with people whose names she doesn't know. She prefers to have lots of sex, with ever-changing partners. She prefers sado-masochism whenever she can get it. She knows her reaction isn't healthy. Her therapist has told her that—and more. "But if I can't get intimate, I might as well get fucked," she says.

Most survivors try harder to be intimate. Many fail. Children abused by priests are hypersensitive to danger. They are unable to trust. So the landscapes of victims' lives become littered with passionate romances that disintegrate at commitment and commitments destroyed by touch.

Calvin Mire, Gilbert Gauthe's victim in Louisiana, was married at the age of eighteen and divorced before he turned twenty.

His wife cheated on him, Calvin insists. By age twenty-three he was on his second marriage—and it was shaky. Sitting in a hotel room in Lafayette, he confessed to irrational jealousy, to paranoia and distrust. His wife, Pam, sat next to him in stony silence as he recited the litany of betrayal he has suffered. She seemed a bit annoyed, but mostly bored.

"I'll be honest with you, and she's sitting right here," Calvin said, pointing at his wife. "I still can't trust anybody."

The marriages of the other five men who were altar boys with him in Louisiana are all either on the rocks or dissolved. They are hardly unusual. Of the sixty-eight victims of Father Porter who first came forward in Massachusetts, only a handful remain married to a first spouse.

Calvin, along with many of the other male victims, is also haunted by a fear ingrained in virtually every victim who has studied the profile of abusers: Will I turn out like him? Because he's read statistics suggesting that many, if not most, molesters were themselves sexually abused, he looks at his children and worries that one day he will want to touch them, that the next day he will. But the numbers that get bandied about—30 percent, 50 percent, even 80 percent—are cruel statistics that are more harmful than illuminating. While it may well be true that molesters were often victims, most victims do not become molesters. Given the rate of abuse in the nation, if they did, no child anywhere could find safety.

David Clohessy of St. Louis has achieved what few survivors manage: a close, loving relationship with his wife. But the damage creeps in when they make love because Clohessy cannot bear to have a woman touch his penis. When the repressed memories of his abuse surfaced in 1988, he began weeping whenever Laura's hand brushed his groin.

SOME PEOPLE LOSE THEIR FAMILIES, WHO CAN'T COPE WITH what's happened and shut them out. Others feel as if they've lost God, or that God doesn't exist. " 'If God is speaking through this person, what the hell is he doing allowing this abuse to go on?' That's the question. That's the way it works itself out in a child's mind," explains Thom Harrigan, a Boston psychotherapist who works with children sexually abused by priests—and is himself the survivor of such abuse.

One fourteen-year-old Phoenix girl explained it clearly in a letter she wrote to the judge who was about to sentence the priest who molested her: "Sometimes I feel Jesus is mad at me." Another victim decided Jesus was cruel. He figured the priest who abused him was going to heaven, so he must be slated for hell. He did not mind. "He wanted to go to hell, away from where the priest and others like him would be," his therapist recounted.

Yet another—abused by a priest who would stand on a chair singing hymns while his altar boys lined up to masturbate him— decided Jesus was a lie. "I don't need prayers, I don't believe in God," he wrote in a four-page, single-spaced suicide note. "It's a farce. Everybody is scared of it. My brother and I were both molested by a Catholic priest when I was seven and he was fourteen. As long as people believe, you're living in a false world. I have to go prepare now, good-bye cruel world."

Then the thirty-two-year-old drove his car into a concrete bridge abutment at more than a hundred miles an hour.

But few actually lose their faith in God. It was God, they feel, who brought them through their trauma. It was the Catholic Church that abandoned them. Tony Kraskouskas of Gardner, Massachusetts, stopped going to Mass when he decided the Church cared less about his daughter, Jennifer, than about the priest who repeatedly raped her from the time she was nine years old to the time she was eleven.

When that priest, Father Robert Kelley, was indicted, other priests rallied to his side. After the Worcester *Telegram & Gazette* ran a front-page photograph of Kelley, weeping and in handcuffs, no fewer than 105 priests banded together to buy a full-page advertisement in the newspaper protesting the picture's use and placement. "For the priest who pleaded guilty and for all those involved, this court procedure and sentence were tragic enough," they wrote. Not one of those priests ever called Jennifer and her family to ask them how they felt.

After the trial, Bishop Timothy Harrington contacted them, inviting them to talk. But his comments made the family feel that his primary concern was not to console them, but to figure out whether they planned to file a lawsuit against the Church. Tony gave the bishop the names of other girls in town who had spent extensive time with the priest and urged the bishop to call their families to ask if they, too, had been abused. The bishop declined. He said he didn't want to dwell on the unpleasant situation any longer.

Tony believes the bishop just didn't want to risk more lawsuits, or more bad publicity. He has determined that the Church puts two values above all others: its bank account and its image. That mission strikes him as perverse. "Maybe there is a God," he says, "but maybe he's not in the Catholic Church."

His wife still attends Mass. But when she listens to the priest read the Gospel of Christ, she often feels rage well up inside her. No one in the Church heeded that gospel when it came to her daughter. "They're not practicing what they preach," she says. She has stopped giving any money when the collection baskets are passed around, and she wonders if she should stop going to church altogether. But she still feels a need to pay homage to God. "I feel that what I have is God-given," she says. "I'm having a hard time separating God from the Church."

MIGUEL CHINCHILLA BATTLED FOR HIS FAITH FOR HALF HIS LIFE. Sometimes when he walked into the peaceful familiarity of daily Mass and heard the priest say "Hallelujah," his heart would leap. Sometimes he simply could not enter a church. Sometimes he was drawn to the confessional, to the joy of the Eucharist. Sometimes he just stopped being Catholic and feigned a cynical, existentialist angst.

"It's tough trying to stay a Catholic when you've been sexually abused by a priest, then raped again by the hierarchy," he said.

Unlike most victims, Miguel kept trying. The Catholic Church was the only safe haven he ever knew. In his childhood, the Church was his refuge from the chaotic home life of a once-wealthy Cuban family trying to re-create Havana 1958 in Miami 1970. In 1960, they had fled the island and taken up residence at the Fountainbleau Hotel on Miami Beach to await Fidel Castro's fall. When their dreams collided with the stark reality of making a living in a country where their last names meant nothing, they drowned their disappointment in tranquilizers and strict obedience to Catholic doctrine. "If the pope tells us to stand on our heads, we'll stand on our heads tomorrow," his father taught him. No evening was complete without a family rosary. Dictator Francisco Franco was much admired for saving Spain from godless communism.

Miguel responded by trying to be the most devout little boy in Miami, to be as much like Jesus as a young Cuban-American could be. He awoke every morning at 5:45 and trudged six blocks in the half-light to The Church of the Little Flower. He prayed fervently for the conversion of Russia. Sometimes he put stones in his shoes, hoping his pain would pay for his unrepented sins. When he was distracted and withdrawn, his father believed he was seeing the Virgin Mary.

When he was five, his parents sent Miguel to his first psychiatrist because he was constantly contradicting his mother. When he was fourteen, they sent him to a psychiatric ward. The immediate excuse for his institutionalization: an overdose of Valium—three, to be exact. The probable cause was that he simply didn't fit in. He embarrassed his younger brothers. He wore scruffy scuffed shoes and wrinkled clothes. He was, in his mother's words, "too dramatic."

Discharged on Thorazine, Stelazine and Elavil, he returned to the solace of the Church—and to Father Ricardo Castellanos, known among the Cuban elite as the right counselor for troubled boys. The thirty-three-year-old priest talked to his young charge about the very books and ideas his parents had banned from his household. He took him to foreign films and fancy restaurants. Father Castellanos became his savior: someone who seemed to understand him, who admired his precocious intellect and individuality.

Miguel was putty in his hands. "He was so sure of himself," he said. "So strong. And horribly wise. There was just something about him which inspired trust. I wanted to please him very, very much." No one thought it strange that a grown man would lavish so much attention on an adolescent. It was just another example of the basic goodness and selflessness of the Father.

In the summer of 1975, Father Castellanos came down with hepatitis and the fourteen-year-old spent his school vacation visiting the convalescing priest. "Why don't you take your shirt off, lie down and take a nap with me," Father Castellanos allegedly suggested one afternoon when the boy visited him at St. Kiernan's parish rectory. That one afternoon became two and then a daily ritual. Father Castellanos would rub Miguel's back and lay the boy's head on his chest. "It seemed almost biblical to me," Miguel said. "You know, St. John often lay with his head on Jesus' chest. It seemed so pure. I never dreamed he had sexual feelings toward me."

At the end of the summer, Father Castellanos invited his young companion to spend Labor Day weekend in Key West with him. It was the priest's thanks for a summer of devotion. What a lovely gesture, Miguel's parents thought. What a kind and holy man.

On their first afternoon in Key West, Miguel lay down to take a nap. He alleged that the priest stretched out beside him and began to stroke his genitals. "I remember being absolutely shocked and petrified," Miguel said. "I wanted him to stop because the relationship, up to that point, had been as close to altruism as you can get. I thought, maybe if I just lie here, and pretend I'm asleep, he'll stop."

Father Castellanos did not, according to Miguel, whose accounts of this and other sexual episodes are denied by Castellanos. Miguel said that without a word, the priest undressed them both. The boy, embarrassed by his semi-nudity, pulled the sheet over his thin frame. The priest removed it and tried to enter him. Miguel made him stop. Then the priest rolled onto his back and guided the boy's penis inside him.

"I didn't know what to do," Miguel said. "This was my pastoral counselor, my confidant. This man was my confessor. I know that I didn't want to do anything that would upset him. After a while, I did become aroused. That made me much more confused. I didn't know what to do next."

That night, Miguel fell asleep in the priest's arms. The next morning Father Castellanos whispered to him, "Now you're my lover."

Two months later, Miguel went into a bathroom in his parents' home and nicked his wrists in a feeble attempt at suicide. He watched the blood flow into the sink, then clot. Terrified, he didn't try again.

Miguel kept up the routine of family religiosity: grace before meals, nightly rosary, Sunday Mass. But the Church had lost its magic. "Once the sex began, I started to view priests and the Church as something cynical and people of my parents' religious bent as naive," Miguel said. "I remember talking about it with Ricardo, saying 'this is all a farce.' He said, 'Do you blame me for that?' I lied and said no."

For two years the man and boy met almost daily, allegedly having sex in Father Castellanos's rectory and the rectories of other priests, where Father Castellanos shared the boy with his own best friend. When Miguel was fifteen, Father Castellanos invited him to Europe. Miguel's mother, Rita, opposed the trip; she had gradually begun to question the priest's intentions and now felt his relationship with her son had gone too far. But her friends dismissed her worries and told her she should not deprive her son of the chance to see St. Peter's, to go to the Vatican. Her husband told her she was being irrational; Father Castellanos was a priest, after all. Other priests accused her of standing in the way of the boy's moral development. Rita started to doubt her own sanity, and relented.

The priest and the boy toasted Miguel's sixteenth birthday on the Champs-Elysées. They attended Mass at St. Peter's, celebrated by the pope. In public and in bed, Father Castellanos treated Miguel like a grown-up. But in most respects, Miguel was still a troubled boy. And that little boy increasingly felt overwhelmed by the conflicts and the hypocrisy in their relationship.

Shortly after they returned to Miami, Miguel snapped under the pressure. He took to his bed, refusing to eat or talk. He had to tell his parents something but couldn't bring himself to confess the abuse. He said he was a drug addict—although he'd never done more than smoke a little marijuana. They sent him to a treatment center where he began to feel that he should break his silence. "The secrecy was killing me," he said.

He told his counselor and, three months later, his parents. "I knew it," his mother screamed. "I knew it. Everybody said I was crazy. I want a gun. Somebody get me a gun. I'm going to kill him." She ripped up every family photograph that included Father Castellanos. Her husband sat in stony silence, disbelieving. Neither reached out to comfort Miguel.

His parents went to the auxiliary bishop of Miami, who declared their son to be a psychotic liar. He never questioned the boy. He ordered Chinchilla's father to be silent on the matter "under penalty of sin," Miguel and his mother said. His father will not confirm the story. He will not break his silence.

Miguel joined the army, fleeing Miami for Munich and commencing a pattern of restless movement, perpetual escape and constant immersion in organizations or behaviors that would allow him to lose himself, to surrender all control and personal responsibility, to shut out any real feeling. His ability to trust anything or anyone—even himself—had been put to an almost impossible test by what had happened with Father Castellanos.

Miguel's therapist, Dr. Robin August, explained: "Here's the one person you should be able to trust, probably, right below God, right? More than anybody in the world, more than your parents. So you open yourself, you make yourself completely vulnerable when you turn to this priest, and he abuses you. A violation of trust like that—how can you trust again? Who can you trust? Maybe not even God."

Miguel hid his pain and confusion behind bold masks and provocative poses. In Munich, he played the hip gay Cuban concerned about nothing but promiscuous sex and a good time. He played the devil-may-care connoisseur of recreational drugs, progressing from cocaine to heroin. He played the existentialist who never stepped into a church and felt content in a world in which God was dead. But in the private corners of his heart and mind, God was very much alive. Miguel yearned to be reunited with Him.

One day, during a sudden rainstorm, he took shelter in the

nearest structure—a Catholic church. A priest was saying Mass. "Blessed are the pure of heart for they shall see God," he read from the Beatitudes. Miguel broke down.

"I didn't feel pure of heart and didn't think I would ever see God," he said. "My desire to see God and be one with God overwhelmed me and I was so afraid. That fear stayed with me for a long, long, long time and those words haunted me. I was so far from being pure of heart."

But he wanted to be. He wanted to do good works, to live as a Christian. So after he left the army and returned home to Miami, Miguel volunteered at a shelter for the homeless run by the Catholic Church. There he began to meet Catholic social justice activists and to join them at Sunday Mass. He still could not regain the fervor of his youthful faith, but he felt at home in the quiet sanctuary of a church, comforted by the familiarity of the Gospel. He joined the Catholic Worker movement and moved to Kansas to work in a shelter there for Central American refugees.

During his years in Germany, Miguel had succeeded in banishing Father Castellanos from his mind. But now, back in the Church, Miguel couldn't stop thinking about the priest and the boy in Key West. After four months in Kansas, he flew to Miami to confront the archbishop about Father Castellanos. "It was important for me to reclaim the Church as my own and I needed the archbishop to reach out to me as a brother, as a Catholic and get this man help," said Miguel. "I desperately needed closure."

His attempt was a fiasco. The archbishop backed out of a prearranged meeting and sent his auxiliary, who greeted Miguel with a lawyer on one side and the chancellor on the other. A videotape camera recorded the meeting. Miguel's fantasy of a gentle, pastoral visit disintegrated.

The lawyer asked Miguel to sign a contract releasing the diocese from financial liability. He agreed. Then the lawyer asked skeptically: "Why didn't you come forward before?"

"I was frightened," Miguel said softly.

He then went on to tell the long story of his relationship with Father Castellanos, to talk about the other victims whose names he knew, about the many more he could only imagine. When he was finished, Father Castellanos was brought in to confront his

Ed Morris with Father Terrence Pinkowski at Morris's graduation from Archbishop Ryan High School in Philadelphia, 1981. Morris, whose story is told in Chapter 4, "Suffer the Children," alleges that Pinkowski began sexually abusing him four years prior to this, when he was fourteen.

Tim Martinez of Albuquerque, New Mexico, in 1980, at age seventeen. Martinez says he was sexually abused by a New Mexico priest for many years. His story is also told in Chapter 4, "Suffer the Children."

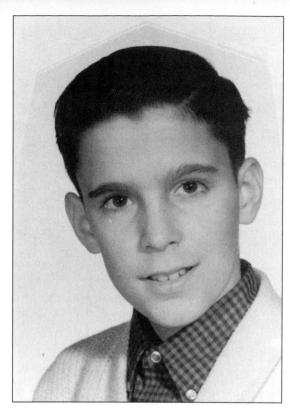

Dennis Gaboury of North Attleboro, Massachusetts, in 1962, at age eleven. A year prior to this, he says, Father James Porter invited him into a church office for butter cookies—then molested him. Gaboury's story is told in Chapter 8, "The Crucifixion of Innocence." Porter's is told in Chapter 1, "While God Wasn't Watching."

Dennis Gaboury, now of Baltimore, Maryland, in 1993, at age forty-one. Gaboury helped lead the crusade to bring James Porter to justice more than two decades after his alleged crimes.

Susan Sandoval (far right), then of Abiquiu, New Mexico, at age fifteen with her mother, brother and a friend. Unbeknownst to all of them, Sandoval had an unorthodox lover—her priest. Her story is told in Chapter 6, "The Silencing of the Lambs."

Susan Sandoval today, with her son and daughter.

James Porter, escorted by law-enforcement officials, steps off a plane at the Minneapolis-St. Paul airport in September 1992. The former priest is returning from an arraignment in Massachusetts to face another arraignment in Minnesota on additional sexual abuse charges. James Porter's story is the subject of Chapter 1, "While God Wasn't Watching." (*Minneapolis Star Tribune*)

David Clohessy of St. Louis, Missouri, pictured in 1967, when he was twelve years old. That's the age at which his sexual abuse by a priest who was a close family friend began, Clohessy alleged two decades later in a civil lawsuit. Clohessy's story is discussed in Chapter 6, "The Silencing of the Lambs."

Father Robert Kelley, convicted of raping a nine-year-old girl in his parish, breaks down in court in March 1990 as he makes a final statement to a Massachusetts judge before being sentenced to five to seven years in the state prison. The publication of this picture on the front page of the *Worcester Telegram & Gazette* provoked a furious response from 105 area priests, who purchased a full-page advertisement in the newspaper to protest what they saw as its sensationalism and poor taste. Father Kelley's story is told in Chapter 4, "Suffer the Children." (*Worcester Telegram & Gazette*)

Jennifer Kraskouskas of Gardner, Massachusetts, in the fall of 1983, when she was nine years old. She was just beginning the fourth grade—and she was already being abused by Father Robert Kelley, a forty-one-year-old priest. Jennifer's story is told in Chapter 4, "Suffer the Children."

Above: Jennifer around Christmastime, 1983. Here she plays with the E.T. doll through which she often spoke.

Jennifer in the fall of 1984, when she was ten years old and beginning the fifth grade. She was receiving the doting attention and countless gifts from Father Robert Kelley, her pastor at her parish and a close family friend. Kelley was also molesting her.

Jennifer at age ten. Father Robert Kelley would sneak up to her bedroom at night, pluck the stuffed animals off her bed—and begin touching her. Her family believes this picture was taken by Kelley.

Jennifer at age eighteen in her high school graduation photo, taken in 1992. More than seven years have passed since the end of her abuse by Kelley, and it has been two years since Kelley was sentenced to prison for his crimes.

Jeanne Miller stands outside her suburban Illinois town house in 1992. Miller founded Victims of Clergy Abuse Linkup (VOCAL), which became the driving force behind efforts to compel the Church to take stricter action against abusive priests. Miller is the subject of the epilogue, "Amazing Grace."
(Timothy P. Boyle for the *Chicago Tribune*)

Robert Kirsch, a former priest of the Archdiocese of Santa Fe, New Mexico, is currently the target of a lawsuit by Susan Sandoval, who alleges he sexually abused her when she was a teenager. Their stories are told in Chapter 6, "The Silencing of the Lambs."
(*Albuquerque Journal*, 1991)

accuser. "I loved Miguel very much," he explained. "I don't understand why he's making these charges." Father Castellanos continues to deny these charges.

The auxiliary bishop and the chancellor pronounced that what the priest and Miguel really needed was reconciliation. The two were left to talk alone. Before they did, Father Castellanos searched Miguel for a tape recorder. "It was so ugly," Miguel said. "I went to them in good faith. I only wanted Ricardo sent to treatment. And he was lying. And I was absolutely convinced that everybody in that room knew that I was speaking the truth. I even knew I hadn't been the first one to complain."

Bitterly disillusioned, Miguel left the Church once again. He moved from Kansas back to Miami, then from Miami back to Europe and a life of sex and drugs and forgetting. But when he began to fall ill with AIDS, to feel his days were numbered, he realized he could not die at peace unless he reconciled himself with the Church. He returned to Miami—and his Church—once again. He demanded a private meeting between just him and Archbishop Edward McCarthy. This time, he insisted there be no lawyers, no cameras. This time, he threatened to go public with his charge.

His Catholic friends and his father tried to dissuade him. "Think of the damage to the Church," they said. "The Protestants will dance in the streets." But Miguel persisted even though his immune system was beginning to disintegrate, his body to grow thin and frail. He needed to force the Church into accountability for what had happened to him, to make the Church recognize its errors and change. "I couldn't die knowing I could have done something to stop this and hadn't," he said.

On a bright day in November 1991, Miguel walked alone into the office of Archbishop McCarthy who began the meeting by talking about his recent trip to Spain and all the pretty ships he'd seen in the exhibition celebrating Columbus's discovery of the Americas and the 500th anniversary of Christianity in the New World. Miguel thought, "This man is out of his mind. I've come here with a serious complaint and this man is making small talk." Then, in fewer than thirty minutes, the archbishop managed to bring up not only Miguel's own history of drug abuse but the litany of his family's problems. He even questioned the young man about his "communist activities," a red flag in a city where human rights work and liberal politics are tarred with Fidel Castro's brush. He seemed to be issuing Miguel a warning. Although the archbishop promised to investigate the accusation, he never specified how or when. "You'll hear from someone soon," he promised.

Miguel was still waiting when he received last rites from his confessor in a stark Miami hospital room and when he died five days later, at the age of thirty-one, on April 7, 1993.

PART III

Let us remember: what hurts the victim most is not the cruelty of the oppressor, but the silence of the bystander.

—ELIE WIESEL

Chapter 9

CARDINAL
SINS

FATHER THOMAS ADAMSON WAS DANGER-
ous. He had a yearning for adolescent boys
that he couldn't control. His first bishop in the
Diocese of Winona, Minnesota, knew it, having discussed it with Adamson in 1964. His
second bishop in that diocese knew it, having
had his own talk with Adamson in 1974, according to Adamson's own testimony years
later in court. And his third bishop—in the
Archdiocese of St. Paul and Minneapolis, to
which he was transferred in 1975—knew it as
well, having heard complaints from at least
one set of parents in 1980 and having confronted Adamson at that time.

But none of them ever told criminal authorities. None of them ever warned parents in
the more than half a dozen parishes to which
Adamson was assigned. None of them ever
kept him away from children. And so Adam-

son claimed victim after victim, for more than two decades, as
Church officials continually granted him forgiveness, gave him
second, third and even fourth chances and looked the other way.
"Adamson was like a mad dog foaming at the mouth," St. Paul
attorney Jeffrey Anderson said later in arguing one of fourteen
lawsuits he filed on behalf of Adamson's victims. "And they
turned him loose in the schoolyard."

Adamson claimed his first victim in 1961. Three years later,
while at a new parish, he confided to Winona bishop Edward
Fitzgerald that he had had sexual contact with a different boy.
Fitzgerald told the priest to control himself and transferred him
to another parish. In 1967, other priests heard that Adamson was
sexually abusing boys and referred him for psychiatric care. But
his access to children was not restricted.

In 1969, Bishop Fitzgerald retired and Bishop Loras Watters
took his place. Watters later insisted that he was never briefed
about Adamson's history. But Adamson testified that he had discussed his problem with Watters in 1974 and was sent to Connecticut for treatment. When Adamson got back to Minnesota,
he was assigned to a new parish. Church officials neither warned
parents there about Adamson's past nor put any limits on his
contacts with children.

In late 1974, the silence and cover-up almost unraveled. By
that time, Adamson's first known victim had become a priest and
was in treatment for alcoholism. Sifting through his emotional
turmoil and its origins, the man decided to tell his brother the
long-held secret of his abuse. The brother probed Adamson's past
and learned that the priest had abused other children as well. He
called Bishop Watters one Saturday and demanded Adamson's
immediate removal from his current parish. "I told him if Adamson ever said another Mass [there], we would be in the pulpit
and tell everyone who and what he was," the man testified.
Bishop Watters called him back at 9 P.M. that night, he said, to
tell him that Adamson had just resigned.

Watters did not, however, move to eject Adamson from the
priesthood. Instead, he found a new home for him in the neighboring Archdiocese of St. Paul-Minneapolis. It is unclear how
much information about Adamson's past accompanied him to the

Twin Cities. Archbishop John Roach later testified that he had simply heard rumors about a homosexuality problem and some psychiatric treatment. But Bishop Watters, in a 1984 letter to Roach, wrote: "I am very sorry that Father Adamson's many talents continue to be compromised because of his involvement with juvenile males. . . . As you will recall, when I asked you to consider helping Father Adamson in January of 1975, I indicated that I could no longer accept pastoral responsibility in the Winona Diocese because of this same type of problem."

In any case, Adamson got a brand-new parish assignment—again, with no public warning about his past and no close supervision. His predations continued until about 1980, when the parents of a new victim complained to archdiocesan officials. When Adamson was confronted, he confessed, and was sent to inpatient psychiatric treatment for a month. Then he was resurrected at yet another new parish.

This time, at least, Adamson was told to stay away from children. He didn't. And on at least two occasions, archdiocesan officials were told that he was keeping steady company with a boy from his previous parish. But Archbishop Roach and his advisers did not yank Adamson out of his new parish or warn the child's parents. Asked why in court, one of Roach's auxiliary bishops testified: "It did not occur to the archbishop that I go see them."

So Adamson, who had begun sexually abusing that boy in 1979 when he was twelve, continued having sex with him until 1987. That year, Adamson's decades of molestations finally came to public light—and he was finally removed from ministry—as past victims began filing lawsuits against the Church. While most of the suits were settled out of court, one actually went to trial in 1990. Church officials admitted negligence, but attorney Anderson sought to prove they had been worse than negligent—that they had been reckless. He asked the jury to grant not just compensatory damages but punitive damages against a church which had placed so many children in danger.

The jury obliged, returning a compensatory judgment of $859,500 and a punitive judgment of $2.7 million. It marked the first time ever that punitive damages had been assessed against the Roman Catholic Church in any type of case, Anderson says.

The jury foreman explained to one newspaper reporter: "They knew they had a priest with problems [and] at no time did they remove the gentleman to an assignment where he would have absolutely no youth contact." He added that in never telling parishioners about Adamson's problems or reporting him to authorities, Church officials "profited by this, not financially, but by preservation of image."

THE TRAGEDY OF CHILD SEXUAL ABUSE IN THE CATHOLIC CHURCH is more than the story of sexually confused or disordered priests acting out destructive desires. It is the story, too, of Church leaders coddling these men, protecting them from criminal prosecution and public exposure and allowing them to continue in ministry despite the threat they posed. Church leaders never purged them from their parishes or the priesthood, never stripped them of their unique opportunity to prey on children. Church leaders thus guaranteed that more and more children would be victimized, until the dimensions of the tragedy became staggering.

Church leaders coaxed into silence parents who complained about a priest's actions, urging them not to go to the authorities and falsely assuring them that Father would never again be allowed to hurt a child. They offered some families money to stay silent. They pacified others by transferring abusive priests out of town, into new parishes. They almost never told parishioners at the former congregation why Father was leaving. They almost never told people at the new congregation why Father was arriving. Parents didn't know to ask their children if Father ever hurt them. Parents didn't know to watch the way Father acted around their kids.

Church leaders disregarded clear warning signs about priests and shrugged off direct complaints, frequently electing ignorance over initiative. They took Father at his word that he would never again misbehave, failing even to keep an eye on him to make sure. They got burned, time and again, and marched straight back into the fire.

There was a pattern in the way Church leaders often dealt with allegations or knowledge about sexually abusive priests. It was distinct, and it was disturbing:

- Church leaders in Boise, Idaho, allowed Father Carmelo Baltazar to work as a hospital chaplain even after he had been kicked out of the U.S. Navy and three previous dioceses for sexual misconduct with minors, allegedly including the fondling of one boy who was on a kidney dialysis machine. They took no action against Baltazar after he was reported for fondling a boy in double leg traction at the Boise hospital.

  Baltazar was eventually brought up on criminal charges, convicted and sentenced to seven years in prison in 1985. The judge said: "I think the Catholic Church has its atonement to make as well. They helped create you." Bishop Sylvester Treinen of Boise later responded: "I've felt all along we've done everything we can do. We've been prudently careful all along for years. No matter how well you take care of your car, no matter how safe your car is, you're still going to have an accident now and then. Or a flat tire."

- Church leaders in the Archdiocese of New York in 1989 transferred Father Daniel Calabrese to a new parish after complaints by parents that he had given alcohol and shown pornographic movies to teenage boys. Parents were allegedly assured the priest would be kept away from kids in the future.

  Two years later, Calabrese was assigned to coordinate the efforts of a countywide Catholic Youth Organization. He was soon charged with sodomizing a sixteen-year-old boy whom he had gotten drunk on vodka. Within one hour of his arrest, another priest in the parish asked an assistant district attorney on the case: "Can we make this go away if we make Father Calabrese go away?" The answer was no. Calabrese pleaded guilty and was sentenced to ninety days in jail.

  Afterward, the district attorney, furious at the Church's handling of Calabrese, wrote a letter to Cardinal John O'Connor saying: "I cannot express to you in any stronger terms the sense of outrage I feel when I look at how the Church responded to these incidents. A grievous wrong was committed in this case and the Church, under the circumstances, must share responsibility for that wrong. I feel the tragic consequences and emotional trauma that occurred in this Dutchess County case could have been averted."

• Church leaders in Orlando, Florida, ignored complaints and warning signs about Father William Authenreith for more than a decade. In 1976, a parish man complained that the priest had touched his son's penis. Church officials transferred Authenreith to a new parish, where he allegedly molested four boys—including three brothers. When their father complained to another priest, he was told: "It's not for you to judge. That's for God to do."

Authenreith remained in that parish until 1983, when an anonymous letter suggesting he was a molester was sent to the pastor who supervised him. Later that year, Authenreith was transferred again. But teachers at the school there became so concerned about the sexually suggestive comments he was making to boys and girls during their confirmation interviews that they complained directly to the vicar general of the diocese. Authenreith was transferred yet again. The game of musical parishes ended only in 1985, when several lawsuits were filed by past victims and he was suspended from duty as a priest.

• Church leaders in Miami, Florida, did not tell child welfare authorities, as required by state law, about any of at least three allegations they received between 1980 and 1988 about Father Ernesto Garcia-Rubio's sexual abuse of refugee youths from Cuba and Central America. The first complaint, brought to an auxiliary bishop, was made by the mayor of the town in which the priest's parish was located. The second came four years later from a social worker, who also took the alleged victim to the chancery. The third was lodged four years after that by two parish couples.

Church officials neither removed Garcia-Rubio from parish life nor restricted his access to youths. When their inaction drew the attention of the *Miami Herald* in 1988 and a reporter called the archdiocese for comment, Chancellor Gerard LaCerra said he knew of no such accusations against the priest.

Over the next few days, LaCerra changed his story and admitted that the archdiocese had received two of the allegations. In one case, LaCerra said, it became clear that "whatever had happened transpired in [the priest's] sleep." In the other, he said, the accusation was "so vague it honestly didn't deserve our concern."

Garcia-Rubio consistently maintained his innocence. The Miami archdiocese authorized his transfer to Honduras, a posting they insisted the priest had long desired. Church officials there were not told about the allegations in his wake. A spokesman for the archdiocese reasoned: "The bishop of the receiving diocese has an obligation to check out very thoroughly the person he's receiving."

- Church leaders in Providence, Rhode Island, persistently ignored complaints that something was terribly wrong with Father William O'Connell. The priest's boozing and fondness for the company of teenage boys was no secret in the quaint seaside town of Bristol, Rhode Island, home to the nation's oldest Fourth of July parade. When another priest, Father Jude McGeough, arrived there in 1977 to serve as O'Connell's assistant, high school students remarked to him that he was working "up with the drunk" or "up with the fag."

McGeough found gin bottles strewn throughout the rectory, which was pungent with the smell of urine from O'Connell's constant companion, an Irish setter named Sean. On several occasions, he expressed concerns about O'Connell's emotional health to both Providence bishop Louis Gelineau and his auxiliary bishop, Kenneth Angell. Nothing was done. In November 1978, McGeough sent a four-page report on O'Connell to Bishop Gelineau that included a section titled "Scandal of Little Boys." He noted that some boys and their parents talked about the need to stay away from the old priest, and that there were virtually no altar boys left to serve Mass.

Two months later, McGeough was told that Gelineau had met with O'Connell but that O'Connell had refused to resign. McGeough, however, was asked by Church officials if he would like to transfer. "If you put a cross on a hot dog stand, I'll apply for it now," McGeough recalls answering. He was given a new assignment.

Parishioners at St. Mary's complained about O'Connell, too. In 1980, one parish woman wrote a letter to Bishop Gelineau saying she would no longer raise money for Catholic Charities because the Church was ignoring problems at St. Mary's. Another wrote saying that O'Connell was "obviously a sick man. Please help him. If he had cancer you would help him."

In 1983, Father Richard Bucci became O'Connell's new assistant and puzzled over all the boys the pastor overpaid to perform chores around the rectory. Once he spotted a boy inside the rectory dressed only in bikini briefs. Bucci relayed these observations and experiences to Bishop Angell. But O'Connell remained in the parish, unsupervised and unchanged, until his arrest by police in February 1985 on charges of child sexual abuse.

When police searched O'Connell's private rooms in the rectory, they found black-and-white memo pads captioned "You Need My Body Parts," a condom, a chain whip and the books *The Young Male Figure* and *Sex Education for Young Boys.* O'Connell pleaded no contest to twenty-six counts of sexual contact with three boys and was sentenced to a single year in prison.

The failures of Church leaders opened the door wide to lawsuits, and in the late 1980s, as America's litigation mania hit a crescendo and child sexual abuse became an acceptable topic of discussion, there were lawyers aplenty ready to rush through that portal. News of one lawsuit against a priest bred five more; those five bred fifteen. Men and women abused as far back as the 1950s and 1960s suddenly recognized that Church leaders had failed to protect them. As state legislatures lengthened the statutes of limitations for civil suits, victims descended on the courts. The Church came under legal siege. And rather than confess errors of judgment and acknowledge victims' wounds, Church leaders fought back.

Often, they immediately distanced themselves from children and families claiming sexual abuse, fearful that any apology or offer of help might seem an admission of guilt for which they would pay in court. Sometimes they even cast aspersions on the accusers. As James Seritella, a lawyer for the Archdiocese of Chicago, said in a private meeting about the issue in 1986: "When one of these situations develops, those people are the enemy."

Church leaders refused to hand over abusers' personnel records, protecting their priests as they denied their parishioners' cries for justice. And they frequently tried to exploit their status as a religious institution to argue for exemption from legal claims. When deposed in connection with a $14 million lawsuit arising from the O'Connell case, Bishop Gelineau repeatedly evaded questions regarding what he knew about the priest's troubles by saying the inquiries violated his free practice of religion as guaranteed in the United States Constitution. He used the same argument when he refused to hand over files. But a Rhode Island Superior Court judge rejected it, ordering Gelineau to submit to another deposition and give responses to 75 of the 128 questions he had not answered.

In other dioceses, Church leaders claimed that the confidentiality of their files came under the same legal protection as words spoken in the confessional. In still others, they leaned on laws that put financial caps on the amounts for which charitable institutions—including religious organizations—could be sued.

Auxiliary Bishop James Quinn of Cleveland even encouraged diocesan officials to send files on priests who had been accused of child sexual abuse to the Vatican Embassy in Washington, D.C., where diplomatic immunity would protect the documents from being subpoenaed. Quinn explained to the Midwest Canon Law society, in an April 1990 address, that this alternative was preferable to tampering with or destroying files, which would be an obstruction of justice.

In one sense, none of those strategies should have been surprising. A wealthy corporation, faced with a potentially costly lawsuit, will defend itself in any way it can—that's the nature of modern litigation. But when the Church did it, the effect was chilling. People expected more from a religious organization than they did from Union Carbide or from Dow Corning. How could Church leaders turn their backs on the pain of victims? How could they evade answers and accountability and tell half-truths about men who had molested little children?

They were supposed to be moral exemplars, last bastions of

pristine virtue. Yet they were acting no better, and sometimes worse, than everyone else. To many people, it was more than a disappointment. It was an outright scandal.

As priests and bishops around the country filed grimly into and out of court throughout the late 1980s and the early 1990s, Father Thomas Doyle sat in his office on an air force base near Peru, Indiana, the site of his exile, shaking his head and seething with rage. He had warned them about this. He had tried to save them from it. And his reward was ostracism and the kind of agonizing frustration known by the Greek prophetess Cassandra, whose ever-accurate predictions of catastrophe were uniformly and tragically dismissed.

Once a rising canon lawyer, one of four assigned to the Vatican Embassy in Washington, D.C., Doyle is now a military chaplain in the middle of cornfields. Once a member of the Church establishment, he is now an outcast, a priest who doesn't own a Roman collar and unabashedly voices contempt for most American bishops. Once a close friend of Cardinal Joseph Bernardin, he is now totally estranged from the Chicago archbishop; a framed photograph of the two of them hangs, on purpose, above Doyle's bathroom toilet.

He says the way Bernardin and other bishops have handled the child sexual abuse crisis has revealed them to be unChristian, arrogant and just plain stupid. "They do this and they still parade around in their funny outfits and demand respect," Doyle bristles. "They have the intellectual depth of a layer of shellac. The phrase 'smart bishop' is like 'military intelligence': an oxymoron."

Doyle's bitterness now is proportional to the determination he felt back in 1985, when he thought he saw a way to help the Church handle a looming crisis. Doyle was then at the Vatican Embassy, where he was suddenly receiving more and more reports of priests accused of child sexual abuse, the most infamous being Father Gilbert Gauthe. He swapped information with two other concerned Catholics: Ray Mouton, the attorney defending Gauthe against criminal charges, and Father Michael Peterson, a priest psychiatrist who had founded a private hospital, the St. Luke Institute in Suitland, Maryland, that treated priests with emotional problems and disorders. The three agreed that child sexual abuse by priests was a burgeoning scandal that needed to be managed carefully, but aggressively. They vowed to make that happen.

They knew that the American bishops, in reaction to the unfolding Gauthe case, would formally discuss child sexual abuse for the first time at their June 1985 meeting in Collegeville, Minnesota. So they decided to submit a report detailing their own observations and recommendations, culled from their three different areas of expertise: canon law, secular law and psychiatry. Just before the bishops' conference, Doyle and Mouton met in Chicago—Peterson couldn't be there but sent his contributions along—and holed up in a room at the Marriott Hotel on Michigan Avenue to accomplish the task.

Neither Doyle nor Mouton was much of a typist, so they recruited a Chicago-area friend of Doyle's to perform that chore. She borrowed a typewriter from the classical music radio station where she worked and stacked several telephone books on the hotel room chair so she could reach the desk. She, Doyle and Mouton worked nearly around the clock for three days, often forgetting to eat meals. Mouton's son, whom he had brought with him, sat quietly out of the way on one of the two full-sized beds, sketching images of men jumping out of military helicopters and tanks as he listened to his dad talk about a "SWAT team" to help the Church handle child sexual abuse cases.

The report, more than an inch thick, stated boldly that child sexual abuse by priests was shaping up to be "the single most serious and far-reaching problem facing our Church today." It mentioned thirty cases in which priests or Church leaders had been hauled into court and predicted that child sexual abuse by priests could, over the next decade, cost the Church $1 billion in civil suits and legal fees and undermine its credibility as a moral institution. It pointed out the many ways in which the Church's response was failing and proposed remedies to ward off disaster.

It was stunningly savvy and, as it turned out, eerily prescient. The report's authors exhorted bishops to push past their disbelief regarding complaints of priest misconduct. "Where there is smoke, there is fire," the authors wrote. They noted that Church officials usually first heard about abusive priests from victims and their parents—and that it was only when officials disregarded their complaints that criminal and civil authorities entered the picture, publicly exposing the Church's failures. "It is simply a legal, social and psychiatric fact that some action must be taken immediately which indicates to the families, legal authorities, reporting agencies, and future litigating attorneys that [Church leaders take] such accusations with great seriousness," they wrote. Accused priests must be suspended, they insisted, while the accusing parties must be consoled. "The welfare of victims . . . is most important and should be given priority."

They warned that in the 1980s, with the heightened public concern over child abuse and the diminished influence of the Catholic Church, law enforcement authorities would not go easy on bishops and priests. "Our dependence in the past on Roman Catholic judges and attorneys protecting the Dioceses and clerics individually is GONE," they wrote. And they warned that as cases multiplied, more and more news reporters would flock to a story with all the right elements: hypocrisy, exploitation, cover-up.

They made other suggestions, too—most significantly, that some kind of national policy guidelines be discussed or delineated and that the National Conference of Catholic Bishops consider the formation of a crisis intervention team of trained legal and psychiatric professionals to assist dioceses in dealing with complaints of child sexual abuse.

By the time they finished the report, Doyle and Mouton were not only exhausted by their efforts but flushed with pride. It seemed to them an exemplary piece of work and a crucial service to the Church they loved. Concerned about leaks to the news media, they made only fifteen copies of the report and distributed them to selected bishops, on the understanding that those men would carry and present the report to their colleagues. That never happened. The report, produced too late to make it on to the official agenda for the Collegeville meeting of the National Conference of Catholic Bishops, was never formally discussed there. It was not formally discussed at the next bishops' conference, either. In the end, many bishops never received a copy. Many who did never read it. And the ones who initially had encouraged Doyle, Mouton and Peterson in their efforts grew silent and remote. The dire predictions in the report went largely unheeded. The bold ideas in it languished.

The reasons remain something of a mystery. Some bishops and other Church insiders say the report wasn't introduced through the proper channels, that it was perceived to be an ambitious bid by three men intent on carving out more exciting careers, that Doyle's bombastic style and Peterson's widely known homosexuality discredited them in Church leaders' eyes. More likely, bishops just didn't want to believe all the bad news in the report. In 1985, before the first wave of lawsuits hit, the report seemed to them overwrought, hysterical. The most seductive thing to do with it was to pretend it didn't exist.

Its authors faded from prominence. Doyle lost his job at the Vatican Embassy, joined the chaplaincy corps of the U.S. Air Force. Peterson fell ill with AIDS and died in 1987. And Mouton—who could never really come to terms with his rejection by the bishops and could never find a way to understand the way bishops were ignoring and dismissing all the victims and their pain—became so disillusioned that he withdrew from much of his previous life, giving up his law practice and refusing, for the most part, to discuss what happened in 1985.

"I just can't take it spiritually," he says. "If I talk about it for an afternoon, I won't sleep for the next three nights. I'm spiritually spent. I just don't have the spiritual strength to do this anymore.

"I'm almost more pained for what they did to Michael and Tom [Doyle]. I can still see Doyle, a very young Tom Doyle, sitting in that embassy on the fastest career track, screening bishops and archbishops and on his way to being a bishop himself. Then something crossed his desk. Not that much later, he was in Greenland."

Mouton no longer considers himself a Catholic. "I no longer believe in it at all. I believe that all institutions are corrupt and the bigger and older they are, the more corrupt they are. The Catholic Church is the oldest and biggest institution in the world. Right now I tell the parents of a victim: Go to the chancery. Go every, every, every, every day. Be a presence. Make the bishop see your pain. Take your grandmother and aunts and uncles. Take turns if you have to. Because nothing filters to them.

"Tom Doyle once said that once you become a bishop, you never again have to speak the truth and you never again have to hear it. They don't. Nothing filters to them."

WHY WERE THE BISHOPS SO INEPT AT MANAGING THE CHILD SEX-ual abuse crisis in the first place? And why, when that became obvious, were they so impervious to the criticisms, both nudging and bombastic, that attended their failures? The answers given by the Church's harsher critics are that bishops are power-mongering misanthropes guilty of a conspiracy to let priests do whatever they want. The truth is less dramatic, though equally sad. The bishops failed because they didn't have the capacity to succeed. They lacked the wisdom, the temperament and the sheer grit to tackle a problem as thorny and discomfiting as priests molesting kids.

The typical bishop is a conservative man in his fifties who was raised by working-class parents and entered the seminary as an adolescent or an older teenager just prior to the social tumult of the 1960s. His education, both informal and formal, focused not on life's messy temporal realities but on its spiritual aspirations. His world was sheltered, his life experience limited. He knew lit-tle, in particular, about human psychology and sexuality. In re-gard to the first, his religion held the view that behavior was the product of moral resolve. In regard to the second, his religion both forbade sexual expression in his own life and discouraged discussion of sex on the whole.

One day, unexpectedly, a priest on his administrative staff walks into his office with a sober, befuddled expression and men-tions a strange call he just received from the pastor at a suburban church, who said a mother had just come to talk to him about his associate pastor, Father Robert. Father Robert had been spending several afternoons a week with her twelve-year-old son, Michael, and one afternoon she found the two of them lying to-gether on the bed in Michael's room. Michael later told her that

Father Robert sometimes massaged the area on his pants just below his belt.

Hearing this, the bishop feels intensely embarrassed and slightly incredulous. He has met Father Robert, an exemplary priest and an articulate man—certainly not the kind who would molest a child. There must be some explanation, some mistake, the bishop thinks. He summons Father Robert downtown and confronts him with the accusation. Father Robert admits, weeping, that on one or two occasions he touched this boy inappropriately.

The bishop, unaccustomed to a cleric talking so candidly about sex, is so moved by the confession that he doesn't doubt its veracity, doesn't ask additional questions, doesn't consider that there might be other boys in Father Robert's past or present. As he listens to the sobbing priest's assurances that this will never happen again, he quickly becomes convinced that it won't. The bishop, like most others in society, does not know how ingrained sexual disorders can be, how difficult they are to change. But perhaps more importantly, the bishop's religion has taught him that repentance paves the road to redemption, that contrition and prayer have the power to heal, and that forgiveness is Jesus' way. He mercifully spares Father Robert from public exposure and humiliation by giving him a new start in a new parish.

This, of course, is a hypothetical scenario, but one that Church insiders and bishops themselves say was undoubtedly played out time and again in dioceses across the country, at least until the late 1980s, when some bishops began to reassess their thinking. "I don't think we understood clearly that we were dealing with a disease," says Cardinal Joseph Bernardin of Chicago. "It was looked upon more as a moral problem."

The bishops' ignorance about sexual pathologies in part reflected society's lack of knowledge, says Bishop Kenneth Untener of Saginaw, Michigan. "The words 'sexual addiction' didn't get used in society until a few years ago," he says. But he admits that the bishops' ignorance persisted longer than other people's. "We were a little behind. And I think it's because of the illusion that we could change behavior through some kind of moral suasion.

We didn't really talk the way we do now about sexual aberrations. In the Church, the advice for those aberrations was: 'Be celibate. You're supposed to anyway, so be celibate.' I think there was some element of our not being able to believe that a person, with God's power, couldn't change this. We should know better. One of our oldest Thomastic axioms is that grace builds on nature. You've got to work on nature first."

Some bishops might have been ignorant about the nature of child sexual abuse. But not all. Documents and witnesses turned up by attorneys representing victims prove that even in the late 1960s some ecclesiastical leaders were receiving clear warnings about the true nature of the pathology from their own experts. In February 1967, for example, Dr. John Salazar, the consulting psychologist for the Servants of the Paraclete treatment facility in New Mexico, met with the archbishop of Santa Fe and the head of the Paraclete order to explain the dangers of allowing the priest molesters brought there from all over the world to return to work with children and to explain the necessity of providing the men with long-term treatment. According to a deposition Salazar gave in February 1993, his contract with the Paracletes was terminated after that meeting.

In his reports on Father James Porter in 1970, provided at least to the bishop of Fall River, Father Frederick Bennett, a clinical psychologist for the Servants of the Paraclete center in Missouri, explained the pathology clearly and succinctly. He issued a special warning about how vulnerable children might be to abuse by a priest.

Bishops seem to have ignored the advice they were given about sexual pathologies in part because they were operating within a long Catholic tradition of conceiving spiritual remedies for sexual problems in particular, a tradition that revealed Church leaders' essential prudery and embarrassment about sex, says Archbishop Rembert Weakland of Milwaukee. Weakland recalls visiting a convent of nuns in the 1960s and learning from the abbess that many of them were experiencing physical discomfort related to menopause. He asked her what, if anything, doctors had advised. The sister, who clearly saw menopause as a sexual problem rather than a medical condition, said she hadn't sent any of the women to a physician. She had told them, instead, to say three Hail Marys whenever they were in pain.

In the context of this culture, it is little wonder that most bishops had a tough time swallowing the Doyle-Peterson-Mouton report, which instructed them that sexual aberrations such as pedophilia sometimes first present themselves in seemingly innocent ways, such as a priest's predilection for tickling the toes of young boys or girls with cotton-tipped swabs.

Many Church leaders' discomfort with thinking or talking about sex colored their responses to incidents of abuse in ways that proved destructive and irresponsible. Projecting their own sense of shame onto victims, they often assumed that those children and their families had no more desire or inclination to discuss what had happened than bishops themselves did. They assumed as well that families wanted the matter handled quickly and quietly, without the intrusion of police officers, lawyers and the news media.

Their reticence and secretiveness left many victims feeling forgotten, discounted, cast away. Victims sensed that Church leaders had little appreciation for how deeply they had been wounded. That sense was correct. Just as Church leaders thought prayer could conquer an abuser's desire, they thought it could vanquish a victim's pain. When they did offer victims counseling, they often suggested a priest as the counselor. It seemed lost on them that perhaps the victim, having just suffered at a cleric's hands, might want to look elsewhere now for comfort.

Bishops felt themselves being tugged in conflicting directions, uncertain how to juggle all their responsibilities and concerns in dealing with abuse complaints against a priest. It was their job to comfort the afflicted among their laity—in this case, the alleged victim or victims. It was their job to nurture and safeguard the priest, whose guilt might not have been immediately established. And it was their job to protect both the financial health of their individual dioceses and the reputation of the Catholic Church on the whole, which to them meant keeping the matter out of the public eye.

The average bishop let the last two concerns eclipse the first. Archbishop John Roach of the Diocese of St. Paul Minneapolis observes: "You are really torn between the need to protect the interests of the Church, whether they are legal or financial. You are torn between your role and relationship to a brother priest. It's very hard not to protect him; Vatican II language calls him a son or brother. You don't know the victim and frequently when victims make their first presentations, they're in so much pain, they don't make a very good case. You have to understand that."

Archbishop Daniel Sheehan of Omaha, Nebraska, concurs: "Down through the years, in the past, a bishop's sympathy probably went more to the reputation of the priest than to the people involved. I think he's been more sensitive to the patrimony of the Church and the priest's good name. Those things were the higher priority."

In an example of tragically short-sighted thinking, the bishops felt that the way to protect the patrimony of the Church was to downplay child sexual abuse by priests, to refute allegations or stand silent in the face of them. They seemed not to appreciate that down the road a bit, if it all came out, their combativeness and silence would tarnish the Church's image in a way that the actions of a limited number of priests—dealt with honestly and harshly—could not. They reacted to the immediate scandal, and created a more serious long-term one.

Bishop Thomas Gumbleton of Detroit explains: "We were taught that the Church is the perfect society and the Church is a divine institution and part of our tasks as bishops was to make sure people respected the institution. If you allowed it to be defamed and tarnished, you were failing as a bishop. You weren't living up to your pledge to protect the mystical body of Christ."

The impulse of Church leaders to protect their institution by challenging charges of child sexual abuse dovetailed perfectly with the counsel they received from lawyers, who gave the Catholic Church the same advice they would give any corporation facing potential litigation and financial loss: Deny responsibility. Evade accountability. Shut up. Archbishop Daniel Pilarczyk of Cincinnati, who served as president of the National Conference of Catholic Bishops from 1989 to 1992, says the instruction that bishops got from lawyers probably explains their failures as well as anything else. "My perception—and I have to say this is my perception and not my own personal experience—is that a lot of bishops said, 'I've got to get to those families [of victims],' and the lawyer said, 'Go ahead. Every conversation's going to cost you a million bucks.' I think every fiber of pastoral sensibility was saying, 'My God, I've got to reach out.' And the legal advice was: 'It's great you feel that, but you don't dare do that.' "

Father Bernard Bush, a California priest who advises dioceses nationwide on how to handle allegations of child sexual abuse, is particularly concerned about the contradiction between lawyers' natural preoccupation with protecting the Church from liability and the Church's moral responsibility to its parishioners. Bush, a Jesuit, recalls crossing paths with a lawyer who waxed proud about his own moral education at a Jesuit university. Bush talked with him about the child sexual abuse crisis, saying he would like to see the day when a bishop, informed that a priest was a molester, asked the priest to provide a full list of victims and sent someone from the Church door to door to tell their families what had happened. Bush asked the lawyer: If you represented the priest, would you encourage him to cooperate—clearly the virtuous course of action? The lawyer replied, "No. I would tell him, 'Don't say anything, and worry about your soul later.' "

The Church's defensive posture also reflected the personality styles and priorities of American bishops who are chosen, for the most part, because they are loyal men who steadfastly defend a Church traditionally suspicious of outside criticism and often contemptuous of any challenge to its divine authority. "These bishops really believe that they are the direct descendants of the apostles," says Eugene Kennedy, a Chicago psychologist who is a confidant of many American bishops and one of the country's most respected scholars of Church culture. "That is still an intact myth: that they have a direct connection to—a line to—the twelve apostles, and that they were chosen specially, from all eternity, to take on this obligation. They will be loyal to the institution. They will suffer misunderstandings."

There was no enforceable national policy to check this thinking in many bishops, no national coordination or supervision as suggested in the Doyle-Peterson-Mouton report. Even today, when many bishops agree that such a unified response might be a good safeguard against mistakes and might prevent one or two backward dioceses from making the whole Church look bad, there is none. The Church isn't set up to allow it, which may be another reason the Doyle-Peterson-Mouton report died. Each bishop in America has complete autonomy over his own diocese and is answerable only to the Vatican in Rome. Bishops cling so tenaciously to this independence that the various dioceses in the United States will not even band together to get a single corporate account for their telephone service—which would save them millions of dollars.

Meanwhile, Rome has done virtually nothing to press the American bishops. Indeed, the Vatican has even been reluctant to give American bishops the only significant help they have requested: more leeway and flexibility in laicizing abusive priests, or ousting them from the priesthood. Only the pope has that power and he has been hesitant to exercise it over priest molesters, leaving this country's ecclesiastical leaders with priests they can either keep in parish work or tuck away in relatively safe administrative or hospital posts. Rome has resisted all demands for a new laicization process, bowing to a long Catholic tradition that once a man is a priest, he is a priest for life. Vatican officials, who sit an ocean away on a continent where child sexual abuse is not yet a burning social issue, cannot fully appreciate the American crisis. "Rome has a way of relativizing everything in its own framework," explains Bishop Untener.

As a result, any change in the handling of child sexual abuse by priests has come gradually and grudgingly. "The Church is slow," observes Father Stephen Rossetti, editor of a 1990 collection of essays, *Slayer of the Soul*, about child sexual abuse by priests. "It does everything slowly. It must be the pasta and the wine. I think every organization has what would be called its corporate culture. And the culture of the Catholic Church is caution. The Church feels a great weight of responsibility: We speak for Christ on Earth. Be cautious about what you say. Don't cause scandal."

A telling contrast, Rossetti says, is the way the United States Navy ultimately responded to allegations of sexual harassment and sexual assault by naval aviators at the 1991 Tailhook Association convention in Las Vegas. "They fired the secretary of the navy. They called people in and said, 'You do it right or you're gone.' Could the Church do that? No. You're a bishop until you're dead.

"You get a certain subtle arrogance, which is always dangerous, toward the people—as long as they keep coming, as long as they put their money in the box."

By 1991 AND ESPECIALLY BY 1992, THERE WERE SIGNS OF REform. Many bishops began drawing up new, more victim-sensitive policies for the way they should respond to complaints that a priest had sexually abused a child. Many began exerting stricter control over the placement and movement of priests who had been identified as abusers, attempting to make certain those men never work around children. And as a group, the American bishops formally discussed child sexual abuse at both of their 1992 meetings and even opened some of their discussions to the news media. If nothing else, they were taking long strides toward acknowledging the extent of the problem.

In October 1991, Cardinal Joseph Bernardin of Chicago held a press conference to announce the convening of a special commission to study the mistakes his diocese had made in responding to complaints of abuse in the past and to devise a policy to make sure those mistakes weren't repeated in the future. Two of the commission's three members were lay people. Bernardin also announced the removal from parish work of five priests in the diocese due to complaints of child sexual abuse. In 1992, the commission released an impressively researched ninety-three-page document that included a section on the care of victims and another that gave readers a brief education about pedophilia and child sexual abuse. And Bernardin announced the removal or resignation of eight additional priests against whom complaints had been made in the past.

In June 1992, at the year's first National Conference of Catholic Bishops, in South Bend, Indiana, Church leaders devoted nearly all of the eight hours of their closed executive session to a discussion of whether priests who had sexually abused children could be returned to ministry. They invited Dr. Fred Berlin, one of the nation's most respected experts on sexual disorders, to make a presentation to them and to field questions. After the session, Archbishop Pilarczyk of Cincinnati met members of the news media to describe the closed session and release a statement of concern by the conference.

In November 1992, at the year's second National Conference of Catholic Bishops, in Washington, D.C., three bishops—including Cardinal Roger Mahony of Los Angeles—took an hour away from their formal schedules to sit down in a small hotel meeting room with women and men who had come to protest the Church's inaction and errors in dealing with abusive priests. Seven of the people were themselves victims of priests; one was a victim's mother.

The group had requested the meeting only the night before, but even so the bishops obliged. It was a stunning move for men who had spent so much time and effort shutting out the pained voices of people who wanted, more than anything else, for Church leaders to acknowledge their hurt and offer an apology.

One of the victims, Ed Morris of Philadelphia, told the bishops that the Church's unwillingness to confront what a priest had done to him had put him in an agonizing bind. Although he wanted desperately to believe in the Church, he felt forced to do battle with it by filing a lawsuit.

"I feel like I'm kicking the crucifix at the Calvary," Morris said as he stared directly at Cardinal Mahony, who was sitting right beside him, so close that their knees almost touched. "I'm shaking my very soul while I'm defending my rights. I was a blue-blooded Catholic, to the heart, and I was abandoned. You've affected my relationship with Christ. I hold that against you. I really do."

When Morris finished, no one in the room spoke for several moments. Then, in a hushed voice, Mahony said: "I'm so sorry." After the meeting, the cardinal made a point of talking privately with Morris for several minutes. When Morris later followed up on their discussion by phoning Mahony in Los Angeles, the cardinal returned the call the next day.

In an interview one week after the meeting, Mahony said it had opened his eyes. "I was impressed by the tremendous sincerity and the real faith there, even though, in many ways, it had been strained and shattered. They have concerns, hurts, and we need to listen to them, as long as it takes. Normally, our meetings are Church business meetings. This allowed the bishops to be pastors."

Some dioceses seem to have learned from their mistakes, although it is impossible to gauge whether their actions will match their tough talk. According to Santiago Feliciano, a lawyer for the Diocese of Cleveland, officials there now take swift action when they receive a complaint that a priest may be molesting kids. They suspend the priest from his parish and send him for an evaluation not to a Church-affiliated treatment center but to Dr. Fred Berlin in Baltimore, Maryland. They immediately visit alleged victims and their families and offer to pay for counseling, even before the veracity of the allegation is established. Feliciano believes this kind of response is not only consistent with the Church's mission but helps prevent lawsuits. People who feel the Church has acted responsibly and treated them well don't take it to court, he says.

But other dioceses still don't have well-developed policies on how to deal with complaints of child sexual abuse. At a meeting of an ad hoc task force convened in St. Louis in February 1993 to advise the bishops on the problem of child sexual abuse by priests, Mark Chopko, general counsel for the National Conference of Catholic Bishops, insisted that all dioceses do have policies. But he conceded that "some are thick; some are thin. Some are many pages; some are one. Some are oral; some are written."

And some bishops still fall prey to their ingrained impulses to protect the Church, avoid scandal and downplay the gravity of child sexual abuse. In an off-the-cuff comment to one newspaper reporter in late 1992, a midwestern bishop referred to a woman who had been sexually abused by a priest when she was fourteen years old as a "little Lolita" who was now trying to milk as much money as possible out of the Church. Equally disturbing were some of the comments made by Bishop John McCarthy of Austin, Texas, in an interview in August 1992. McCarthy was describing and defending his handling of the following case, which never came to public attention:

In 1987, a priest who was working in an administrative post in the diocese asked McCarthy if he could return to work as a parish pastor. In the past, the priest had admitted to child sexual abuse and had been sent away for six months of psychiatric treatment. McCarthy agreed to give him a second chance—the only decision he admitted regretting. But he first made the priest sign a document stating that if he ever molested again, he would immediately ask for laicization.

A year later, the priest called McCarthy from a police station. He had just been arrested for child sexual abuse. McCarthy phoned the district attorney, arranged a meeting and pleaded for the priest not to be charged. "You can move against him," McCarthy said to the D.A., "and my Church in that area will be hurt." McCarthy pulled out the document with the priest's signature. "Look," he said, "he's out of the priesthood." The D.A. acquiesced.

McCarthy never told the priest's parishioners why he was leaving—never suggested that parents should ask their own kids if anything had happened to them. One of his reasons: "I know of a particular action that has occurred that is abhorrent, at least sinful and possibly very sick. Because someone committed that action, that by itself doesn't entitle me to destroy that person's reputation and disrupt an entire community. If a person comes out on Sunday morning vested as an ordained minister of Jesus Christ, he's supposed to be an example of a struggle toward holiness. This is an abhorrent act. If you read on Monday morning that Father is guilty of this crime, it's agonizingly disappointing."

By intervening to help the priest evade criminal charges, McCarthy sent a potentially dangerous man out into society with no record of his crime, no way for employers or anyone else to know about his problem. "He's still got his reputation and he's got a right to it," McCarthy reasons. "If I find out you committed adultery several times last week, I don't have a right to destroy your reputation by talking about that. That's a private act.

"It may be a potential problem," McCarthy conceded of his decision to help keep the priest out of jail. "But it isn't my problem."

Chapter 10

UNSPOKEN COVENANT

No human institution, no matter how noble its ideals or moral its leaders, is immune from abuse. Power creates self-interest, self-interest the urge for self-preservation. Even the most decent men and women go on the defensive when the stakes are high and their privileged positions are challenged. They deny. They lie. Sometimes they cheat. Then the remarkable human creative instinct for self-justification kicks in and blinds them to their deeds.

Closed, highly secretive institutions are in special danger. They turn in on themselves, carefully guarding information from outsiders. Their own collective reality becomes undisputed truth. Nobody is permitted to rock the boat. Those at the bottom fear the wrath of those at the top. Messengers of bad tidings go unheeded.

An open society can minimize the danger. The crimes of a Watergate or Irangate are revealed by whistle-blowers and investigative reporters. Bankers are protected from the instinct to embezzle by watchdogs from the Federal Deposit Insurance Corporation. Men of wealth and influence are imprisoned because nobody is above the law. Police and journalists and regulatory agencies watch and warn and report. They nudge the powerful away from defensiveness and into accountability.

They have failed the Catholic Church miserably in its child sexual abuse crisis and, in the process, allowed the problem to fester—and mushroom. Police have been too timid to investigate, prosecutors to press charges and judges to sentence. Reporters and their editors have been skittish about shining the same harsh investigatory light on priests and the Church that they do on other individuals in positions of community trust. Mental health professionals have held priests in special reverence, making optimistic predictions of recovery that added, time and again, to the growing roster of victims.

It was not a conspiracy of lawyers and judges and journalists and cops paid off by the Church or even knowingly trying to protect it. It was a more subtle collusion borne of respect bordering on awe for an institution whose power seems to transcend the temporal. It was willful, but rarely conscious.

Perhaps its origins can be traced to an era when popes sent crusaders to deal with unruly civil leaders, when inquisitors led even the mighty to the torture chamber—and the stake. Perhaps it is a vestige of the centuries when Church and State divided up social power, agreeing to each other's hegemony in its own domain. Clearly, it is reminiscent of an epoch—until the late Renaissance in Europe—when clergy stood exempt from civil law entirely, falling exclusively under the jurisdiction of ecclesiastical courts.

In Europe, even today, it's not so different. The Church still wields enormous influence over secular authorities. In fact, when American bishops began talking to Vatican officials about civil suits against the Church for the sexual misdeeds of its clergy, one was asked, point-blank: "Can't you just talk to the judges?"

In modern America, the pope cannot order a newspaper

burned to the ground or a police officer flailed to death. The State is purportedly supreme over the Church in civil matters. Priests are expected to obey the law because their collars, theoretically, accord them no legal immunity. Yet the shadow of medieval relationships hangs over the interactions between bishops and secular authorities. It is reinforced by fear of the Church's wrath—even though most of the real power behind that wrath disappeared centuries ago. "The myth of power is, of course, a very powerful myth and probably most people in this world more or less believe in it," explains anthropologist Gregory Bateson. "It is a myth which, if everyone believes in it, becomes self-validating."

It is a myth that has made the job of a cop like Gary Costello almost impossible. For seventeen years Costello has walked the child sexual molestation beat in the Maryland suburbs of Washington, D.C., confronting schools, athletic leagues and churches with the abuses of their employees. He's faced them all down successfully, with a single exception: the very Church in which he was raised.

Costello first saw what happens in cases of child sexual abuse by Catholic priests when Father Peter McCutcheon was arrested in 1986. By his own admission, the priest had been abusing children for more than five years before he was caught. As the case wound through the civil and criminal courts, Costello watched one judge seal all the records of the case to spare the Church embarrassment and another judge reduce the priest's twenty-five-year jail sentence to simple probation.

Costello hoped these events were anomalous. He was wrong.

In 1990, Costello heard about Father Thomas Chleboski, a priest assigned to a Maryland parish who was arrested by Arlington County, Virginia, police for sexually abusing a thirteen-year-old boy there several years earlier. Costello needed to see if the priest had committed similar offenses in his jurisdiction. It was easier said than done. When Costello tried to interview parishioners, he was frozen out. "People told us that they were told by the archdiocese not to say anything to the police," he recalls.

But Costello knew the turf too well to be stymied. He found the victims—and the witnesses. He filed his own complaints against the priest. The next morning, he picked up the *Washing-*

ton Post to read the news that would surely bring in more victims. Or so he reasoned. But the front page of the Metro section carried an article about two rottweiler dogs that had mauled a Maryland woman and been condemned to death by lethal injection. The arrest of Chleboski was consigned to a brief paragraph in the Around the Region news—inside the Metro section, page 3.

"I don't know what it is," Costello says. "Whether the media are intimidated or what. But these cases of priests never receive the attention they deserve, the attention they'd get if the molester were a politician or a cop or a teacher. Newspapers just won't cover them fully, so parents never get warned."

In his efforts to get priest molesters off the streets, Costello has even run into brick walls in his own station house. The worst experience began just after the McCutcheon case, when Paul Interdonato, the lawyer for the archdiocese, called the detective to ask a favor: Could he run a background check on yet another priest in the diocese? Interdonato wouldn't say why, although Costello warned the lawyer that if his search turned up any information, he expected to be told what was going on. Costello ran the priest's name through his computers and discovered he had a record of child sexual abuse in another state.

The next day, he called Interdonato. "I need to know more," he said. But Interdonato would not elaborate on the reason for his request, saying only that the archdiocese had received letters complaining about "inappropriate conduct." Costello asked to see them. Interdonato refused. "I'll have to get back to you," he insisted. Costello waited for three days, with the file on his desk. When he broke down and placed a call to Interdonato himself, the attorney informed him that he had been instructed by the archdiocese to give the police no cooperation.

Costello barged into the office of his superiors and asked for a warrant to search archdiocesan offices for the information. "What are you, crazy?" his superior replied. "No way." Costello tried for a compromise: "Could somebody higher up in the department at least make a phone call?" he asked. The response was identical: a forceful no. A few weeks later, Costello discovered that the priest had been relieved of his duties but was freely walking the streets of the nation's capital in secular clothes.

Costello's experience is hardly unique. Detectives working in child sexual abuse units around the country have found that the Church refuses to cooperate with them—and that when they turn to other law enforcement authorities for what should be routine help in overcoming that resistance, they are stonewalled again. "It's very hard to work on priest cases because if the Church finds out before we do, they cover it up and no one will stop them," says Bill Dworin of the Sexually Exploited Children's Unit of the Los Angeles Police Department.

Dworin is still seething from the case of Father Nicholas Aguilar Rivera. One Monday morning in 1988, Dworin and his partner, Gary Lyon, received a call from the Archdiocese of Los Angeles informing that a complaint of child sexual abuse had been lodged against the priest. Initially the detectives were elated at what seemed to be a rare and responsible example of cooperation from the Church. But they soon learned that diocesan officials had talked to Aguilar Rivera about the complaints against him three days earlier. By the time they got around to calling the detectives, the priest had already crossed the border into Mexico.

Then Dworin and Lyon asked Church officials for lists of the altar boys who had served the priest so they could locate all of Aguilar Rivera's victims. The officials refused. And when the detectives made a routine request of their superiors for a search warrant, it was denied. The pair persevered and ultimately found ten altar boys who alleged they had been abused by Aguilar Rivera. The priest was charged for those crimes in absentia. But no judge was willing to try to extradite the priest, no Mexican official willing to assist them.

Cases like Aguilar Rivera's have sent a clear message to detectives working in child sexual abuse units: you have to play hardball with the Church from the beginning—and not tell anyone what you are doing. That's precisely the approach Los Angeles detective Patti Rodriguez took when she received complaints about Father John Salazar from families in the barrio of East Los Angeles. She tried to deal with the Church civilly. Once. When she got no cooperation, she charged into the offices of the Archdiocese of Los Angeles and threatened to arrest everyone in sight.

"She never had any trouble after that," remarks Kenneth Wullschlager, associate district attorney of Los Angeles.

Even when police can—and do—investigate priests, they are frequently thwarted by prosecutors unwilling to take Catholic clergy to court. Prosecutors, after all, are usually elected—and thus often shy about confronting institutions known to exercise influence over the votes of their members.

In 1992, a furor erupted in Chicago when State's Attorney Jack O'Malley refused to prosecute Father Norbert Maday. Five allegations had been lodged against the priest, but O'Malley, who was facing reelection, insisted that in each case there was either not enough evidence or the criminal statute of limitations had expired. When officials in Oshkosh, Wisconsin, where Maday had allegedly molested children on a field trip, filed their own charges against him, Father Andrew Greeley, noted Catholic sociologist and novelist, used his column in the *Chicago Sun-Times* to call for a special prosecutor to be appointed locally to investigate obstruction of justice in cases of child sexual abuse by priests in Chicago.

"Out of respect for the clergy and the Church, police and prosecutors who are Catholic are reluctant to drag a priest into court and would rather leave him to the discipline of the Church, such as this may be," Greeley wrote. "Prosecutors are not eager to bring to trial a case that they might have a hard time winning. They are not convinced that they could gain a conviction against a priest in Chicago. A much publicized trial of a priest could do enormous political harm to a state's attorney in the heavily Catholic Chicago area."

Sometimes prosecutors simply hand errant priests over to ecclesiastical officials as they did, by law, in the Middle Ages. In 1988, for example, Maryland police arrested Father William Q. Simms for molesting two altar boys by dressing them in sheer nylon swim suits and women's clothing and enacting ritualistic sexual fantasies with them based on the torture inflicted on Jesus and several saints. But when the Archdiocese of Baltimore agreed to send Simms into therapy and pay for his victims' treatment, the Maryland state's attorney dropped all charges. Father Simms is still an active member of the Catholic clergy.

But the most dramatic example of prosecutorial stonewalling was based neither on confidence in the Church's abilities to police its own ranks nor on reelection jitters. It was simple religious conviction. In 1988, in New Orleans, a priest found a stash of child pornography in the St. Rita's rectory room of Father Dino Cinel, a faculty member at Tulane University: photographs and videotapes and books with titles like *Little Brother Wants a Kiss* and *Yes, A Minor Is Loads of Fun.*

Possession of child pornography is a serious crime in Louisiana, a crime carrying a mandatory jail sentence—thanks, in part, to the efforts of New Orleans' district attorney Harry Connick, Sr., a devout Catholic and member of St. Rita's. It is an even more serious crime to make your own kiddie porn, which is precisely what Cinel seemed to have done—on 160 hours of videotape. The tapes, many of them shot in the rectory, showed Cinel having sex with boys, boys having sex with one another, Cinel encouraging boys to have sex with their sisters and mothers and Cinel bringing his white lapdog into the sexual diversions.

Church officials hung on to the materials for three months before turning them over to the district attorney, as required by law. But even then, no charges were filed against Cinel. Although Connick, the father of singer Harry Connick, Jr., had cultivated a reputation as an ardent crusader against pornography, strip joints and dirty movies, he admitted unabashedly that he would take no action that might embarrass the Church. One year after he received the tapes, Connick was confronted by a private investigator who had been asked by the D.A.'s office to review the materials. "When are charges going to be filed?" the investigator asked Connick. "Never, not as long as I'm district attorney," Connick replied.

More than two years after Connick received the tapes, a local television reporter aired the story of Cinel and Connick. The district attorney finally filed charges. But it was a classic case of too little too late. A judge threw the case out of court, ruling that the district attorney's long delay in charging Cinel constituted an implicit contract with the priest that no charges would ever be filed. "The judge ruled that the actions of the district attorney were basically a cover-up," said Arthur Harris, clerk for state district judge Frank Marullo.

Cinel's alleged victims had no more luck with civil courts. In response to one of their lawsuits against the Church, Orleans Parish judge Yada Magee, who had listed God as one of her endorsements when she ran for the bench, rejected the argument that Cinel's collar gave him special influence and that those who had vested him with his priestly powers were thus implicated in his abuse. She ruled that the Church had no liability in the case.

Finally, some prosecutors are subject to clear intimidation. Robert Craven recalls how, when he was assistant attorney general for Rhode Island, the Church tried to influence his handling of the prosecution of Father Paul Henry Leech, who had been charged with abusing four boys. Craven encountered evidence that the Church had probably known about Leech's predilections for at least five years and had done nothing to safeguard children. Craven, who keeps a hand-lettered Irish blessing on his office wall, was incensed.

"I was raised Catholic," he explains. "I spent twelve years in Catholic school. The priest was THE PRIEST. He was the guy you went to. He was the guy who, when you sinned, forgave you. Now he was the guy to take advantage of that role with a child. Although I've been told on many occasions that priests are human beings, it's unforgivable. There are precious few occupations given more power and trust than being a religious leader. I defy anyone to explain this to me. I realize there are a few bad apples in any barrel. But even the grocer throws out the bad apples."

Craven prepared to prosecute the case vigorously and even considered trying to hold Church officials criminally liable for the cover-up. Then he walked into court. "When that day of reckoning came, suddenly all the penguins came out of nowhere," he says, referring to the flock of men in black suits and white collars. "Dozens of them. And that was a lot of priests for one small courtroom."

One priest walked up to him and said: "Paul Leech is a good guy. Whatever consideration you can give him would be great." Craven was livid. "Of all the priests in Rhode Island, they picked my nephew's godfather to come up to talk to me," he says.

"That's either an incredible coincidence or they went out and found the only person in a collar in this state who might be able to have an influence on me. And they took the step of having this guy come up to me and, as I see it, put the arm on me. What about the facts? What about just common decency, for Chris-sakes? You hold yourself out as being a light in the fog that people should follow. And this is the way you conduct business?"

Craven sent his nephew's godfather away. And Father Leech was sentenced to three years in prison.

The collusion ascends the ladder even to judicial benches where judges frequently ignore the best efforts of the least timid policemen and prosecutors. Perhaps swayed by defense descriptions of the priests' years of good works and community service, they bow to men in Roman collars, hesitating to send priests who molest to jail. Perhaps moved by the presence of bishops and crowds of faithful parishioners in the courtroom, they treat priests with a level of mercy even Protestant clergy do not enjoy. In a study of 190 clerical child sexual molesters tried in 1988 and 1989, the average Protestant cleric sent to prison got 11.5 years, the average Catholic priest received only 3.6 years.

Even more shocking is the sentence of a priest compared to that of a layman. In July 1989, a judge in Phoenix, Arizona, sentenced Father George Bredemann to one year in prison and life-time probation for molesting three children—although he acknowledged having abused at least twelve more. The year before, a Phoenix man convicted of trying to molest one of those same children received a twelve-year prison sentence—with no chance for early parole. Two weeks after Bredemann's sentencing, another Arizona man accused of molesting a single child was sentenced to 120 years in jail.

Three months after his release from jail, Bredemann violated parole and fled Arizona. He was found in a Miami Beach hotel room with a ticket to Rio de Janeiro in his pocket.

The judge in Phoenix was hardly unique. In 1984, Father Eugene O'Sullivan was found guilty of molesting a boy over a two-year period. The Massachusetts prosecutor asked for a two-to-five-year jail sentence. The judge gave him probation. Three years later, Father Patrick Weaver pleaded guilty in a New Jersey court to endangering three children. The crime: making them disrobe in his rectory office. The sentence: probation. Less than a year later, Weaver was back in court, this time for fondling a twelve-year-old boy. The priest insisted the molestation was innocent; he explained that he had touched the boy's penis because it seemed to be swollen. The sentence: probation to run concurrently with his first probation.

Brother Andrew Hewitt of Newark, New Jersey, was indicted in August 1988 for aggravated sexual assault, criminal assault and endangering the welfare of a minor. When he was evaluated by the State Adult Diagnostic and Treatment Center, he was classified as a compulsive and repetitive sexual offender. But he was contrite in court. "I swear by Almighty God I won't do it again," he told the judge. The sentence: five years of probation.

Orange County (California) Superior Court Judge Luis A. Cardenas remembers how he succumbed to the influence of a priest's stature when he sentenced Father Andrew Christian Andersen in November 1986. Father Andersen was a young, dynamic priest at a wealthy and active Orange County parish. He knew how to crack a joke—or crack open a bottle of beer—with the laity. He drew dozens of converts to his classes. When he was charged with molesting three altar boys, the community rose up against the victims, accusing them of trying to toss a holy man to the lions.

"Let me be candid," Cardenas says. "I was initially tempted to come down very hard on Father Chris because I'm a Catholic and I'm embarrassed for the Church. The hierarchy was rude and irresponsible in dealing with the investigators. They tried to sandbag the case. I thought that was immoral. They swept the first case under the rug and when the second case came along, they gave the police the runaround. It was not handled in a way people who are advocating the precepts of Christianity would handle it."

Then Cardenas was besieged with letters from Andersen's followers insisting that the boys had misinterpreted the priest's affection or that his behavior was more sick than criminal. There were missives from physicians and social workers written on professional letterhead, from couples the priest had married or counseled penned on flowery stationery. Cardenas was moved by what he believed to be the spontaneous outpouring of love for the priest, unaware that the campaign had been orchestrated by Andersen's attorney.

Wherever the judge went, he was badgered by loyal parishioners. One day, when the owner of a local camera store waited on Cardenas, he delivered a lecture on why the judge should send Andersen to a treatment center rather than jail. At a neighborhood meeting in a private home, a woman pulled the judge aside and told him flat out that Andersen was being railroaded by the criminal justice system. No one wanted to remember that Andersen had pleaded guilty.

Cardenas had received court-ordered psychiatric reports suggesting that Father Chris had long-term emotional problems: "a mixed personality disorder with narcissistic, schizoid and sociopathic characteristics." But the priest's attorney argued that those problems could be dealt with most effectively in a Church-run treatment center in New Mexico. The information on the program stated authoritatively—although falsely—that none of their patients had ever reoffended. The defense attorney also argued that the ninety days Andersen had served in the state prison in Chino for evaluation had scared him straight.

On November 24, Cardenas entered his courtroom to deliver his sentence. "It was like a damned circus had come to town," remembers Don Howell, the police detective in charge of the case. "There was Monsignor Duffy, the parish pastor, in full regalia there to support Father Chris. There were dozens of parishioners demanding that the priest be sent off to some treatment facility on some New Mexico mountaintop instead of jail. They had to bring in extra bailiffs and remove people from the courtroom because they were screaming at each other. Then the prosecutor starts outlining the case and a woman in her forties jumps up and starts yelling, 'Shut up, shut up. This is not a trial. Shut up.' It was a total zoo."

Although he might have sent the priest away for fifty-eight years, Cardenas sentenced Father Chris to probation at the New Mexico treatment center. The courtroom erupted in cheers and applause. Fifty parishioners leapt to their feet to embrace their favorite priest. Two years later, the priest was back in Cardenas's courtroom for parole violation. After finishing his treatment, Father Chris Andersen had been arrested in Albuquerque for sexually molesting a seventh-grade boy.

"I was devastated, queasy in my stomach," Cardenas says. "My decision came back to haunt me. My critics were quick to point out I should have sent him to jail. I gambled and lost. The next judge down the line isn't going to gamble. He's going to be gun shy."

Perhaps the most powerful influence on judges is exerted when parents who would cry for blood if the molester did not wear a collar join other devoted parishioners in demanding leniency for priests. When Father Richard Henry was charged with abusing six siblings in Los Angeles, the victims' parents refused to cooperate with the prosecution and helped the priest's defense attorney instead. When the priest asked to be sent to a Church-run treatment facility prior to sentencing, the mother supported his petition in open court. The judge deferred to her request.

Prior to the sentencing of Father Thomas McLaughlin in Bellefontaine, Ohio, dozens of parishioners spoke out on behalf of the strapping Irish priest, whose rectory room was littered with boys' underwear and a collection of child pornography, including books such as *The Boy: A Pictorial Essay*. Even the mother of the twelve-year-old victim rose to beg for leniency for the priest. "I was flabbergasted," prosecutor Gerald Heaton told the local newspaper. "I can't recall, in my seven years of prosecuting cases, having the parents of a victim, especially a sexual abuse victim, speak in support of the perpetrator."

It's not just judges and police and prosecutors who seem to have special rules covering Roman Catholic clergy. All kinds of people who hold public trust, from child-care workers to elected officials, seem to cower when dealing with child sexual abuse by a priest. Teachers in Catholic schools—nuns or lay people—rarely notice that Father is always pulling Johnny or Mary out of class or that children seem to vanish when he approaches.

In New Hampshire, it was the state's Division of Child and Youth Services that received a complaint against Father Gordon MacRae but never called the police after the bishop promised to "handle the matter." The issue came to light five years later when MacRae was arrested for abusing yet another child.

In South Florida, it was the mayor of the town of Sweetwater who received a barrage of complaints that a local priest was molesting the Central American boys he was sheltering but reported him to an auxiliary bishop instead of the local child welfare authorities.

In Houston, it was a social worker who walked into the kitchen of the home of an elderly client and found his granddaughter on the floor with a priest atop her, his pants down and collar askew. It turned out that Father Noe Guzman had been raping the girl for two years while her blind and deaf grandfather lay in the next room. The social worker never contacted the police or the child welfare authorities—as required by law. She did, however, meet with her priest, who informed the bishop. No action was taken to remove Guzman from contact with children.

Perhaps public officials don't act because they, like the Church, are rarely called on the carpet for neglecting the welfare of Catholic youth. Until the last two years, newspaper and television reporters have been remarkably shy about taking on the Catholic Church for the criminal misconduct of its clergy. The very media that showcased the sexual activities of Jim Bakker and Jimmy Swaggart, who were involved with adult women, turned a blind eye when accusations of criminal child sexual abuse were leveled against priests.

Carl Cannon, writing for Knight-Ridder newspapers, was one of a handful who didn't. In late 1987, he became the first mainstream journalist to report the story of child sexual abuse by priests on a national level. Others had written news stories about single instances of abuse in their hometowns, but Cannon penned a series that illuminated a national pattern of transferring abusers from parish to parish, of using hush money to cover up allegations of molestation, of blaming the victim for embarrassing the Church.

As he went about his reporting, the people he interviewed expressed skepticism that the stories would ever get published. "There was a presumption that the Church would make it difficult," he recalls. "Lawyers would say: 'I wonder if they'll ever really let you write about it.' As if the Catholic Church has some kind of power to kill stories, or was a force to be feared. There was sort of that feeling in the press that this was taboo, that the Church was a powerful institution and you dare not attack it. It struck me as a very faint-hearted attitude."

It did not seem faint-hearted at all to the editors and publishers who had watched the travails of *The Times* of Acadiana, an alternative weekly in the bayous of Louisiana, the first paper to print the full details of the Gilbert Gauthe case. *The Times* became the target of an advertising boycott organized by a diocesan official and egged on by a rival paper that branded its work "yellow journalism." By the time a truce was negotiated, the paper had lost more than $20,000 in advertising revenue.

Reporters knew they would win neither prizes nor friends if they dared report on child sexual abuse by priests with the same objectivity they leveled against offenders in other institutions. They learned that from the experiences of the few intrepid reporters who wandered into a minefield they never could have imagined. Eleanor Bergholz, religion reporter for the *Pittsburgh Post-Gazette*, is one of the walking wounded. In 1985, she heard about a lawsuit alleging child sexual abuse by a priest in western Pennsylvania. A good story, she thought. An important one. But it was difficult to uncover because the case had been sealed by the courts to protect the Church. Bergholz dug. Then she went to court, insisting that the public has a right to know the names of rapists in its midst.

But when the story appeared, she received no thanks. Instead, she got venomous hate calls and an avalanche of furious mail accusing her of being anti-Catholic and anti-Church. She even lost friends among fellow reporters who were Catholic. "I thought I would get stoned out of Pittsburgh," she recalls.

When Home Box Office television aired a fictionalized account of the Gauthe case, Catholic officials throughout the country went wild. Father Faymond Goedert, Vicar of Priests for the Archdiocese of Chicago, told the *Chicago Tribune*: "It's going to destroy the trust that the average person has in their minister or priest or rabbi. I think it's diabolical."

Perhaps the high point of hysteria was reached in Boston in May. The *Boston Globe* had been covering the mounting scandal of James Porter aggressively. Day after day on its front page it detailed how Porter was transferred after each complaint of child sexual abuse. Porter's face was splashed across the state, encouraging new victims to come forward, which fueled the cycle of reporting. By May 23, the archbishop, Cardinal Bernard Law, was in a rage. At an antiviolence march in Roxbury, he blew up and declared: "The papers like to focus on the faults of the few. We deplore that . . . By all means we call down God's power on the media."

No one has accused newspapers of lying about the cases on which they reported. But in strong, often vicious language, Catholic readers have made it abundantly clear that they simply don't want to know about priests molesting their children. When confronted with the truth, they cry foul and attack the messengers as Catholic-bashers. They have been encouraged by their church leaders, who routinely refuse to talk to the news media about accusations and allegations that surface, then demand editorial space in which they complain bitterly that their side of the story was not represented. In feigned innocence, or a stunning unfamiliarity with the role of the news media, they have consistently berated reporters for pointing to the misdeeds of the few rather than reporting on the good works of the many.

Until very recently, few newspaper reporters and editors resisted the chilling effect of such venom. Some admit they are unwilling to bear the brunt of the Church's wrath. Others seem to convince themselves that the evidence of abuse presented by victims and their lawyers—evidence that would clearly have passed editorial muster if the accused were not a priest—simply is not compelling.

In May of 1992, for example, when the tale of Father James Porter escalated overnight from the story of a priest who had molested nine children to the story of a molester of pathological proportions protected by the Church, the major newspaper near the scene of the crime refused to give its readers full information about what was being uncovered, or even Porter's name. They read about it in the *Boston Globe* and the *New York Times*. They saw it on the national news and on "PrimeTime Live." But readers of the *Providence Journal*, one of the nation's most respected papers, were protected by their hometown press from what its editors were convinced was a questionable story, if not a downright hoax.

Even though Massachusetts law limited the Church's liability to $20,000, *Journal* editors worried that the press was being manipulated by alleged victims looking to make a quick buck. They refused to acknowledge the credibility of audiotapes produced both by victims and other media, tapes in which Porter admitted his crimes. Thus, despite the statements of more than seventy men and women about their abuse as children—and corroboration from parents who had reported the abuse—the paper grossly underplayed the story until criminal charges were filed against the former priest. Rhode Island is the most densely Catholic state in the nation.

Even four years after the suit was filed, the *Philadelphia Inquirer* had never printed a single word about one of the longest running court battles between an alleged victim and any diocese in the country. Ed Morris filed suit against Father Terrence Pinkowski, the Archdiocese of Philadelphia and the Franciscan fathers in 1989. While the *Inquirer* ran thousands of words about the perversion of Eddie Savitch, a child molester whose crime was primarily buying boys' dirty underwear, it ignored Morris's legal battles, including the Archdiocese of Philadelphia's insistence that Morris's parents were responsible for his abuse because they had allowed the boy to spend so much time with his confessor.

David Crumm of the *Detroit Free Press*, one of the most respected religion reporters in the country, believes some of the problem is the nature of the religion beat. Few religion writers are trained in the type of investigative techniques the broader story demands. Few have the time to weed through court documents scattered in dozens of cities. Finally, even when they try, they run up against Church officials who insist they have no information on the number of cases nationally or the financial damage suffered by the Church—information vital to good reporting. And they feel intimidated.

"In hindsight you can look back and say that secular newspapers and secular reporters missed a major story," Crumm says. "It is fair to say that we didn't tell the story for many years. But you felt that if you went too far down that alley you'd be picking on the Church."

FINALLY, THE KEY PEOPLE TO WHOM THE CHURCH HAS TURNED for advice on child sexual abuse, the mental health professionals, have let it down badly, providing bishops with wishful thinking that was just plain bad advice. To some extent, that advice has reflected the still primitive state of psychological understanding of child sexual abusers. "For a long time, a lot of professionals signed off on people who later went on and abused again because they simply didn't understand the nature of the disorder," explains Gary Schoener, a Minneapolis therapist. "They were ill-informed, often naive."

But the problem had also stemmed from the belief by many therapists, particularly those affiliated with Church-run institutions, that priests are more amenable to treatment than are other offenders, that a rapist in a Roman collar is less likely to rape again than one who has never been ordained. "Priests are good candidates for therapy," says Stephen Rossetti, a priest psychotherapist on the staff at the St. Luke Institute. "They're usually high-functioning. They're usually not fixated pedophiles. They usually have a job to go to. They usually have some support system. They're a bunch of guys who are somewhat good-willed. So they're usually good risks for treatment."

Dr. Frank Valcour, medical director at the St. Luke Institute, insists there is a positive story to be told about the treatment of priests who molest. Of the hundred priests treated there for child sexual abuse since 1985, he says that only six have relapsed into their earlier behavior. Dr. Jay Feierman, consulting psychiatrist for the Servants of the Paraclete in Jemez Springs, New Mexico, put it simply: "Our worst patients are the best patients in most secular programs."

But therapists not affiliated with Church-run institutions tell a different story. Listen to Dr. James Pedigo, the Philadelphia psychiatrist specializing in the treatment of professionals who sexually abuse children: "Priests are difficult to work with. For therapy, patients must recognize the events leading up to the abuse as part of the cycle. The Catholic clergy have a harder time doing this because they're less sophisticated sexually. And a lot of them have not had close intimate relationships with others. They don't learn about what they themselves are like emotionally, inside. It's very difficult if they believe, as one of the priests I work with believes, that even thinking about these issues is sinful and therefore he should not even think about the things I'm asking about. For him, engaging in psychotherapy is sinful."

Richard Sipe, the Baltimore psychotherapist, suggests that the very culture in which priests live and work so warps their sense of reality that they cannot be good patients in therapy. "There's no doubt that priests are harder to treat. I think they have more intellectualized defenses and more denial. Also, the cover is so perfect, you see. You go around and everybody gives you discounts, everybody says 'Good Morning, Father.' You're in garb at the airport with your luggage. If you weigh over the limit, they waive it. You get seated more quickly in restaurants. You take that for granted. You're held in respect and you're held in honor regardless of what you're like on the inside. The whole world is one of privilege. And then you get up on an altar in front of people and you preach and YOU tell THEM what's right and what's wrong. And then you hold up the Eucharist. 'This is my body, this is the divine incarnate here that I hold, and I alone can touch it.' It's a tremendous, in a sense, burden, and it can be very seductive to people. And it can be very seductive to split the supernatural from the natural. It doesn't help you keep any sense of reality."

The same Church-run institutions that are so optimistic about the prognosis of priests who molest are, in fact, handicapped in treating them by problems inherent in combining psychiatry and religion. Therapists in those institutions do not have the range of treatment possibilities open to therapists in secular settings. Dr. J. A. Loftus, the Jesuit psychiatrist who is the director of Southdown, a Church-run treatment program near Toronto, explains the primary problem in helping priests who molest. "You could encourage them to delve into fantasies and masturbation and more genital contact, but that becomes difficult if they're living a professedly celibate life," he says. "It's difficult to encourage them to explore age-appropriate sexual fantasies and age-appropriate sexual partners. It's very delicate."

Other experts insist that those institutions are also handicapped by their naïveté. "They've relied on the perpetrator, now in therapy, to want to come clean," says Schoener. "In the end, they were counting on the milieu and the treatment to bring it out. What blows me away is that these outfits never interviewed victims as part of their evaluation, that none of these outfits got solid background data. It's amazing they did as well as they did because they can be totally and utterly snookered."

In the end, bishops across the country have been systematically snookered by therapists into believing that errant priests could safely return to parish work and regular contact with children and judges into believing that Church-run treatment centers could "rehabilitate" child molesters. The Diocese of Crookston (Minnesota) insists that it accepted Father James Porter as a priest only because the Servants of the Paraclete never told told them he had abused children and had assured them that he had been cured of a nervous disorder. Judge Luis Cardenas sent Father Chris to that same group because their literature led him to believe that the priest would find something close to a "cure" there.

In 1992, after a group of men alleged they were abused by James Porter while he was there in treatment, the Servants of the Paraclete facility in Jemez Springs became the target of mounting concern over Church-run treatment centers. Much of the suspicion grew from the repeated assertion of their psychiatrist, Dr. Jay Feierman, that only a handful of the patients he has treated there have reoffended—an assertion most experts find almost unbelievable.

"I don't know what cemetery he's talking about," was the blunt response of Sipe. When asked about Feierman's claim, Loftus said simply: "My gut wants to say, No way. I'm being honest. I can't tell you what our rate of recidivism is. I can't imagine how anyone else can either." According to Loftus, the problem is that too many institutions like the Paracletes base their numbers on arrest and self-reporting. Their thinking, he explains, is: "If I haven't read about him in the newspaper, he must be okay."

"I'm fond of saying to people: This is Southdown. It's not Fátima. We don't specialize in miracles."

The Paraclete miracle is, in fact, a myth created by the order and its staff, a lie which has led bishops to reinstate priest offenders and moved judges to suspend sentences and place priests who abuse on probation. In a 1986 letter to the Reverend Michael Jamail of the Diocese of Beaumont, a copy of which was sent to Judge Cardenas before his sentencing of Father Chris Andersen, Dr. Jay Feierman asserted: "Our recidivism rate for behavior which would be considered criminal is 0% to the best of our knowledge."

Yet, by then the Paraclete center had treated James Porter and seen him return after he had molested even more children. They had treated Father Arthur Perrault, whose continuing abuses were reported both to the police and to the Archdiocese of Santa Fe in the mid-1980s. They had watched the return of Father Jason Sigler, the Canadian priest who was sent there on at least three occasions before he was charged criminally. There was simply no way that Feierman and the Paracletes could not have known about these men—and other of their alumni who also left New Mexico and abused again.

The Paracletes insist that most of the criticism leveled against them stems from the 1960s, when few therapists understood the difficulty of treating child sexual abusers. Yet their own psychologists warned them as early as 1968 that releasing molesters prematurely was hazardous to children. And even in the late 1980s, the Paracletes were hardly engaged in sophisticated treatment. While they made some use of Depo-Provera—a drug used for suppressing the sexual appetite—their use of psychotherapy was extremely limited. The daily schedule of the "guests," as they called the patients who lived in the compound nestled in the hills of New Mexico, was heavy on prayer and light on therapy. They offered them wilderness experiences and classes in pottery, but no more than one hour a week of individual counseling.

In an interview with the *Rocky Mountain News* in 1987, Father William Perri, one of the directors of the program, explained the center's approach: "What we do here is forgive. That means sometimes making some very hard decisions because some things are very hard to forgive. But I think ultimately that forgiveness is what leads to healing." When asked how the program directors decide when a priest needs no further treatment, Father William Foley, head of the Paraclete order, responded simply: "We just get an intuition that they're going to work out."

Even after they were besieged by lawsuits, the Paracletes, who refer to themselves as the M.A.S.H. unit of the Catholic Church, still retained—or feigned—a startling naïveté about the gravity of child sexual abuse. They insisted that they had become more sophisticated since the 1960s, when they treated Porter, as late as the fall of 1992 they continued to allow men in treatment for pedophilia to leave the facility unaccompanied, often to serve as weekend fill-in priests in neighboring communities. In an open letter last year to the people of Jemez Springs, they decried "media misrepresentation" of their work and asserted that no priest in the program posed any danger to the community. But they were letting diagnosed and often convicted pedophiles wander the playgrounds and swimming haunts of the small town.

IF 1992 AND THE EXPLOSION OF THE PORTER CASE MARKED A watershed in the public's awareness of child sexual abuse by Catholic priests, it also marked a change in the reactions of secular authorities to cases of priests who molest. For two or three years the silent collusion had been eroding in some cities and states across the nation. But last year, America's prosecutors and judges and reporters seemed to awaken on a national level to the price that Catholic youths had paid for that collaboration. Authorities stopped trusting the Church to handle its own malfeasants. The news media stopped hushing it up.

In the summer of 1992, the district attorney of Worcester, Massachusetts, resurrected the case of Father Joseph Fredette, which had been dormant for eighteen years. In 1974, Fredette had been charged with sexually assaulting a boy—and fled to Canada. Authorities simply dropped the matter. When the Porter case exploded, Worcester officials suddenly reopened the case. Fredette was indicted in September and a request for his extradition placed before the Canadian government.

In July 1992, a Missouri judge took an unusually hard line against Father Donald Heck, who was tried for assaulting an eleven-year-old altar boy on a single occasion. The boy charged that Heck had held him down and fondled him after Mass. Judge Dennis Kehm received the usual outpouring of letters from friends and former parishioners begging for mercy for the priest. But he insisted that "a person in a particular position of trust who took sexual advantage of a vulnerable child in a place of sanctuary and caused that child immeasurable injury is morally, culturally and legally reprehensible"—and sent Heck to jail for four years.

After years of silence about the problem of priests who molest, Chicago's states' attorney Jack O'Malley accused the archbishop, Cardinal Joseph Bernardin, of covering up decades of complaints by parishioners. In June 1992, when Bernardin publicly acknowledged a number of cases of which secular authorities were unaware, O'Malley requested archdiocesan records. When Bernardin refused to comply with his request, O'Malley slapped him with a subpoena. When Bernardin's attorneys found a Catholic judge willing to quash it, O'Malley appealed the decision to the state supreme court.

The news media made similar strides. Back in 1985, when the Gilbert Gauthe case gave the nation its first fleeting glimpse of child sexual abuse by Catholic priests, the *Chicago Tribune* ran only five articles on the problem, despite the fact that a local priest was arrested and tried on similar charges. In 1988, just after the trailblazing Carl Cannon series exposed the Church's pattern of cover-up and denial, the paper made no mention of the topic whatsoever. In 1992, however, sixty articles ran on the growing scandal—nine of them on the front page.

A similar awakening took place at large and small newspapers across the country. The *Boston Globe*, which before 1992 had made virtually no mention of any of the cases in Massachusetts or elsewhere, suddenly latched onto child sexual abuse by priests as a scandal demanding tenacious reporting. As the story of Father James Porter unfolded, they assigned two reporters to cover the story virtually full-time. By the end of the year, they had printed ninety-eight articles on every conceivable angle of the problem. Thirty of those stories appeared on the front page.

The *Globe* was inundated with irate letters criticizing the paper for overplaying the Porter story. To many Catholics, accustomed to their Church being subject to only half-hearted scrutiny, the erosion of decades of collusion felt like the rise of Catholic-bashing. Why are you singling out Catholic priests? some complained, as if the *Globe* were not reporting abuse by non-Catholic clerics or non-clerics as well. Why are you refusing to write stories about all the good the Church does? queried others. Still others came out and accused the newspaper of trying to smear the Church. Cardinal Bernard Law encouraged the campaign, publicly asking God to bring his wrath down on the media.

The *Globe* countered that it was covering the news in precisely the same way as it did with other institutions wracked by scandal. They pointed out they had run twenty-one front-page stories and a Sunday magazine piece about the troubles of the Christian Science Church, and that second-mortgage scams had received the same treatment.

But few believed them. In fact, the president of the National Conference of Catholic Bishops for 1992, Archbishop Daniel Pilarczyk, saw the end of collusion as the media's—and society's—vengeance against the Church for its exacting moral strictures. "I think our culture in general sees this as a chance to get a little bit even with the Church in the context of unpopular prophetic things the Church says about society," he says. "Maybe it's really a kind of implicit acknowledgment of the relevance that people, even unconsciously, find in the Church.

"The Church is saying you don't have to be sexually active, that homosexual behavior is not acceptable," he said. "These are all unpopular issues the Church is taking on. Then along comes the Church and it is being badly sexually embarrassed. It gives everyone a chance to say: 'Look at that. We told you so; it was all a front. These guys are misbehaving with little kids while the Church is posturing against society.' One could submit it's a kind of corporate vendetta."

C h a p t e r 11

BITTER
FRUITS

SCENES FROM DAILY LIFE IN THE ROMAN CATH-
olic Church, in the United States, 1992:

- A priest ambles down the street in suburban
  Boston, treading the short path from his
  church to his rectory. A car filled with teenagers pulls up beside him. They have never
  met him and know nothing about him. But
  his black suit and white collar shape their
  judgment. "Rapist!" they shout, then speed
  away. The priest's stomach tightens into a
  knot, and he has to fight the impulse either
  to scream in rage, or to cry.

- A formerly devout woman in Phoenix sits at
  home on a Sunday morning, unable to make
  herself attend Mass or to bring her two teenage sons to church. She used to go every
  week, always placing a check for twenty-five

dollars in the collection basket. She was raised by a father so pious he took advantage of idle time in his car by praying, steering with just one hand so he could rub his rosary beads with the other. But now she sees more corruption than grace in the Catholic Church. One of her parish priests has just been imprisoned for molesting three girls, and while she can accept that individual priests commit sins, she cannot abide the silence and disbelief with which the Catholic Church met the initial accusations against him. When the church sends her an envelope requesting donations now, she throws it away. "I'm real torn up," she says. "You know that movie *Man Without a Country?* I feel like the Man Without a Church."

- Cardinal Joseph Bernardin of Chicago, head of the second largest Catholic diocese in the country, meets members of the news media for what will be his best remembered and most widely chronicled public appearance of the year. The subject is child sexual abuse by his priests. He announces the results of an eight-month review of the problem in his diocese, saying thirty-four priests over four decades have engaged in sexual misconduct with minors. He announces a toll-free phone number for complaints about sexually abusive priests. What he doesn't announce is that dealing with the public alarm over sexually abusive priests is now taking up nearly a quarter of his work time. At moments, it has reduced him to tears. And it is costing his diocese millions of dollars in legal fees, lawsuit settlements and psychiatric bills. Some priests in the Chicago area are beginning to express doubts—only half-jokingly—that there will be pension funds left for them when they retire.

- The editorial cartoonist at the *Arizona Republic*, the largest daily newspaper in Phoenix, decides to target the Catholic Church with his sarcastic humor. He eschews such familiar points of controversy as the Church's positions on birth control, homosexuality, and the ordination of women for more fertile soil. This is the image he draws: A priest stands on the front steps of his church, waving at a young boy and girl. Little cartoon bubbles intended to reveal what the priest is really thinking contain a duplicate image of the boy and girl—only they aren't wearing any clothes now. The priest has a lecherous smile on his face. Next to him is a sign that spells out the title of the day's sermon: "Suffer the Little Children."

Discouraged priests. Disillusioned parishioners. Money trouble. Image problems. The failure of Church leaders and others in society to confront child sexual abuse by priests is costing the Catholic Church all of this and more. It is exacting a price much greater than the cumulative pain of the children directly victimized. It is demoralizing an entire institution and everyone who cares, or once cared, about it.

Father Andrew Greeley—novelist, noted university sociologist and professional Church critic—calls child sexual abuse by priests and the Church's attempts to cover it up possibly the most serious crisis in Catholicism since the Reformation. He also calls it the savings and loan scandal of the Catholic Church. In truth, both assessments are more than a bit extravagant: Child sexual abuse by priests is neither cleaving the Church in two nor threatening it with financial collapse. But it is, without a doubt, creating the greatest public relations fiasco the Catholic Church has faced in recent memory.

Even most bishops say so. They protest that they have acted honorably and in good faith when dealing with abusive priests and abused parishioners. They complain that the news media have made too much of the problem. But they do not argue about the impact of it all. "I have not seen anything that has concerned me as much about the image of the Church," says Archbishop Daniel Pilarczyk of Cincinnati. "It's just saddening. And discouraging. And enervating. The cost to the Church is that all of a sudden, what was perceived to be totally trustworthy is now a source of suspicion."

ON THE MOST SUPERFICIAL LEVEL, CHILD SEXUAL ABUSE BY priests is causing financial damage, leeching at least tens of millions—and more likely hundreds of millions—of dollars from Church coffers. Victims of sexual abuse and their families have filed a flurry of lawsuits against the Church, alleging it failed to monitor troubled priests and safeguard parishioners, and many of those lawsuits have carried hefty price tags. It has not been uncommon for a diocese to pay a victim between $100,000 and $500,000 to settle a case out of court.

The Catholic Church's vulnerability to sexual abuse litigation is much greater than that of other faiths. In most Protestant denominations and in branches of Judaism, pastors or rabbis are hired by individual congregations. But in the Catholic Church, a priest is assigned to a congregation by the geographic diocese to which he belongs, and that diocese dictates his movements and placements with full knowledge of his prior performance. If he commits abuses in a given parish, the diocese can be grilled about his prior record and held accountable if there were any suggestions that the priest was heading for trouble.

"It's called the liability trail," says Ken Wooden, a child sexual abuse expert from Vermont. "You get a Doberman pinscher attorney, he sniffs the trail. Who does it lead to? It leads to the bishop who reassigned the priest. Then they pay."

The first such case in the Catholic Church to garner national publicity was that of Father Gilbert Gauthe, who abused scores of children in southwestern Louisiana. As victim after victim came forward in 1983 and 1984, the Diocese of Lafayette deflected lawsuits by offering each of them an average of $450,000 for damages and therapy. A few victims and their families, however, either refused a quiet payoff or were dissatisfied with Church officials and insisted on being heard in open court. One family was awarded $1.25 million by a jury; another was awarded $1.8 million. To date, victims of Father Gilbert Gauthe have received more than $20 million.

Using the Gauthe case and several others around the country as barometers of the financial threat posed by child sexual abuse litigation, the 1985 Doyle-Peterson-Mouton report predicted that by 1995, Church losses to child sexual abuse—to lawsuits, legal fees and psychiatric bills for priests—would total $1 billion. In the years following the report, journalists, Church critics and other observers became fixated on the question of just how high the bill had climbed. Often, they ventured estimates using the following formula: They assumed the $1 billion guess to be prophetic, looked at the current calendar date, figured out what fraction of the ten-year period between 1985 and 1995 had elapsed, and then multiplied that fraction by $1 billion.

The math was neither scientific nor reliable. In fact, any attempt to estimate how much money the Church has lost to child sexual abuse is ridiculous. There's just no way to know. Attorneys' fees represent a significant portion of the bill, yet it's impossible to guess the hours worked and rates charged by different lawyers defending different dioceses at different times. It's also impossible to know how much it costs a given diocese to send an abusive priest away to a treatment facility. In some cases, medical insurance picks up part or all of the tab; in others, the diocese foots the entire bill.

Most significantly of all, it's impossible to tally what probably represents the biggest component of the Church's losses: the amount of money paid directly to victims either to ward off litigation, settle it, or satisfy the judgment of a jury. The Gauthe case is exceptional; financial figures came to light because several lawsuits came to trial. In a few other cases, the sums leaked out to the news media: In 1987, the Diocese of Springfield, Illinois, reportedly paid out $2.5 million to three victims; and the Diocese of Orlando, Florida, paid about $3 million to the families of four. But usually, such figures are shrouded in secrecy. Deals are struck before suits even get filed; if a suit is filed, it is settled before trial, and the settlement includes the condition that no one involved disclose the amount.

So there's no public record of the Church's losses. And the Church may not even have a private one. The Roman Catholic Church in the United States is entirely decentralized; each of the 188 dioceses manages its own finances and is not obliged to share information with others or with any kind of central administrative body, such as the National Conference of Catholic Bishops. The heads of dioceses are answerable only to the Vatican, and it's quite possible that Vatican officials have not even tallied the molestation bill. For one thing, Rome has been desperately slow to grasp the severity of the child sexual abuse problem. For another, it's the dioceses—not Rome—that are writing the checks.

The current estimates that Church observers throw around—

$400 million, $500 million—seem plausible at first glance, given the volume of litigation against the Church. The number of child sexual abuse lawsuits may well exceed five hundred; one St. Paul, Minnesota, attorney who specializes in this has filed more than seventy-five. His clients alone have been awarded a total of $30 million. But much of the money lost to these suits hasn't been paid out by the Church; it's been covered by diocesan insurance policies. For example, in the Gauthe case, the vast majority of the bill fell to the Diocese of Lafayette's insurers.

After that case, there was a period of two to three years when insurance companies considered sexual abuse by priests to be such a high financial risk that they stopped offering the coverage altogether. (Insurance companies also stopped offering that kind of coverage for many day-care centers, schools—any businesses or institutions entrusted with the care of children.) In the last few years, the coverage has again been made available, but at rates so exorbitant that many dioceses simply take a chance and don't buy it. An executive with the Michigan Catholic Conference says that when he last reviewed sexual abuse insurance options for the combined dioceses of Michigan, the best deal he could find was a policy with an annual premium of more than $200,000, an annual deductible of $500,000 and an annual limit of $1 million. He decided not to purchase it.

Mark Chopko, general counsel for the National Conference of Catholic Bishops, says that most of the lawsuits filed against the Church in the past few years refer to abusive incidents that occurred before dioceses lost insurance around 1986, so the policies from back then still pay for damages. For the past decade, Chopko has been the Church's point man on child sexual abuse by priests nationwide, yet he insists he has no idea how much money the Church has lost.

He guesses that dioceses and their insurers combined have paid out about $50 million as the direct result of civil litigation —a figure that seems crazily optimistic, given the price tag of the Gauthe case alone. He says he cannot guess how much dioceses have paid in legal fees and psychiatric bills, although he added that it's possible each of those categories would be as costly as litigation payouts. Assuming they are, Chopko's estimate would seem to be $150 million for the total cost of child sexual abuse to the Church before deducting what the insurers paid. But Chopko is hardly an objective observer—his salary is paid by the Church. The Church's losses are undoubtedly higher, though how much so is a matter of pure conjecture.

How keenly are these losses being felt? Probably less so than Church critics would like to think. For example, the Archdiocese of Los Angeles, the largest in the country, had a total operating revenue of $361.4 million in 1991, plus $1.4 billion in assets. Spending one, two or even three million dollars on child sexual abuse in a year would wound the diocese, but not critically.

A smaller diocese is more vulnerable. If hit with a particularly explosive case that insurance doesn't cover, it might not have enough of a cash flow to pay the bills. Neither larger dioceses nor the Vatican would be in a position to bail out the diocese, Chopko says, so it would probably have to sell off stocks, and maybe even some property. That's never happened, according to Chopko, although many wonder where the Diocese of Fall River raised almost $5 million to compensate the victims of Father James Porter. The diocese's insurers are refusing to ante up, arguing that Church officials' utter irresponsibility in repeatedly transferring Porter was hardly what the policy covered.

MONEY, HOWEVER, ISN'T THE WORST OF THE CHURCH'S WORRIES. Far more costly than any financial loss is the damage the child sexual abuse crisis is inflicting on the morale of Catholic priests, the vast majority of whom are innocent of any crimes. Loyal, hardworking, self-sacrificing men, they watch helplessly as the reputation of a profession they love is torn to shreds and cast under chilling suspicion. They wear their collars less comfortably than ever before. They stand on the pulpit some Sundays, look out into the pews and wonder: Will these people ever trust me completely again?

The question could not have come at a worse moment. Even before the child sexual abuse crisis, the Catholic priesthood was in dire straits.

The most basic and biggest problem was the continually diminishing number of Catholic priests in the United States over recent decades. The decline began in the late 1960s, when forces both inside and outside the Church combined to trigger an exodus of priests. The Second Vatican Council wrought changes that allowed priests, for the first time ever, to quit without facing utter disgrace and exile from institutional Catholicism. At the same time, the priesthood began attracting fewer recruits. Organized religion's influence in American society was waning, and the Catholic Church's rigid stands against birth control, abortion and the ordination of women made it seem increasingly out of touch with modern realities. In addition, the sexual revolution forced many men contemplating priestly service to doubt whether they could really live a celibate life. Many wondered why they were even being asked to try. Many felt vaguely embarrassed about doing so.

In 1970, there were 6,426 students enrolled in Catholic seminary programs in the United States. By 1990, the number had dwindled to 3,609. That decline, coupled with the resignations and retirements of ordained priests, has led some observers to predict that by the year 2005, the number of active Catholic priests in the United States will be 40 percent lower than it was in 1965. To make matters worse, those priests would be expected to serve a population of Catholics swelling rapidly, primarily as a result of Hispanic immigration.

In response to the situation, the Catholic Church has resorted to some previously unthinkable recruitment tactics that hardly make priests feel like the elite class they once were. Church leaders have put signs on billboards beckoning the devout to consider a life in vestments. They have placed advertisements in newspapers declaring that the Church is looking "to collar a few good men." They have searched the pews after Mass to see if any of the prayerful lingerers were adult men without wedding bands.

The shortage of priests has transformed priestly life entirely. More priests run parishes by themselves, with little or no help. More priests live alone in rectories that once housed half a dozen clergymen who ate dinner together and played poker late into the night. They endure heavier workloads and more loneliness. Yet they are less revered than ever before. As the ranks of priests winnowed and the appeal of the priesthood waned, this way of life lost much of its luster. Priests once had the aura of elite cultural heroes—Bing Crosby in *Going My Way*, Spencer Tracy in *Boys Town*. Through the 1970s and the 1980s, they acquired the aspect of curious cultural relics.

Now, with the child sexual abuse crisis, priests are coming under suspicion as dangerous cultural aberrations. In the Boston and Providence, Rhode Island, areas in the summer of 1992, as the story of Father James Porter regularly grabbed front-page headlines and top billing on television newscasts, every priest felt the sting of that publicity. One was sitting in his car at a stoplight when the driver of a truck beside him rolled down his window, stretched his head out and shouted: "All of you guys are pedophiles!" Another, dressed in plain clothes, was browsing in a Radio Shack when he overheard two men joking with each other. "Why don't you become a priest?" one man suggested to the other, who replied: "Nah—I don't like little boys enough."

Even a few years before the Porter case, one Providence priest, Father Jude McGeough, had a chilling conversation with one of his best friends. McGeough was friendly with the man's high school son and once, when the priest had a spare ticket to a classical music concert, invited the boy to come into the city to accompany him. Several weeks later, the man came to McGeough with this confession: "I don't know how to say this, because I'm so ashamed of myself. But when I was putting my son on the bus, some cold feeling grabbed my heart, a nervousness: He's going with a priest." Although the man couldn't bring himself to say the words, it was clear to McGeough he was talking about child sexual abuse.

In Chicago, where cases of child sexual abuse by priests have received as much news media attention as in the Boston-Providence area, priests have suffered similar indignities. One priest stood outside his church on a Sunday morning, mingling with the parishioners for whom he had just said Mass, when he casually remarked to a man: "I suppose your son will be an altar boy one of these days." The man answered: "No, he's not going to be an altar boy, and you're not going to talk to my boy unless I'm present."

Although most priests have not been subjected to such direct insult, they sense that people are eyeing them warily, standing at arm's length. And it tears them apart. These priests know that to be effective ministers, people must feel totally safe with them, must be willing to share their deepest secrets and confess their gravest sins. "We cannot function as priests without the trust of our people," says Father Dominic Grassi, chairman of the Association of Chicago Priests and pastor of St. Josephat's church in north Chicago. "And this erodes our trust. Unless the People of God can trust and believe us, we might as well close the doors."

FATHER DOMINIC, FORTY-SIX, WHO WAS ORDAINED MORE THAN two decades ago, typifies countless priests across the country. He entered the priesthood at a time when it still seemed like one of the most respected life paths a young man could follow. Then he witnessed a vast shift in people's attitudes toward priests. He cherishes mightily the nurturing, inspirational role that he, as a priest, can play in people's lives, but agonizes over the thought that he might lose that privilege as the crimes of a minority of priests sully the reputations of the majority.

Dominic's devout Roman Catholic parents immigrated to Chicago from southern Italy. His mother, Immaculata, bedecked their home with statues of different saints to whom she prayed on different occasions. His father believed so unquestioningly in all the rules the Church laid down for him that when he discovered he could not bring himself to follow one of them, he stopped going to Mass, feeling unfit to take Communion. His sin was wearing condoms because doctors had warned Immaculata that any more pregnancies would endanger her health.

When Dominic was ordained in 1973, his mother, following southern Italian tradition, gave up her wedding ring so that the diamond could be laid into the base of her son's silver chalice. Other relatives also offered up gems to gild the sacred cup in which Dominic would transform wine into the blood of Christ whenever he celebrated Mass. Its rim was plated with gold melted down from his grandparents' wedding bands.

Dominic reveled in the unique place he held in people's lives,

the special comfort he gave them. Baptisms, weddings, funerals—
he presided at all these events, guiding people through their moments of greatest joy and most profound sorrow. He gave first
Communion to his nephews and nieces, married good friends. He
administered the last rites for his own father. Out on the streets
of Chicago, he wore his collar with pride. Seeing it, people waved
and smiled. Restaurant owners gave him good tables. Police officers scratched out speeding tickets.

But gradually, his honeymoon with the priesthood ended. In
the late 1970s and 1980s, the Church's conservative stands on
most social debates alienated many parishioners and put many
priests like Dominic in the tense position of being expected to
defend edicts with which they didn't fully agree. Although the
Church condemned homosexual behavior, Dominic couldn't find
it in his heart to pass judgment on committed, responsible gay
couples. Although the Church opposed the ordination of women,
Dominic felt they should be allowed to celebrate the Eucharist.

At the same time, the news media began increasingly to portray priests as hypocritical, particularly in their sexual behavior.
Reporters asserted that many priests led active sex lives that broke
their celibate commitment. Reporters chronicled the deaths of
some gay priests to AIDS. And finally—the worst blow of all—
reporters exposed the growing number of priests arrested or sued
for child sexual abuse. Toward the late 1980s and early 1990s,
it seemed that every few months brought a new molestation
charge, a fresh disgrace.

Dominic's collar began to feel like an albatross. Whenever he
went out to dinner, whether with a female or male friend, he
debated whether to wear it. If he did, he worried, he might attract
quizzical stares from strangers wondering if that priest over there
was out on some kind of romantic liaison. If he didn't, he worried, he might run into a parishioner who would think that Father
was trying to disguise himself in plain clothes because he was up
to no good. It was a lose-lose proposition.

When he took his twenty-one-year-old niece out for a birthday
dinner to a restaurant just a few blocks from his parish, he felt
compelled to announce to the many diners who recognized him
precisely what he was doing and whom he was with. "This is my

niece," he said, emphasizing the last word. "It's her birthday," he explained, even to those diners who didn't ask or indicate any curiosity.

For Dominic, the low point came in October 1991. That month, Cardinal Joseph Bernardin held a startling press conference to announce that he was forming a special commission to study the problem of child sexual abuse by priests. As responsible as that action was, it made many priests around Chicago feel as if the image of them as potential child molesters was now seared into people's brains. In addition, Bernardin instructed priests to read aloud from the pulpit one Sunday a letter he had written to parishioners. It said, in part: "Words cannot adequately express my distress over the tragedy of child sexual abuse, especially by priests or other Church personnel. In dealing with the issue of child sexual abuse, Catholic parishioners have shown a healthy openness and appropriate concern. They have a right to expect that their trust and faith will not be taken for granted."

As Dominic read this to his congregants, he blinked back tears. (Later, most of his fellow priests would tell him they too cried that day.) He wondered how his people could hear this and still have confidence in him or any other priest. When he finished the letter, he added a few comments of his own, telling parishioners that most priests had never molested children and still merited trust. He said: "If you can't trust any of us, don't give up on God. Don't give up on God."

Ever since that month, which some priests in Chicago refer to as the "October massacre," the child sexual abuse crisis has hovered over Dominic's every day, and sometimes his every hour. He retires to his room in the rectory at night, turns on the local TV news, and there it is, on every channel—another story about a priest removed from a parish amid molestation rumors. During his days, Dominic senses disappointment, anger and a sense of betrayal in some of his parishioners. One man recently called him to ask about the procedure for an annulment and, irritated to learn how intricate and lengthy the process was, blurted out: "With all that's happening with you priests today, you think you'd be more understanding."

Many priests in Chicago feel that the intense climate of suspicion around them could lead easily to false accusations, false arrests, and Dominic has watched some of them grow paranoid and suffer acute anxiety around children. One friend who ministers to juvenile offenders—kids given to fibbing and acting out to get attention—actually has nightmares that one of them will cry sexual abuse. Another friend dropped plans to take a sabbatical in Africa because he feared that acquaintances would assume he had really disappeared, like so many other priests, because he had been hospitalized or incarcerated for child sexual abuse. When yet another priest friend did take a leave of absence, the man's aunt approached Dominic's mother with a question: "Can you ask Dominic if my nephew is one of those guys?"

Dominic feels anxious, too. When he told a mercurial woman that she had to take her daughter out of the parish school because the girl was racist and hostile, he thought: What if she becomes so angry she decides to get back at me by accusing me of child sexual abuse? He watches himself around children. He won't even hug one unless an adult is present to witness the innocence of the gesture.

Beleaguered by bad press, beset by self-consciousness, Dominic wonders if he and other priests aren't bound to lose all of their spontaneity, and much of their warmth. "When you can't be one hundred percent yourself, when there's that consciousness that you can't do anything that would even mislead people's thoughts, I think that what's lost is a degree of our humanity," he says. "What makes us most effective as priests is when people can identify our humanity, when they see that we can love them."

Although he finds much of the attention that's been focused on priest molesters to be overwrought and alarmist, he recognizes that a fair share of priests have engaged in child sexual abuse and that the problem must be discussed. "One priest said that every family has an Uncle George who nobody wants to talk about," Dominic says. "This is our Uncle George, and we've got to talk about him. We've got to make sure he doesn't hurt anybody else."

But the discussions aren't easy. In August 1992, Dominic invited three priests who had sexually abused children to address a meeting of the Association of Chicago Priests. His goal, in part, was to discover where these men went wrong and how others like them might be helped and healed. But some of the priests present at the meeting, particularly the older ones, found it impossible to listen dispassionately and sympathetically to the very abusers who, they felt, had dragged their beloved profession so far down.

One veteran priest sat with his head in his hands, not looking up from a spot on the table before him. Another excused himself to go to the bathroom—and vomited. Dominic watched their reactions with a sinking heart. "These were two of my heroes in the priesthood," he says. "And they were in so much pain."

THE NATION'S ROUGHLY FIFTY-THREE THOUSAND PRIESTS ARE SO worried about what child sexual abuse is doing to their profession that priest delegates to the April 1992 convention of the National Federation of Priests' Councils voted clergy sexual misconduct to be their top concern. The concern isn't solely about the priesthood's plummeting image. Many priests fear that the prevalence of child sexual abuse in their ranks says something important and alarming about their emotional well-being, their mental health. They wonder what role loneliness plays in all of this, and what relevance their level of sex education, or lack of it, has. They wonder about celibacy: Does it retard sexual maturity, create a dangerous vacuum of need? Indeed, the child sexual abuse crisis has triggered in many priests an unprecedented soul-searching around sexual issues, and it has added fuel to the already fiery debate over mandatory celibacy for priests.

Listen to Father Kevin Clinton, forty-four, a suburban St. Paul priest who has witnessed four colleagues, two of them friends, fall to charges of child sexual abuse over the past decade:

"This is the consequence of an institutional structure that thinks it can handle sexuality so flippantly that it won't suffer consequences. One of the most dangerous things you can do with sexuality is repress it. When you repress it, it splits off and becomes this separate part of you that you don't deal with. And if you don't deal with it, it deals with you.

"Very early in my life, I set my sights on the priesthood. That means you take your sights off the opposite sex. You put this part of your life in a box. This part of my life has been in the ice box since I was twelve. In my seminary preparation, it was a void. It was as if we weren't sexual beings. When I was twenty-nine, I fell in love for the first time. I didn't follow through with it. I kept my vows. But I remember the feeling of turning on the radio and all of a sudden, here at age twenty-nine, these songs now made sense to me.

"About a decade ago, I did a marriage encounter, and I was in a room surrounded by husbands and wives who loved each other very much. I remember couples holding hands. I remember wives running their hands through their husbands' hair. I remember all of the body language that goes with a married couple who are deeply married, and I remember feeling just very lonely, very cut off from something that was just deeply human and very natural and very profound.

"If the Church is going to mandate men to be celibate, they have to provide an environment that those men can survive in. Today's priests—the bishop takes them, and he's trying to fulfill the needs of the diocese, and he assigns them to a parish alone. What does the priest do but work, and try to keep this vast system going, and work, work, work, work. Then he goes back to an empty house, plops down on an easy chair with his TV changer, and flicks from one channel to another.

"The Church can't not be in touch with the reality of human sexuality and not get in trouble for it. We are reaping the seeds that the system has unconsciously sown. The key for me isn't celibacy—it's the mandating of it. The presumption that you can control something as slippery as human sexuality without doing violence to a person is crazy. The heart is not a place of logic. It's a mystical place. It's the center of existence."

For Clinton, as for other priests, the child sexual abuse crisis has brought misgivings and downright anger over the mandatory celibacy requirement boiling to the surface. He blames the mandatory celibacy requirement for the severe shortage of priests, a shortage that will only get worse as the image of priests as sexual miscreants gains wider currency. He questions the institutional Church's values. With fewer and fewer priests, there may soon come a day when the celebration of the Eucharist won't be readily available to all the Catholics who want to partake in it. And yet,

Clinton asserts, that celebration is the core of Catholicism—not some sexual shackling of priests. "We're placing the traditions of man higher than the law of God," Clinton says. In that sense, he adds, "The system is immoral."

PRIESTS ARE LOSING ESTEEM BECAUSE PARISHIONERS ARE FEELING less of it—both for them and for the institutional Catholic Church. This, too, is a consequence of the child sexual abuse crisis far more costly than any financial damage.

It's difficult to gauge just how severely the faith and trust of Catholics has been shaken. Such sentiments aren't easily quantified. But Father Stephen Rossetti, a priest psychotherapist then working in Chestnut Hill, Massachusetts, tried to glean some sense of how Catholics were feeling through a survey conducted in the late spring of 1992. He polled 1,013 Catholics—86 percent of them from the United States, the rest from Canada. "The effect among parishioners was even worse than I imagined," Rossetti said upon the survey's publication in the September and October 1992 editions of *Today's Parish* magazine. "They are very angry, very sad and very disappointed. It is not just the victims and their families who have been harmed by these incidents of clergy-child sexual abuse. The entire community has been wounded."

Rossetti sought to determine whether Catholics familiar with incidents of child sexual abuse by priests had dismissed them as freakish occurrences or were more deeply affected. To do so, he asked respondents to separate themselves into three groups: those whose diocese had never been rocked by a public accusation against a priest; those whose diocese had; and those whose own parish priest had been accused of child sexual abuse. Remarkably, a full 10 percent fell into that last category, which means one out of every ten Catholics worshipped in a church where a priest had been alleged to be a molester. Another 55 percent said a case or cases had popped up in their dioceses. Only 35 percent said they didn't know of a case in their area.

Rossetti asked those surveyed to respond to statements indicating their level of confidence in priests and in the Church. And he found, consistently, that confidence waned sharply among people whose dioceses or parishes had been affected by child sexual abuse. Consider the responses to the following statements and questions:

When someone wants to be a priest, I wonder if he has sexual problems. Just 19 percent of people in dioceses not affected by child sexual abuse agreed, but that number climbed to 27 percent among people in affected dioceses and 42 percent among people in affected parishes.

Would you let your son or daughter go on vacation with a priest? Even among people in dioceses not affected, just 43 percent said yes. That dropped to 33 percent in affected dioceses, and 26 percent in affected parishes.

The Church's current response to the sexual abuse of children by priests is adequate. In the first group, just 57 percent agreed; in the second, just 34 percent; in the third, only 20 percent.

I trust the Catholic Church to take care of problems with its own clergy. First group—53 percent. Second—33 percent. Third—25 percent.

And finally, this stunner: *I believe that the Church will safeguard the children entrusted to its care.* Even in the first group of people—those in dioceses not affected by abusive priests—only 50 percent answered yes. That dropped to 38 percent of people in affected dioceses, and 28 percent of people in affected parishes.

Behind these numbers are thousands of individual Catholics whose encounters with abusive priests have caused them to take their first tentative steps away from the Church—or flee it completely. Gerardo Gamez, a Houston police officer, is but one example. One night, while on patrol, he happened across a seemingly unoccupied van, looked inside, and saw a man having sex with a boy. When he ordered the man out of the van, the man protested: "I'm a man of the cloth." When he brought the man in for booking, the man laughed: "They won't do anything to me. I'm a priest."

The man was indeed a priest. In fact, he was Gamez's priest —although the officer at first didn't recognize him in the darkness, out of his clerical garb. Once Gamez did, his horror and disillusionment made it impossible for him to go to Mass. "I had two boys in catechism class with him," Gamez said seven years later. "I thought about what I'd seen in that van and I just lost a lot of faith. My wife and my sons still go to church, but not me. I haven't been to church since that night."

Clearly, Catholics aren't shrugging off incidents of child sexual abuse by priests. They are reexamining their confidence in Church leaders, reassessing their trust in the Catholic Church. When Rossetti asked the people in his survey if they were generally satisfied with the Catholic Church, 63 percent in dioceses not affected by abuse said yes, but just 47 percent in the next group and 34 percent in the final group agreed. The decline was the work of abusive priests and unresponsive bishops.

Rossetti's survey delved into attitudes and thoughts rather than actions. A July 1992 poll commissioned by the *Boston Globe,* however, asked 401 Catholics in the newspaper's circulation area whether, as a result of the child sexual abuse crisis, they were attending Mass less frequently. One of every ten said yes. Two of every ten said they now worry about sending their kids to church alone. And half said they had actually sat down with their children and discussed sexual abuse by priests.

To be fair, the results of both polls must be viewed in the context of two important trends. One is the growing skepticism Americans feel toward institutions in general. The other is the decline in recent decades of many Catholics' sense of allegiance to, and investment in, the Church as an organization that dictates the terms of their lives. Increasingly, they separate their faith from the institution that houses it.

"People already pay no attention to the bishops," says Eugene Kennedy, a prominent Catholic scholar and psychologist who has written numerous books about the modern-day Church. "When the Church serves the people well, they're really glad. But when the Church says things that don't resonate with their sense of Christianity, they don't pay attention. I think the bishops have no authority when they try to use it. It's a house of cards, and as long as nobody blows on it, it'll stand."

The child sexual abuse crisis, to extend Kennedy's metaphor, is probably not a strong enough gust to bring the walls down.

But it's adding velocity to the winds of change, and forcing at least some people who hadn't already done so to remark on the faults in the structure and seek shelter elsewhere.

ARCHBISHOP THOMAS KELLY OF LOUISVILLE, KENTUCKY, WAS VA-cationing on the west coast of Florida in July 1992 when he turned on the television set one night and watched one of the most disturbing programs he had ever seen. It was an episode of the ABC news show "PrimeTime Live," and the majority of it was devoted to the case of Father James Porter. Diane Sawyer intoned the words "rape" and "molest" as images of little Catholic girls in their white Communion outfits and little Catholic boys in their altar-server cassocks flitted across the screen. It went on for nearly forty minutes.

At some point, Kelly began to weep. He cried for the victims, whose pain he could not begin to imagine. And he cried for his Church, which had made some grievous errors and was now paying so dearly for them. "It just blew me away," Kelly says. "We've had our share of embarrassment and small scandals, but I don't think anything that would rival this."

The leaders of the Catholic Church in the United States are hardly unaware of all that the child sexual abuse crisis is costing their Church, and they are hardly unconcerned. In fact, many feel as much pain and frustration as priests do. They realize that they are often portrayed in the news media as aloof, even callous men. They appreciate just how crippling this publicity is to the Church's mission, and to its good standing in society.

So they are spending inordinate amounts of their time and energy working to control the damage. Former Archbishop Robert Sanchez of Santa Fe, New Mexico, estimated in late 1992 that he was devoting 30–40 percent of his working hours to matters related to child sexual abuse by priests. (His bungling of those matters would lead to the revelation of his own failure to live a celibate life and his resignation.) Archbishop John Roach of the Diocese of St. Paul-Minneapolis says that whenever two bishops talk, no more than five minutes goes by before one of them mentions the problem.

Bishop Kenneth Untener of Saginaw, Michigan, says these discussions are marked by a mood of "gloom and heartache and great concern. You're watching something that you're a part of, and something that you love very much, being twisted and broken. This looks so malicious. You've got victims, years and years, all these kids, cover-up. There's no point in trying to defend it, or to explain it."

Bishops wonder how the Church can ever retain any credibility on sexual matters, how it can preach effectively about such important virtues as monogamy and commitment in this atmosphere. They wonder how they can recruit the next generation of priests under such a pall. And they wonder how long the image of the Church as a place that harbors child molesters will linger, now that it is so deeply ingrained.

A joke made the rounds among many Catholics in 1992 about a priest who has to go the bathroom while he's hearing confessions. The priest, Father George, asks Joe the janitor to take his place for a few minutes. He shows Joe a list on the confessional wall of sins and their appropriate penances. He tells Joe simply to give people whatever penance the list says.

The first voice Joe hears through the dark screen separating him from the person confessing is a man's. "Forgive me, Father, for I have sinned," the man says. "I had sex with a twelve-year-old boy."

Joe consults the list, but cannot find that sin. In a panic, he leans out of the confessional to look for help. He spots Mikey the altar boy. "Mikey," he whispers. "What does Father George give for sex with a twelve-year-old boy?"

"Usually," Mikey responds, "I get a dollar bill and a candy bar."

Chapter 12

A PATH TO REDEMPTION

Once the gravity of the child sexual abuse crisis was established as irrefutable fact—and Church leaders began to taste, and choke on, the bitter fruits it was reaping—pundits scurried forth with solutions that ranged from the absurd to the shallow. Father Charles Fiore, a priest writing for the ultraconservative Catholic weekly *The Wanderer*, raised the possibility that left-wingers had planted pedophiles in the priestly ranks to undermine Christianity and that, by implication, a purge of communists would save the day. Writer Jason Berry, misunderstanding the difference between child sexual abuse and homosexuality, suggested a purge of gay priests instead. Father Thomas Doyle, convinced the problem was the nation's bishops, wanted to fire them all—and maybe even the Holy Ghost, who is believed to have selected them. And hundreds of Catholic women who dreamed of consecrating the Eucharist insisted that the immediate ordination of women would bring salvation.

Meanwhile, Church leaders fixed on less drastic approaches. They set up twenty-four-hour hot lines to facilitate the reporting of abusers. They deputized posses to investigate complaints. They rewrote their internal policies, convened seminars on child sexual abuse for all priests, mandated psychological screening of seminary applicants and designed classes in sexuality for those accepted. Where major surgery was called for, they prescribed Band-Aids.

Neither set of solutions—the pundits' or the bishops'—held much promise. Weeding out homosexuals was unlikely to have even as much impact as weeding out heterosexuals since abusers don't always fit neatly into one sexual orientation. Screening was a mirage since psychologists had yet to develop a "test" for pedophilia. And the ordination of women pivoted on the naively sexist assumption that only men molest kids, abuse their power and cover up scandal.

These flaws were lost on solution-peddlers, who in fact had their own agendas. Those castigating the Church for inaction frequently had other axes to grind—mandatory celibacy and the ordination of women, to mention but two—and latched on to the victims' rights movement to further those causes. The bishops themselves were entrenched in a hierarchical Church over which they had virtually no doctrinal control and thus could not, realistically, propose solutions they were helpless to implement. Thus one group bent the situation to fit its view of reality while the other bent reality to fit the dogma prescribed by Rome.

It was not a hopeful scenario for the resolution of what many observers considered to be the most serious crisis in the history of the Catholic Church in the United States.

At heart, the problem is that the Catholic Church, in its structure and mentality, is a medieval institution trying to cope with modern problems in a very modern world. The Church thinks in centuries, even millennia; secular society demands to be dealt with in real time. Bishops are princes in their own domains, unaccustomed to being questioned or challenged; that gloss is wearing thin for victims and judges and attorneys. Ecclesiastical authori-

ties live in a world of confidentiality and secrecy; they are surrounded by a society that thrives on the exposure of every hidden
truth. Strict doctrine almost demands that the bishops insist that
prayer and adherence to Church teachings will resolve the di-
lemma; the nature of modern society makes that prescription as
realistic as ending the AIDS crisis by wearing red ribbons.

While proponents of a dozen solutions look for answers in the
upstairs bedroom, the back den or on the porch, they fail to consider the possibility that the entire structure may be tilting on its
foundation. The Church, as currently designed, simply does not
have the flexibility to deal with a crisis that lingers at the intersection of sexuality, secrecy, patriarchy and blind obedience.
Child sexual abuse has become a scandal within the Church not
as the result of conscious, or even unconscious, error or evil, but
because it is embedded in the very structure of Roman Catholicism.

That reality has begun to creep into the discussions of child
sexual abuse by priests in the Canadian Conference of Catholic
Bishops. They were forced into a serious consideration of the
problem in 1989 when the people of the remote maritime province of Newfoundland discovered that the archbishop had known
for years that children at a local Catholic orphanage were complaining about routine molestation by priests and brothers—and
had done nothing. As the scandal rocked a devout Catholic community, Sister Lorraine Michaels, director of social action for the
neighboring diocese of St. John's, predicted that it would strike
to the core of the institution. "What has happened here will force
the Church to examine its own hierarchical system to see whether
the fact that it is a male-dominated one, with no accountability
to the rest of the [Church] body, contributed in any way to what
happened," she said. "The rules are going to have to change and,
first among them, the rule that gives male clergy all the decision-
making powers without any participation by the laity or the rest
of us [nuns]. This, I think, will be the key change. Then, we will
have to look at the rules governing celibacy, married priests and
female clergy."

In a forty-page report to the Canadian bishops, Paul McAuliffe, a social worker specializing in the development of programs

for the investigation and treatment of child sexual abuse and an adviser to bishops on the matter, went even further. He argued that dealing effectively with child abuse by clergy would not so much demand better guidelines and procedures as it would the realization that there is something fundamentally wrong with the "way we have been doing things.

"It is true that misuse of power over those we consider less powerful is part of our human condition—the pyramidal pecking order," he wrote. "This is all the more reason why we must structure ourselves as a church in a way that does not provide an environment which supports this human failing, as our present structure seems to do."

McAuliffe insisted that any credible response to the crisis must address the issue of power within the present church structure since sexual abuse is, at its core, an abuse of power. He noted that the abuse of power was not just sexual, but included the "secrecy, denial, collusion and pressure" he saw as the Church's dominant response to reports of sexual abuse by clergy and religious. He ended by suggesting the upending of the pyramidal power structure that now exists in the Church. "We need to find a new model of church, one which, while retaining the Church's doctrinal purity, also recognizes the needs of a church approaching the 21st century."

In their 1990 report on the problem, the Canadian bishops accepted much of what Michaels and McAuliffe argued. They noted that until recently, "Catholic priests could, on account of their ministry and their status as priests, exercise considerable authority over the day-to-day lives of their communities. This excessive power, unchecked by any kind of social control, placed certain individuals beyond the reach of legitimate questioning and made it possible to prevent detection. The fact that priests were placed on a pedestal was actually a kind of trap." While they recommended changes in seminary education, and changes in the handling of abuse complaints, they also mandated steps to encourage the development of a more communal church in which ecclesiastical officials concern themselves more with service than with power.

Perhaps unknowingly, they were mandating a revolution.

———

NOT SO ON THE OTHER SIDE OF THE BORDER. OUTSIDE CHICAGO, in October 1992, Richard Sipe, psychotherapist and former Benedictine monk, greeted the first national gathering of victims of sexual abuse by clergy with a call to arms: "My friends, welcome to Wittenberg," he said, referring to the German town where Martin Luther helped to launch the Protestant revolution. "We stand on the brink of the most profound reformation of the Catholic clergy and its celibate/sexual system since the time when Martin Luther challenged clerical integrity on October 31, 1517."

But even there—before a group of men and women who regularly applied socially unacceptable epithets to the names of the nation's bishops—Sipe found few takers for his crusade. Although conference participants were hell-bent on holding the Church accountable for crimes against children, few saw forcing bishops to deal energetically with child sexual abuse as a revolutionary act that would shake the foundations of two millennia of Catholicism.

Most survivors and their supporters don't get it. They picket and bargain and holler and petition for precisely the kind of tiny, timid adjustments the bishops are now offering—largely in response to victims' demands. But they remain touchingly convinced that those adjustments will do the trick, so long as the nation's bishops are honest and consistent in implementing them. They naively believe the problem will disappear if the bishops simply straighten up and fly right.

This is what they want, and this is what the bishops are starting to give them: psychological screening of seminarians; savvier sex education in seminaries; laicization of proven molesters. All of which is well and good. All of which would help—a bit. A few potential abusers might be denied collars. A few active ones might lose theirs. But none of these solutions strikes anywhere near the heart of the problem. They sound and look good. But examine them a little more closely and the illusion disintegrates.

The notion of screening out potential child abusers is a chimera: a nice concept, but meaningless in a world without an effective test for who is—or might turn out to be—sexually attracted to children. It is what Gary Schoener, the Minneapolis psychologist who consults with the Archdiocese of St. Paul-Minneapolis, calls "diving for a quick fix." Researchers can't administer a standardized test to ferret out hidden desires or sexual immaturity. It's like trying to divine a man's genital endowment without getting him out of his clothes. Even if tests could detect desires, they would have no way to gauge who might act on those feelings and who might overcome them.

Some researchers believe that child sexual abusers tend to be outwardly conservative about sexual matters, vehemently opposing any sexual activity outside of marriage. Some researchers believe that abusers tend to interpret the world in a hierarchical fashion, comfortable with certain people claiming power and license over others. But that description probably fits a third of the people in the world—and, certainly, the vast majority of those who come knocking on seminary doors. The Church could choose to turn them all away, but that would leave most of the nation's Catholic pulpits empty.

Many of those who harp on screening as a clerical cure-all aren't really after child molesters, anyway. They think they are, but get them talking for a few minutes and they start ranting about all those fussy and effeminate young men, stuck on priestly drag, who think the all-boy seminary atmosphere is the next best thing to a gay bar. They want the homosexuals out because it must be those queers, after all, who are causing all this trouble.

To some degree, their confusion is understandable. Just before the child sexual abuse crisis hit, several studies and much discussion began to focus on the priesthood's disproportionately high percentage of men with homosexual orientations. To the thinking of many uninformed observers—including both Church critics and the bishops they criticize—the twin phenomena could hardly be coincidental. They had to be linked.

And they are, but not in the way many observers and some bishops think. The common ground is that the same forces drawing men who desire children to the Church also attract men who desire other men. Members of both groups have sexual interests that run smack up against society's taboos. Members of both groups may respond to those taboos by denying their desires. And members of both groups may choose the priesthood, with its pledge of celibacy, as a way of formalizing and buttressing that denial. But the groups remain distinct, separate.

No credible research links child sexual abuse with homosexuality. Men molest more little girls than little boys. And men who molest little boys are more likely to be heterosexual than homosexual in their adult involvements. So screening out suspected homosexuals from the priesthood would have no more—and maybe less—effect on the child sexual abuse crisis than screening out suspected heterosexuals.

Another hopeful fantasy which is equally flawed is giving seminarians better instruction about sexuality and training for celibacy. The theory: If a man understands his sexuality, he can live with celibacy not merely as a practical and even spiritual necessity, but as part of his own growth and development. He can live without repression or personal harm. Or, early on in his training, he will realize that celibacy simply isn't for him.

The reality: How can a man with little or no sexual experience explore his sexuality? How do you investigate your desires in the abstract? Is there something—anything—seminaries can teach that might actually be a substitute for experience? Father Anthony Kosnik, former dean of a Detroit-area seminary, isn't convinced there is. "I used to tell students not to take their vow until they were thirty-eight," Kosnik says. "Or until they'd fallen in love."

And even if seminaries could find a way to teach Celibacy 101, it's unclear what effect that curriculum would have on those men who enter seminary with already-ingrained sexual desires for children.

So the Church is—and will be—stuck with a certain number of child molesters. Even worse, the Church is unlikely to find out who most of them are. The best reporting policies in the world cannot change the fact that the Catholic Church has encouraged in its parishioners an almost blind faith in its servants.

"It's a hierarchy, and the consumers of the service are not supposed to question it," explains Mic Hunter, the St. Paul therapist specializing in male victims of sexual abuse. "Nobody's going to go and say: 'The priest fucked me.' The system is set up so that God speaks through the priest. You confess to the priest, who forgives you in the name of God. Then he tells you what you need to do in order to be forgiven. The priest is higher than you—so accusing him would bring more shame to the family than the priest. The Catholic Church isn't a Ralph Nader–approved organization."

Even if children do lodge complaints and a priest is proven to be an abuser, bishops are caught in a bind, trapped by their own rhetoric of forgiveness. A school administrator is supposed to fire an abusive teacher, a hospital director to get rid of a nurse who molests. But a bishop cannot treat a priest as a simple employee. It's antithetical to Catholic theology. Once you're a priest, you're a priest for life. "The very situation of the priest is singular," Cardinal Joseph Ratzinger, head of the Vatican Congregation for the Doctrine of Faith, wrote in a controversial series of interviews published in 1985. Priests represent Christ on earth and have "supernatural 'authority of representation.' "

Antithetical or not, defrocking abusive priests—or laicizing them has become the American bishops' most ardent crusade in their attempts to make the problem of child sexual abuse by priests disappear. Since only the pope has the authority to do that, they have been lobbying him for a change in the rules. For four years, they have been sending representatives to the Vatican to plead, beg, explain and cajole the pope into ceding them a bit of his turf—to no avail.

"There is a long tradition of trying to protect priests from dictatorial bishops," explains Bishop John McCarthy of Austin, Texas, who has discussed the matter directly with the pope. Archbishop Daniel Pilarczyk of Cincinnati adds: "Laicization is generally a privilege. It's a favor that somebody asks for and is given. Laicization as a punishment is the highest punishment. And you can't do it if there's any mitigating circumstance. And psychiatric disability is a mitigating circumstance."

Even if bishops succeed in this quest, it could well come back to haunt them. IBM can dump errant accountants on society with no fear of embarrassment. But the Catholic Church is expected to safeguard not only its own reputation but the welfare of society. If it dumps molesters onto the secular streets, where they might molest again, is the Church living up to its own and society's expectations? Archbishop Rembert Weakland of Milwaukee thinks not. "I know we can't reassign anyone who's a great risk, and in most pedophilia cases, there is a grave risk," he says. "On the other hand, I don't know if I have the right to throw someone like this out into society when I might be able to exercise some control or supervision over him if he remains part of the Church."

Weakland's crowd opts for tucking selected abusers away in safe corners of chancery offices, Catholic charities and old-age homes. But that's hardly a perfect solution either. Priests leave those posts at the end of the day, and there aren't enough eyes in all of the Catholic world to monitor their every movement. They wander past playgrounds. They visit friends with small children.

So bishops are faced with an agonizing quandary.

DR. RICHARD MCBRIEN NEVER MINCES WORDS. THE FORMER HEAD of the Department of Theology at the University of Notre Dame has managed to provoke every conservative Catholic from Chicago to Rome—and a healthy percentage of moderates as well. In 1985, the priest got his wrist slapped by the nation's bishops for doctrinal deviationism. His appearances on "Nightline" and the "CBS Evening News" and his comments in *Newsweek, Time* and the *New York Times* inspire letters promising that he'll rot in hell.

McBrien's sin in 1992 was to attack the litany of purportedly aggressive measures that the nation's bishops paraded as proof that they were vanquishing child sexual abuse. McBrien was not impressed. Corporate damage control, he dubbed it.

"In the final accounting, no matter how many teeth there are in the new guidelines for dealing with these cases," he wrote in a syndicated newspaper column in November 1992, "no matter how many Catholics work up the courage to come forward and accuse their predators, no matter how many priests are exposed, defrocked and even sent to prison, the problem is not going to go away. Why not? Because the problem isn't only in the pool; it's in the pipeline. The seminary pipeline. And at the root of the seminary problem is celibacy, the church's requirement that a priest must remain unmarried for life.

"Under Pope John Paul II, the Catholic Church remains firmly committed to its law of celibacy for priests. And so sexual abuse by priests will continue—at least until the money runs out."

McBrien's focus on celibacy as the root of this evil is wildly popular. Researchers, victims—and even some bishops—have seized on the abolition of mandatory celibacy as a panacea.

"My argument now is as subtle as a train wreck," says McBrien. "The fellow who doesn't think celibacy is going to be a problem is the fellow who is a problem. Obligatory celibacy has the effect of excluding a lot of healthy men who are called to the priesthood. It has the effect of attracting a lot of unhealthy men into the system. The celibate priesthood is a magnet for people who are psychologically and especially sexually disturbed."

But the call to abolish mandatory celibacy ignores a crucial fact: No one is proposing mandatory non-celibacy. The Catholic Church would inevitably retain a core of men pledged to celibacy—men who, if Church history provides any indication, would be exalted as holier than their more worldly counterparts. That core would continue to act as a magnet and refuge for abusers.

So while permitting priests to marry might attract a greater number of sexually healthy men to the priesthood, it would hardly turn the sexually unhealthy away. The percentage of them in the priesthood would dwindle. But their absolute numbers might not change at all.

In any case, it's a moot point. Mandatory celibacy shows no sign of retreat. Church leaders have clung tenaciously to it despite the violence necessary to its original imposition, despite centuries of unpopularity and despite its seeming irrelevance to the Gospel of Christ. They have come to view the celibate commitment of priests as proof that the Catholic Church's servants are more like Jesus than the men—and especially the women—who labor on behalf of other Christian groups. Whenever challenged, Church leaders respond: "This is how Jesus lived."

But in the beginning, there was no mandatory celibacy. Saint Peter, the first pope, was married. Pope Anastasius I was the father of Pope Innocent, Pope Sergius III begat Pope John XI and Pope Theodore I was the son of a bishop.

Celibacy was imposed gradually—and bloodily—as ascetic monks, ever suspicious of the material world, triumphed over secular priests. The Synod of Elvira ordered priests to stop having intercourse with their wives in 305. When the monk Jovinian resisted the new movement, he was driven out of Rome, thrashed with a lead thong and exiled to the desolate rock of Boa. In 952, when German bishops gathered at the Council of Augsburg and decreed that priests could no longer live with their wives, they declared that women who had sex with priests should be marked with stripes and have their heads shaved. In 1022, Pope Benedict VIII ordered that children of priests be taken as serfs—a decision included in the imperial code by King Henry II of Bamberg. Three decades later, Pope Leo IX and the Council of Rome ordered the wives and mistresses of priests seized and enslaved in Lateran palaces.

That willingness to incur the wrath of loyal clerics for a principle not even mandated in the gospels gave testimony to the weight that Peter's heirs to the papacy placed on mandatory celibacy. They considered it essential to the preservation of Church property, as Pope Pelagius I made clear in the sixth century, when he ordered all married candidates to the priesthood to sign contracts waiving their children's rights to inherit Church land. And they saw it as key to the consolidation of their own power. In fact, the culminating moment for mandatory celibacy occurred in a fight between Pope Gregory VII and King Henry IV over nobles granting lucrative bishoprics to their sons—an early sign of the beginnings of a hereditary nobility of bishops the pope was determined to stop. (He ultimately faced down the king, forcing him to set aside the trappings of royal power and stand barefoot before the papal gates imploring Gregory for his soul.)

Mandatory celibacy not only gave the Church tight control over its lands and power but also endowed the Church's servants with an aura of holiness and purity that placed them above other mere mortals. By imitating Jesus in giving up intimate attachments, they became what Saint John Chrysostom declared a priest should be: "Purer than the very rays of the sun, so that the Holy Spirit will not abandon him, and so that he may be able to say, 'It is no longer I that live, but Christ that liveth in me.'"

In consolidating the Church's wealth, shoring up its power and exalting its priesthood above the rest of society, mandatory celibacy lay at the heart of the Church's historic bid for power. And it still, in the eyes of the Church, lies at the heart of its power today. Mandatory celibacy allows the Church tight control over its priests, who have no dividing loyalties to wives and offspring and thus require minimal salaries. And it envelops those priests in a mystique that bolsters the idea of Catholicism as the one and only true faith. Church leaders are not going to let go of mandatory celibacy easily.

In the end, mandatory celibacy is relevant to the current child sexual abuse crisis not just because its culture attracts abusers, but because it facilitated the rise of the rigid Church hierarchy that may, in the end, be the most formidable obstacle to a solution of the crisis. If there is a single truth on which virtually every expert on child sexual abuse agrees, it is that abuse thrives in hierarchical, authoritarian institutions—particularly sexually repressive ones. When experts describe such institutions, they seem to be characterizing the Catholic Church.

"I think any institution that emphasizes infallibility, that emphasizes a hierarchy, a patriarchy, that is a closed system, where there is a great deal of secrecy and lack of accountability, is an environment where abusers are more likely to be able to function without being caught," says Mike Lew, author of the classic book on male survivors of child sexual abuse. "These are systems that are breeding grounds for abuse." In creating a clear and rigid pecking order, they teach people that they owe blind obedience to those who rank above them, yet have unchecked license over those below them. People compensate for their subservience to superiors by exploiting inferiors. They feel entitled.

Consider priests. Under canon law, they owe their bishops obedience. They have very little say in where they work. They have no influence on their Church's doctrine, but are expected to enforce it as the wisdom of a pope who can declare himself infallible. Any dissent could cost them exile. "Suffer for the truth in silence and prayer," Catholic theologians were told in a 1989 Vatican pronouncement, or face "serious measures."

So they suffer. Some make private truces. They are publicly

obedient, but privately loyal to their own consciences. But others find consolation in the power the hierarchy grants them over those on a lower rung—namely, parishioners. If their sense of self-importance is precarious, they may take advantage of that power. If they're at all inclined to sexually abusing children, that is the way they may do it. Their victims, trained to be subservient and obedient to them, will likely acquiesce.

And their superiors, learning about this, aren't likely to act. If they allow a priest's moral authority to be questioned by someone below him, they open the door to challenges to their own moral supremacy. They're worried about the moral dominoes falling, until the Church itself is toppled. So they ignore or veil the transgressions—and they get away with it because they control the closed system, because they occupy the pinnacle of the patriarchy.

IF EXPERTS ARE RIGHT ABOUT HIERARCHIES BREEDING ABUSE, THE prescription for change in the Catholic Church is indeed major surgery. It is to turn a dictatorship into a democracy, the modern Church into the early one. After all, before all the cathedrals, before all the wealth, before all the dogma and before mandatory celibacy, there was simply a community of believers following Jesus' path. Power was not supposed to be concentrated in the hands of any one man or group of men. That was not Christ's command:

"You know that among the pagans the rulers lord it over them, and make their authority felt. This is not to happen among you. No, any one who wants to be great among you must be your servant, and any one who wants to be first among you must be your slave." (Matt. 20:25–27)

But the Church has evolved through wars and schisms, visionary leadership and sheer corruption in the two millennia since that pronouncement. It is now stitched together with an intransigent hierarchy that traps the American bishops trying to solve the child sexual abuse crisis. They are powerless to take the fabric of modern Catholicism and pull out the one thread that is celibacy, the other that is priestly privilege or the other that is obedience.

Today's Church is governed by the sixth canon of the Council of Trent: "If anyone says that in the Catholic Church there is not a hierarchy, instituted by divine ordination and consisting of bishops, priests, and deacons, let him be anathema." And despite Vatican II's declaration that the Church is "the People of God," on his visit to the United States in 1987, Pope John Paul II was brutally frank about the true nature of the Catholic Church: "The Church is a theocratic institution, not a democratic one."

As long as the pope sings that tune, the nation's bishops are helpless unless they want to break up the band. Trapped by the very structure of the institution as defined by the Vatican, they can mandate screening—and perhaps keep a few potential abusers out of their ranks. They can respond with open, pastoral concern to victims—and perhaps keep a few more Catholics in the pews. They can laicize offending priests—and keep at least some children out of harm's way. But ultimately, they cannot address the underlying problems of power and hierarchy that make their Church a breeding ground for abuse.

But some of the changes essential to the protection of Catholic children are occurring despite them. Victims silenced for decades are finding their voices in mounting numbers. Intent on reclaiming the power ripped from them by the abuses of individual priests and their bishops, they are humiliating the Church that broke faith with them before they even reached puberty—and sending a powerful message to Catholic parents who are now refusing to let their sons spend weekends alone with Father Smith or their daughters pass endless unaccompanied hours at Father Jones's rectory. They are telling their stories in lurid detail to the news media—and embarrassing prosecutors and judges into treating priests who abuse just like other child rapists. They are persuading juries that decades of transfers of abusive priests merit multi-million-dollar punitive awards against indifferent dioceses—thus warning bishops to take their stories seriously.

In Albuquerque, they are showing up at churches on Sundays handing out buttons declaring: "Forgive You Father for You Have Sinned." In Chicago, they are filling collection baskets with fake dollar bills reading: "I gave my money to support victims of clerical sexual abuse."

As their demand for justice reaches into every nook and cranny of American Catholicism, the victims are creating the very revolution the bishops cannot lead: a revolt by the laity against the perils of hierarchy. Catholics in the pews on Sundays may not be able to change the nature of that system or its instinct for cover-up, the kind of men it attracts to the priesthood or the impulses it breeds in some of them. But they can control the size of the purse of a Church already strapped for cash by considering the price of children's souls when they reach for the collection basket. They can—and have—changed their attitude toward their clerical leaders and, by withholding blind deference, make their children less vulnerable.

In a response that mirrors how American Catholics have re-acted to the Church's positions on birth control and homosexu-ality, abortion and divorce, they are not breaking away from the Church in great numbers over the child sexual abuse crisis. But they are bowing out of their assigned positions in the hierarchy, refusing to grant priests and bishops and even the pope the au-tomatic respect that makes that structure dangerous.

They are teaching their children that a Roman collar is no safer than any other kind of uniform behind which an abuser might hide.

They are telling their children that priests are human, that their Church is flawed. They are finding in themselves a more mature faith—less dependent on deference than on conscience, tethered not to what they see as an out-of-touch hierarchy but to their own sense and experience of God in their lives.

EPILOGUE

*Children have neither power nor property.
Voices other than their own must speak for
them. If those voices are silent, then children
who have been abused may lean their heads
against window panes and taste the bitter
emptiness of violated childhoods.*

—JUSTICE FRANCES T. MURPHY

AMAZING
GRACE

O N A CHILL OCTOBER WEEKEND IN 1992,
nearly three hundred people poured into
a hotel in the suburbs of Chicago and gave the
Catholic Church notice: We won't stand this
any longer. We won't let tomorrow's children
suffer the way yesterday's did. And we won't
trust your ready-made promises to make sure
that doesn't happen, because we know too
well the bitter fruits of a trust that's unearned.

It was the first annual conference of a
group called VOCAL (Victims of Clergy Abuse
Linkup), now renamed The Linkup, and it
marked a definite turning point for the survivors of child sexual abuse by Catholic priests.
Freed from shame, unshackled from silence,
they revealed bitter histories of victimization
and Church indifference. They did so in clear
and strong voices, without apology or equiv-
ocation, as they stood under harsh klieg lights

set up by TV news crews that recorded their every word. One adult female survivor set the tone in the opening session, when she rose, her entire body trembling with anger, and declared to a hushed audience: "The first kiss of a young woman should not come from a middle-aged priest."

As the stories overlapped and the voices merged, something remarkable happened. The isolated experiences and the lonely battles of individual men and women from different corners of the country coalesced into a single crusade, a cohesive movement that held the possibility, finally, of wielding enough power to wrest Church leaders away from denial and inaction.

This was happening in part because time inevitably brings together scattered soldiers fighting the same war and carrying the same scars. It was happening in part because the public furor over the case of Father James Porter lent this battle crucial momentum and because the survivors of Father Porter's abuse had taught other victims a lesson about the stunning results of unified action. And it was happening in particular because of the passion and pluck of a striking redhead who darted from one meeting room to another in the Woodfield Hilton that weekend and who sneaked Parliament 100 cigarettes and wiped away people's tears in the corridors.

Her name was Jeanne Miller. She was forty-five years old, a legal secretary and divorced mother of four with a comfortable condominium in the Chicago suburbs, a gentle demeanor, a musical laugh and an affinity for bright lipsticks and dangling, jangling earrings. She was also a woman whose name aroused anxiety and dread in many Church leaders around Chicago and, indeed, much of the country. In her crusade to force them to protect children before priests, to minister to victims instead of shutting them out, she seemed indefatigable, almost superhuman. By the time of the VOCAL conference, she had been at it for more than a decade.

Back in 1982, her oldest son, then thirteen years old, came home from a weekend outing with their parish priest and several other boys and told her and her husband an astonishing story. He said the priest had offered the boys alcohol and marijuana, used profanity in their presence, shown them pornographic mov-

ies, walked around naked in front of them and attempted to fondle one of them.

For Jeanne and her husband, whose lives revolved around the
Catholic Church, it was almost too incredible to believe. But other
boys on the outing gave identical accounts. And Jeanne quickly
learned that the priest had a long history of sexual misbehavior
around boys, a history that had been reported to Church officials.
She began to reel with confusion and pain. There must be some
mistake here, she thought. There must be some explanation.

She went to Church officials with a simple request: Get the
boys and the priest some counseling and restrict his access to kids.
Those officials refused to do either. They said the priest denied
the boys' charges, and that his denial seemed honest. They suggested she was an overprotective mother misinterpreting a series
of innocent events. They advised her to forgive and forget, apparently confident that she would.

They did not know Jeanne Miller very well at all.

When the Church failed to take any kind of action against the
priest, she filed a lawsuit. When poverty and exhaustion forced
her family to settle the suit for a meager sum—and without any
formal guarantee the priest would be kept away from children—
she found other ways to register her anger and lobby for change.

She wrote a fictionalized account of the episode under a pen
name, convinced one friend to use a small press he owned to
publish the book, recruited another to help her with publicity,
and got herself booked on radio and TV talk shows nationwide
to discuss the Catholic Church's coddling of dangerous priests.
She researched child sexual abuse in the Catholic Church as part
of a master's thesis, eventually compiling a list of hundreds of
priests across the United States and Canada accused of molesting
teenagers and children.

She turned her home office into a veritable clearinghouse of
information on abusive priests and her home telephone number
into a veritable hot line for their victims. She gave birth to
VOCAL, becoming the unofficial spokeswoman for victims and
survivors nationwide. And in October 1992, she summoned these
people to the Woodfield Hilton, along with detectives dedicated
to putting an end to any collusion by the law enforcement com-

munity in Church officials' negligence, mental health professionals determined to help sound the alarm about priests' unusual power and their victims' heightened vulnerability, and lawyers eager to haul Church officials into civil courts to make them atone for their failures.

To some eyes, her commitment borders on the fanatical. Her zeal seems disproportionate to the crime that spawned it. Her son, after all, was not raped or physically brutalized. Neither were the other boys on that fateful summer trip.

But Jeanne Miller's quiet rage and steady determination have almost nothing to do with the specifics of that event. Rather, they spring from the devastating betrayal of a sacred trust she placed in her Church, which was the source of her most unshakable assumptions about what was right and wrong in the world, what was good and bad. It was her anchor and beacon.

And when she felt that it had abandoned her, an illusion shattered, and she saw at once how dangerous that illusion was, not just for her but for all the other mothers and all the other children who might be rendered vulnerable by it. So she fights to warn and protect them. And she fights because if she wins—if Church leaders confess the sins she has documented, accept her suggestions for openness and reform, and give her voice a weight equal to that of their own self-interest—then she will be able to rediscover a respect for the Catholic Church that matches her humble awe at the Gospel of Christ it preaches. Then she will be able to feel at home in the Church once again.

ONE MAY DAY WHEN JEANNE WAS JUST FOURTEEN YEARS OLD, she arrived home from school to find police cars outside the small Chicago building in which she, her mother and her sixteen-year-old brother shared a two-bedroom apartment. Her brother was walking away from the front door, toward the street. He had a look of disgust and sorrow on his face.

"What happened?" Jeanne asked him.

"I'm out of here," he said, shaking his head. "Go inside. You'll find out." He disappeared down the street.

Jeanne walked toward the door of the first-floor apartment.

Her grandmother opened it. And then, without any delay or soothing reassurances, the old woman blurted out: "Your mother shot herself."

Jeanne had lived in fear that something like this would happen, that it was only a matter of time. Her mother had been an unstable, desperately unhappy woman ever since her divorce from Jeanne's father two years earlier. Both parents were alcoholics, and her mother's drinking had worsened since the marriage dissolved. Some days, her mother would take out a shotgun she kept in the house and carry it around with her, threatening to kill herself. Other days, she would prop it up against the bed as she lay there for hours on end. Jeanne would sometimes sit outside the door, trying to hear what her mother was doing and trying to banish the dread in her heart.

On this day, while Jeanne was at school, her mother finally made good on her threats. She stood the shotgun up on the floor, leaned into the barrel with her chest and pulled the trigger.

Jeanne's father was not in any kind of position to raise her, so she was sent to a girls' boarding school at a Catholic convent. She immediately formed a deep attachment to the nuns and to the rituals, to the whole community of faith. Life there was serene and predictable: no surprises, no fears. It was tinged with a certain rapture at the mysteries of faith, and it held out a solid promise that eternal joy could be purchased with simple piety and virtue.

After graduation, Jeanne went to college for a year, but she missed convent life. "It was a life that had structure and my life hadn't had any structure," she recalls. "I really wanted to belong to a family that had structure, coherence, that represented some goodness." She left college and entered a convent in Dubuque, Iowa, on a track to become a nun.

For the two years she stayed there, her instincts constantly warred over whether she belonged in religious life. On the one hand, she felt deep devotion. On the other, the exacting rules and ascetic traditions of the convent seemed to her unduly repressive, even nonsensical. She wanted to belong to a much broader community of people, and she wanted to taste the full flavor of life —to dance, to laugh, to date men. As she stood on a bluff overlooking the Mississippi River during a July Fourth celebration, a hot summer's wind tugging at her white veil, she made her decision. "I was holding a sparkler in one hand and a lemonade in the other," she remembers. "I looked at them and thought, 'I'd rather be holding a cigarette and a martini.' " She left the convent the following morning.

But she stayed close to the bosom of the Church. The man she married a year later back in Chicago had a piety and devotion that matched hers. The couple baptized each of their four children in the Church and made certain those children partook of the sacraments: Communion, confession, confirmation. Their family not only attended Mass every Sunday, but also played active roles in the life of their parish, St. Edna's in Arlington Heights, Illinois. Rick Miller was a Eucharistic minister. Jeanne was a master cate-chist who also developed special materials and lessons to teach children about the Bible and the Catholic faith in lively, innova-tive ways. Her oldest son, Tom, became an altar boy the moment he turned twelve.

Shortly after that, in 1981, a new priest arrived at the parish. His name was Father Robert Mayer, and one of the duties he took on was supervising the altar boys. Mayer, forty-two, was more casual and playful with them than most other priests Jeanne knew, but she didn't see any harm in that. When he invited her son Tom, along with three other boys, to go to his lakeside cot-tage to water-ski in July 1982, Jeanne's answer was immediate and enthusiastic: yes. Tom had been making comments that led Jeanne to believe he might want to become a priest; maybe spend-ing more time around a priest would help nudge him in that ex-alted direction.

But when Tom returned from the two-day outing, his behavior disturbed her. He used swear words she had never heard from him before. He talked back to her and her husband, questioning anything they said to him. Jeanne couldn't figure out what was happening—until another mother from the parish, whose son had also been on the outing, shared her son's shocking account of the trip with Jeanne. Jeanne asked Tom if that account was true. He said yes.

There were even bigger shocks to follow. When she went to the pastor at St. Edna's, Father Walter Somerville, with the boys' story about Father Mayer, he admitted that Mayer had a problem with young boys. Somerville and the parish's director of religious education, Marilyn Steffel, confessed that similar allegations had been swirling around Father Mayer since his arrival at the parish a year earlier, and that officials with the Archdiocese of Chicago had been told of them. But Mayer consistently denied the accusations, dismissing them as vicious rumor. And the parents who brought the allegations to parish administrators always backed down as soon as they were told that to force any concrete action against Mayer, they and their children would have to file formal complaints either to archdiocesan leaders or the police. The prospect of confronting the Church in such a manner intimidated them, as did Mayer's fierce denials of any wrongdoing and angry, threatening phone calls to accusers.

It intimidated Jeanne, too, but she was not going to be scared off. Her son had been exposed to something disturbing and damaging, and she expected her Church to reach out to him and to her family. She expected her Church to exhibit genuine alarm over the possibility that Father Mayer was hurting other children.

In the months that followed, those expectations were dashed. Her continued appeals to archdiocesan officials that they get Mayer away from children—at least temporarily, so he could be evaluated and counseled—were denied, even after Jeanne produced written statements from children and parents at Mayer's previous parish that he had supplied alcohol to some children and attempted to fondle others. As she wrangled with officials over her son's credibility and Mayer's future, she kept thinking that at any moment some Church leader was going to step in and apologize for the way these other officials were acting, was going to show her that her Church was filled with the goodness and concern she had always attributed to it. Her hopes surged when two representatives of the archdiocese agreed to meet with her and the parents of three other boys who had been on the outing.

But when the parents began reciting their demands, the archdiocesan officials cut them off. "Let's all let go of the past and move on," one of the officials said. He later added: "We have come to heal you."

Could Cardinal Joseph Bernardin, the archbishop of Chicago,

really know what was going on? Jeanne wondered. She found it hard to believe. But after Father Somerville went to see Bernardin, he told her the Cardinal had said that Father Mayer adamantly denied all of the allegations, and that he had to take Father Mayer at his word.

Meanwhile, as word of Jeanne's charges flew around St. Edna's, other parishioners began to sneer at her when she attended Mass. Jeanne's best friend at the parish, a woman she spoke with almost daily, cut off all contact with her. And one day, Jeanne answered the phone and heard an anonymous man's voice tell her: "A lot of your fellow parishioners think you're being too hard on Father Robert Mayer. Just remember, if something happens to you or a member of your family, you were warned. Is that clear?" Then the line went dead.

As she reeled from the hostility, Jeanne began to wonder: How many other people had been treated this way, and how many other people had been silenced by it? Jeanne felt a moral imperative not to back down.

She, along with one of the other mothers, went to the police. The police promised to investigate, but warned that proving a case against Mayer would be tough: A priest's word carried considerable weight. Finally, the Millers and one other family filed a lawsuit against Father Mayer and the Archdiocese of Chicago. The news broke on Christmas Day, 1982.

The battle lines were definitively drawn. She was told that by filing suit, she was in violation of numerous tenets of canon law and could be excommunicated. As the Church defended itself, Jeanne was plagued by self-doubt: By going against her Church, was she going against God? No, she answered back. God would hardly protect Father Mayer at the expense of innocent children.

"I have to believe someone in the Church cares!" she cried out to her husband one night.

"Jeanne, they're a corporation," he answered. "And in the corporate world, you spend any amount of money to defend your product. The product here is their image. Their image brings in revenue. They will do anything they can and use any resources they have to protect it."

The Millers lacked those same resources. Their legal fees—

which mounted steadily, from $1,000 to $10,000 to $20,000 and up—threatened to bankrupt a family that survived on her husband's $28,000-a-year salary. Jeanne sold off all her good gold jewelry. She took in other people's laundry, washing it at night, while her husband slept, so he wouldn't know she had been reduced to this. She accepted food donations from several parish administrators who quietly supported her fight, hiding the cans in the far corners of the cupboard, so her husband didn't see them and ask any questions. She cooked the cheapest meals possible, losing count of the number of times she served her family macaroni and cheese.

Jeanne and her husband were edging toward financial ruin and their stamina was waning when, more than a year into their fight, the Archdiocese of Chicago offered to settle the case for $15,800—half the attorneys' fees she and her husband had incurred by that point in 1984. The Millers refused at first. They wanted some therapy money for their son; it wasn't forthcoming. They wanted a written agreement that Father Mayer would be kept away from children and that he would receive a psychiatric evaluation. Archdiocesan officials wouldn't give them one.

But Cardinal Bernardin seemed achingly sincere when he said to Jeanne: "Trust us." Moreover, the electricity and phone bills were months overdue, and a mood of gloom had descended on the Miller household. Grudgingly, the Millers changed their minds and took the money.

Reasoned Jeanne to her husband, with a sigh and a tear: "My principles are going to eat us alive."

ON A BALMY JULY DAY IN 1992, JEANNE MILLER SAT ON THE raised deck off her kitchen smoking a Parliament 100, sipping iced tea and basking in the rays of a setting sun. It was a rare moment of relaxation. It didn't last for long. The phone started ringing. Once it started, it never stopped.

There was a call from Wisconsin. Then from Alaska. Then from Missouri. Each caller told a tale of sexual abuse by a priest. Each caller needed to know that someone understood, that someone believed.

"I hope you've come to the right place," Jeanne said in a soothing voice to one of the callers. "I should tell you about myself." She related the story of her son and her lawsuit, then fast-forwarded to the present. "So about a year ago, I started this group. I don't know if you're aware of how pervasive this problem is."

She paused to listen. "Oh, I see," she laughed. "You're becoming aware!" She paused again, listening awhile, then said: "Particular dioceses have been able to get away with that because they're reacting only to little brushfires. What we need—what we really need here—is the ultimate bonfire."

Jeanne began laying the kindling almost as soon as her lawsuit was settled. To purge the pain and disillusionment she felt over the way the Church had treated her, she began writing a book about what happened. She changed all the names and various details and fictionalized all the settings to protect the privacy of her children. She felt it wasn't fair to them, at least until they were adults, to decide to make the family's name and ordeal so utterly public.

Gradually, she stopped going to church. The words she heard priests speaking from the altar were suddenly hypocritical, and the sense of community she had felt in the pews had vanished with her knowledge of how quickly some of her fellow Catholics might dismiss anyone who questioned their Church's actions. Her husband's reaction was the opposite: He thrust himself back into parish life with a newfound vigor, defiantly reclaiming his place. He wanted to return to the life their family had led before Father Mayer came along. Jeanne felt that there was no going back, that that life had been founded on a myth, a lie. The couple grew further and further apart, until they eventually divorced.

Jeanne's book, which she titled *Assault on Innocence*, was published in 1987 under the pen name Hilary Stiles. She hit the talk show circuit as Stiles, hiding her hazel eyes beneath blue contact lenses and wearing a hundred-dollar wig of straight black hair that made her look Asian. In the beginning, she appeared mostly on local TV networks and radio stations, but she eventually worked her way up to the Larry King show on CNN and even Oprah Winfrey. And everywhere she went, people pulled her aside to whisper that they, too, had suffered similar experiences in a Catholic church, that this was much bigger than anyone realized.

Jeanne was seeing that for herself in the research she was doing for a master's thesis in theological studies. After she stopped attending Mass, Jeanne had felt a deep void in her life and a need to investigate the origins of Catholicism, to delve into the core of her faith and separate it from the man-made, modern institution of the Catholic Church. So she enrolled at a local Catholic university, studying for a master's degree. When it came time to choose a thesis topic, she picked child sexual abuse by Catholic clergy.

She conducted elaborate searches of newspapers and magazines for stories that referred to priests being arrested or sued for molesting children. She found hundreds of such articles, documenting scores of cases. That research laid the groundwork for the vast well of information—file drawer after file drawer, computer disk upon computer disk—that she would create under the auspices of VOCAL/The Linkup.

In late 1990, with most of her children grown and the Mayer lawsuit far behind her, she dropped her pseudonym, discarded her contacts, ditched her wig and began appearing on talk shows and giving interviews to the news media as Jeanne Miller, activist and advocate. She spoke with impressive knowledge and authority about child sexual abuse by priests and the Church's pattern of stonewalling and cover-up. One public appearance led to another; one interview bred two more. She quickly became a sort of unofficial spokesperson for survivors nationwide.

In the summer of 1991, she got a call she had long expected: Father Robert Mayer had just been arrested for the sexual abuse of a thirteen-year-old. Since Jeanne's lawsuit, Mayer had changed parishes four times, and twice over the years police from different towns had appeared on Jeanne's doorstep to say that they were investigating current complaints against Mayer. But Mayer was never removed from parish ministry, and now another child had been hurt. (In December 1992 Mayer would be convicted of abusing the child.)

To Jeanne it felt like the time had come to confront the Church with new force, to up the ante. What was needed, she thought, was an organization to unite people concerned about the child sexual abuse crisis. She started by calling four men whom she had never met, but whose names she associated most closely with discussion of that crisis: Father Thomas Doyle and attorney Ray Mouton, coauthors of the 1985 Doyle-Peterson-Mouton report that first sounded alarms for the Church; Richard Sipe, who had done extensive research into the sexual behavior of priests; and Father Andrew Greeley, whose columns in the *Chicago Sun-Times* occasionally lambasted Church officials for the mishandling of allegations against priests.

She felt a stab of nervousness as she dialed each number, worried that the person on the other end of the line would be bothered by her call or dismiss her as an amateur activist. She reached Doyle first and launched into a long introduction of herself.

"I know who you are," he said.

She reached Mouton next and repeated her history.

"I know who you are," he said.

Her calls to Sipe and Greeley yielded the same response. It seemed that everyone concerned about the problem of child sexual abuse by Catholic priests knew who Jeanne Miller was.

Each man voiced respect for her work and applauded her idea for a national organization. Elated and emboldened, she forged ahead with her plans and on August 19, 1991, VOCAL was officially born. Its existence, along with Jeanne's home phone number, was announced in a few TV reports and newspaper articles. In a matter of months, the calls started pouring in.

The most surprising one came just before Thanksgiving of that year. It was from Cardinal Bernardin. He had just announced, at an October news conference that garnered national media attention, the formation of a special commission to review the Archdiocese of Chicago's handling of complaints against allegedly abusive priests and to formulate new policies. Now the cardinal asked Jeanne to visit him. In fact, he suggested she come see him that night. Jeanne could hardly believe her ears.

The two sat by the fireplace in the cardinal's private residence. They talked about Father Mayer's recent indictment, with the cardinal confessing: "I made a mistake. I'm sorry." They talked about the medical center where priests in Chicago received psychiatric evaluations, with the cardinal encouraging Jeanne to visit it, talk to the doctors and tell him what she thought of the place. They talked for three hours in all. At the end, Bernardin personally escorted Jeanne out to her car and invited her to come talk to him again soon.

She did—in January 1992. And she made a special request of him: Would he come and address the first annual VOCAL conference, scheduled for the third weekend of October? Would he come and show everyone that he shared their concerns, that Church leaders and abuse survivors were not enemies in this fight?

Bernardin said yes. And Jeanne walked away from that meeting holding tight both to a hope that she hadn't felt in years and to a reborn conviction: Her Church, in the end, was going to do the right thing.

THE MONTHS LEADING UP THE VOCAL CONFERENCE WERE DIZzying, exhausting ones. Jeanne was receiving dozens of calls every night from victims across the country and dozens of requests every month from reporters who wanted interviews, information, insight. She would come home from her 6 A.M.–2 P.M. job at a law firm, descend into the basement office where she kept her computer and laser printer and two photocopiers, and return calls and answer mail until 11 P.M. Sometimes, in the middle of her work, she would pause for dinner with her romantic partner and housemate, Andy Kagan, a lawyer, who learned that to love and live with Jeanne was to share her with this crusade. Sometimes she didn't take a break.

The conference was shaping up to be an extraordinary event. Jeanne's list of confirmed speakers included Doyle, Sipe and Greeley; Jeffrey Anderson, the St. Paul attorney recognized as the nation's foremost authority on suing the Catholic Church for the child sexual abuse by its priests; and Kenneth Lanning, the FBI's resident expert on child molesters. A group of the survivors of Father James Porter—including Frank Fitzpatrick and Dennis Gaboury, whose names and faces had been splashed across TV screens and the pages of periodicals nationwide—were planning to attend. So were several important news media organizations, including the *New York Times*, the *Chicago Tribune* and cable TV's Arts & Entertainment network, which was producing an hour-long documentary on the crisis gripping the Catholic Church.

About three weeks before the conference, Jeanne placed a call to Cardinal Bernardin to go over some of the security arrangements for him at the conference. He wasn't available, so she left a message. For several days, it went unreturned.

Then she received a letter from him by messenger. In it he said he would not come to the conference, explaining that while he intended for his appearance to be a moment of healing, Jeanne's ongoing criticisms in the news media of his evolving sexual abuse policies led him to believe that healing was not her goal. "My appearance would be counterproductive for you and me," he said. "I'm not sure my appearance would be helpful."

While it was true that she had been critical of Bernardin's proposed policy reforms—she believed there were a few crucial loopholes in the guidelines—she felt it was her right, even her duty, to be a watchdog. She felt that the cardinal's rejection was not merited. And she felt he should not let down all the other conference participants who were eager to see him join them, who craved the important symbolism of that gesture.

She wondered if the reason the cardinal stated for not going was the true one. Was he really just bowing to pressure from Chicago-area priests, who were becoming more and more frightened of the files Jeanne kept of complaints her callers brought to her? Was he scared away by the inevitable news media presence?

Jeanne messengered a letter back to the cardinal, writing: "I'm afraid it would appear an atrocity if you denied the attendants at this conference your presence because you are miffed at me. While we may have our differences, I believe you are sincere in your concern for victims." She left telephone messages for him. Bernardin never responded.

When it became clear that there was no reaching him and no reversing his decision, Jeanne cried for hours. She was shocked that she could still be this hurt and this disappointed, that she could still nourish such high expectations of the Church. "I wanted to be wrong about them," she says. "For all these years, I wanted somebody to come along and prove me wrong. For all these years, I knocked on all these doors to prove to myself and to others that somebody cares."

She still struggles to prove that. She still believes that. And she still prays for a day when she can walk back into a Catholic church and feel that it is a house of pure faith and community, not a business, not an arcane fraternity of aloof men.

But for now, the work she does on behalf of victims is both her church and her prayer. Through it, she says, she practices the love and the sacrifice that she believes are at the core of Catholicism. As she told the people who gathered at the first VOCAL conference, in explaining Bernardin's absence: "It's not as if the Church didn't come to us tonight. The cardinal didn't come to the Church."

NOTES

CHAPTER 1: WHILE GOD WASN'T WATCHING

3 The opening section dealing with the story of Frank Fitzpatrick is culled from interviews with Fitzpatrick broadcast on "PrimeTime Live" (July 1992) and published in the *Boston Globe*, the *Boston Herald*, the *Providence Journal*, the *Los Angeles Times* and *People* magazine.

5 The victims' remembrances of life at St. Mary's are based on author's interviews with Patty Poirier Wilson, Judy White Mullet, Dennis Gaboury, Dan Lyons, Fran Battaglia and Peter Calderone, as well as on interviews with them and other victims published in the *Boston Globe*, the *Providence Journal*, the *Los Angeles Times, People* magazine and broadcast on "PrimeTime Live."

10 The section dealing with, and quoting from, Patty Poirier Wilson and Judy White Mullet about the beginning of the movement to have Porter brought to justice is based on author's interviews with the two women in North Attleboro, Massachusetts, in November 1992, as well as on stories published in the newspapers cited above between May 8 and December 1, 1992. Information on the first days after the WBZ broadcast came from interviews with Dennis Gaboury.

15 Information on the meetings of the Survivors of Father Porter was culled from author's interviews with the members of the group noted above.

18   The details of the unfolding of the story are based on author's interviews with the victims cited above, as well as newspaper accounts published in the *Boston Globe*, the *Boston Herald*, the *Providence Journal*, the *St. Paul Pioneer*, the *Star Tribune* (Minneapolis) and reports sent out on the Associated Press wire.

20   The information on the letter from Bishop Connolly to the archbishop of Santa Fe is taken from the letter itself, dated October 9, 1968.

21   The quotations from Bennett are pulled from his letter to Msgr. Reginald Barrette, dated November 3, 1970.

22   Information on the negotiations between the Diocese of Fall River and the victims is based on author's interviews with Dan Lyons and Peter Calderone in North Attleboro, November 1992, and with George Hardie in February 1993. Financial settlement between the church and the victims was reached in October 1992.

22   Details on the indictment—both public and behind-the-scenes—were culled from accounts published in the newspapers mentioned above. In December 1992 Porter was sentenced to six months in jail in Minnesota for molesting his children's baby-sitter. As of the summer of 1993, he was awaiting trial on the Massachusetts charges.

CHAPTER 2: REVELATIONS

28   The historical background on child sexual abuse in the Church comes from the following sources: The description of the celebration of Spain's victory over the Moors comes from William Manchester, *A World Lit Only by Fire* (Boston: Little, Brown, 1992). The Gauch information is taken from M. Killias, *Jugend und Sexualstrafrecht* (Adolescence and Penal Law in Relation to Sexual Activities) (Bern: Paul Hauplt, 1979). The information on cases of child sexual abuse by clergy in the nineteenth century is from Mark Chopko, "Restoring Trust and Faith" published in the American Bar Association's *Human Rights*, Fall 1992.

28   The literary references are to Denis Diderot, *Amour religieuse*, and Clorinda Matto de Turner, *Aves sin nido*. A more recent example would be Iris Murdoch, *Henry and Cato* (London: Chatto & Windus, 1976).

29   There is a large body of historical literature devoted to the history of childhood—and the history of sexuality—in Western society. See, for example: M. Foucault, *The History of Sexuality* (London: Allen Lane, 1979); Philippe Aries, *Centuries of Childhood* (New York: Alfred A. Knopf, 1962); Guido Ruggerio, *The Boundaries of Eros: Sex Crime and Sexuality in Renaissance Venice* (Oxford: Oxford University Press, 1984).

30   The information from Bishop Gumbleton is from author's interview in September 1992. The information from Bishop Weakland is from author's interview in September 1992.

30   Figures on the number of priests evaluated for sexual problems at the St. Luke Institute come from authors' interviews with Richard Sipe in Baltimore, June 1992.

30   The story of Scott Gastal is based on authors' interviews in Lafayette, Louisiana, in July 1992 with J. Minos Simon, his attorney; authors' review of the records of Gauthe's criminal charges and proceedings; the records of the civil proceedings against Gauthe and the Diocese of Lafayette; and reports published in the *Times of Acadiana*, the *National Catholic Reporter*, the *Times-Picayune* (New Orleans), the *Providence Journal*, the *Houston Post*, the *Dallas Morning News* and the *Daily Advertiser* (Lafayette, Louisiana) and the *San Jose Mercury News*—in 1985 and 1986. Gauthe, imprisoned for the abuse of numerous boys, did not respond to repeated requests for an interview, nor did the current bishop of Lafayette.

31   Information on the Engbers case comes from authors' interviews conducted in Lafayette, Louisiana, in July 1992 with Anthony Fontana and Bonnie Butaud Bonin; personal letters, photographs and other private documents provided by Ms. Bonin; correspondence between Fontana and officials of the Diocese of Lafayette; and media reports published in the *Times of Acadiana*, the *Times-Picayune* (New Orleans), and the *National Catholic Reporter* in 1985. Shortly after Bonin filed suit against Engbers, the priest returned to his native Holland. He is deceased. Bonnie's lawsuit never reached court and no settlement was made. The bishop of Lafayette did not respond to repeated requests for an interview about this case.

31   Information on the Fontenot case comes from reports published in the *Times of Acadiana*, the *National Catholic Reporter, Spokane Chronicle, Port Angeles Daily News* and the *Seattle Post-Intelligencer* in 1986 and the *Seattle Times*, May 24, 1988. The bishop of Lafayette did not respond to repeated requests for an interview about this case. In July 1986, Fontenot was sentenced to one year in prison, two years in an inpatient treatment program and three years' probation.

32   Information on the media event staged at the 1989 National Conference of Catholic Bishops is based on authors' interviews with Michael Schwartz, its organizer; Jeanne Miller, the woman in the wig; David Crumm, a reporter who covered the event for the *Detroit Free Press*; statements released by Catholics for an Open Church, the coordinating group; and press accounts published in the *San Jose Mercury News* and the *Providence Journal*, November 1989.

32   The editorial in *L'Osservatore Romano* is cited in John Crewdson, *By Silence Betrayed: Sexual Abuse of Children in America* (Boston: Little, Brown, 1988).

32   The story of Father Alvin Campbell is based on reports sent out by the Associated Press and United Press International in 1984. In 1985, Campbell pleaded guilty to molesting boys and was sentenced to fourteen years in jail.

32   The story of Father Paul Margand is based on reports in the *Lincoln Journal* (July 1987) and the *Lincoln Star* (November 1987).

32   The story of Father Robert Kapoun is based on reports in the *St. Paul Pioneer Press Dispatch*, May 1990. Kapoun was never charged criminally. A civil lawsuit against him for the molestation of a twelve-year-old boy was settled out of court in May 1990.

33   The story of Father Anthony Corbin is based on a report published in the *Philadelphia Inquirer*, February 1989. Corbin pleaded guilty to sexually abusing one boy and was sentenced to five years in jail. All but sixty days of the sentence were suspended.

33   The story of Father Anton Mowat is based on reports published in the *Atlanta Journal* and the *Atlanta Constitution* (April 1989 through June 1990). In May 1990, Mowat was sentenced to six years in prison. After serving eighteen months, he was paroled and barred from the United States until 2005.

34   The bulleted cases are from the following sources:
    Smart: *The Missoulian* (January 1991).
    Ball: *St. Paul Pioneer Press*, the *Milwaukee Journal, Wisconsin State Journal* (December 1991 through May 1992). In September 1992, Ball was sentenced to five years in prison for abusing a twelve-year-old.
    Ubaldi: Interviews with the woman, who is anonymous, and her San Diego attorney and news reports published in the *San Diego Union* in March 1992. Ubaldi, who left the country, did not respond to requests for an interview about this lawsuit.
    Kelly: *Los Angeles Daily News*, April 1992; *Los Angeles Times*, September 1992. Kelly was given three years' probation after pleading no contest to the charges. He fled to Ireland in 1992.
    Lehman: The *Arizona Republic* and the *Phoenix Gazette* (May 1992) and authors' interviews with the family of those and other victims. For full references see notes to Chapter 7, "Casting Out Lepers." Lehman, who was sentenced to ten years in prison in 1992, refused to be interviewed about his case.
    Lavigne: The *Boston Globe* and the *Boston Herald* (October 1991 through June 1992) and *Boston Magazine* (July 1992), the *Springfield Advocate* (April 1992). In June 1992, Lavigne pleaded guilty and was sentenced to probation and inpatient therapy. Lavigne did not respond to requests for an interview about his case.
    Monaghan: The *Sacramento Bee*, July 1992.
    White: The *Chicago Tribune*, August 1992.
    Provost: (Worcester) *Telegram & Gazette*, September 1992.
    Calabrese: The *Orlando Sentinel* (October 1992) and the *New York*

Post (February 1993) and author's interview with William Grady, the district attorney, in October 1992.

Malsch: The *Wisconsin State Journal* (November 1992).

Holley: The *Boston Globe, USA Today* (December 1992) and authors' interviews with Bruce Pasternack, the attorney filing the cases.

Institute officials have given contradictory responses to the events at St. Luke on January 29, 1993. After Father Canice Connors's description of the event, Father John Geaney, spokesman for St. Luke, offered yet another version: that the police appeared without a warrant and "violated protocol" by appearing at 5:45 P.M. He insisted that Holley was turned over quietly to police after the institute's lawyer was contacted. The various accounts of these events are based on interviews with Irv Smith, spokesman for the Prince Georges County Sheriff's Department; Gary Costello, head of the pedophilia unit of the Montgomery County Sheriff's Department, and documents about the events submitted to the members of the Think Tank co-chaired by Father Connors.

38   The section devoted to the number of Catholic priests who molest is culled from a variety of sources. The figure of two hundred is a minimum based on cases the authors have discovered in newspaper reports, court documents and from interviews with lawyers, prosecutors and victims. The denial that the Church keeps centralized records was issued by Mark Chopko, general counsel for the National Conference of Catholic Bishops during authors' interview in July 1992. Information on non-reported cases mentioned by bishops comes from interviews with the bishops of Chicago, Rochester (New York), Louisville (Kentucky), Savannah, Los Angeles, Austin (Texas), Cincinnati, St. Paul-Minneapolis, Omaha, Saginaw, Milwaukee, and the auxiliary bishop of Detroit.

The percentage estimates are from Richard Sipe, *A Secret World: Sexuality and the Search for Celibacy* (New York: Brunner/Mazel, 1990), and from authors' interviews with him.

The estimates for the percentages among mainline Protestant clergy are based on a study of 1,000 clerics by Lloyd Rediger, a Presbyterian pastor-therapist.

The information on the arrests of other Massachusetts clergy comes from the *Boston Globe* (May 11, 1992); the arrest of Frey from the *Commercial Appeal* (Memphis, October 1992). Chilstrom's quote was cited in the *Dayton Daily News* (December 8, 1991). Other background on Protestant clergy was provided by the Reverend Marie Fortune in author's interviews.

39   Loftus quote from author's interview in August 1992.

39   Rossetti quote from author's interview in July 1992.

40   Observations on the difference between Protestant and Catholic clergy based on author's interviews with the Reverend Marie Fortune. The policies of various denominations were obtained from the appropriate administrative bodies. See, for example, *If You Have Been Sexu-*

ally Abused or Harassed: A Guide to Getting Effective Help in the ELCA (Chicago: The Evangelical Lutheran Church of America, 1991).

41   The nationalities of foreign priests accused of or arrested for child sexual abuse is based on the authors' case files compiled from newspaper accounts and court records.

41   While information on the Newfoundland scandals was culled from newspapers across Canada, the most comprehensive treatment of what occurred is from Michael Harris, *Unholy Orders* (Ontario: Viking, 1990). Information on Canada's continuing problems with child sexual abuse by Catholic priests was pulled from the following newspapers and magazines: The *Toronto Star*, the *Hamilton Spectator*, the *Winnipeg Free Press*, the *Windsor Star, Montreal Gazette, Compass* and the *National Catholic Reporter* through 1992. Further information came from "From Pain to Hope," the 1992 report of the Ad Hoc Committee on Child Sexual Abuse of the Canadian Conference of Catholic Bishops and "Breach of Trust, Breach of Faith," the materials they prepared for discussion groups.

41   Information on the Archdioceses of Melbourne and Wellington was provided to the authors by Father Thomas Doyle, a consultant for both dioceses.

42   Information on the reaction to the broadcast of the program on Dutch Catholic Television was provided to the authors by the program's producer, Stijn Fens.

42   The general discussion of child sexual abuse, pedophilia and ephebophilia is based on authors' interviews with the country's leading experts in the field, including: Dr. Gene Abel, director of the Behavioral Medicine Institute in Atlanta; Dr. Judith Becker, clinical psychologist and professor in the department of psychiatry at the University of Arizona's College of Medicine; Dr. Fred Berlin, a Baltimore therapist and professor at the Johns Hopkins University School of Medicine; Anne Cohn Donnelly, executive director, National Committee for the Prevention of Child Abuse; Dr. David Finkelhor, codirector of the Family Research Laboratory at the University of New Hampshire; Dr. A. Nicholas Groth, director of Forensic Mental Health Associates in Orlando, Florida; Kenneth Lanning, supervisory special agent, Federal Bureau of Investigation in Quantico, Virginia; Dr. Robert Prentky and Gail Ryan of the Kempe Center in Denver, Colorado.

The discussion is based as well on articles and research published in a variety of national publications and on the following books, among others: David Finkelhor, *Child Sexual Abuse* (New York: The Free Press, 1984); David Finkelhor, *A Sourcebook on Child Sexual Abuse* (Newbury Park, Calif.: Sage, 1986); John Crewdson, *By Silence Betrayed: Sexual Abuse of Children in America* (Boston: Little, Brown, 1988); Mike Lew, *Victims No Longer* (New York: Harper & Row, 1990); Ellen Bass and Laura Davis, *The Courage to Heal* (New York: Harper &

Row, 1988); and Stephen J. Rossetti, *Slayer of the Soul* (Mystic, Conn.: Twenty-Third Publications, 1990).

43   Quote from the Reverend Margaret Graham comes from author's interview in August 1992.

44   Quote from Dr. Groth comes from author's interview in June 1991.

45   Quote from Dr. Berlin comes from author's interview in June 1991.

45   Quote from Dr. Berlin comes from author's interview in July 1992.

47   The *Los Angeles Times* poll was conducted in late July 1985 and later published both in the pages of that newspaper and in scholarly journals, including *Child Sexual Abuse and Neglect* (1990).

CHAPTER 3: GENESIS

49   The idea of a celibate culture as a possible magnet for people with sexual immaturity, confusion or disorders is derived from authors' 1992 interviews with a variety of experts on sexual disorders and child sexual abuse, including the following: Dr. Judith Becker, clinical psychologist and professor in the department of psychiatry at the University of Arizona's College of Medicine; Walter Bera, Minneapolis psychologist; Dr. Fred Berlin, a Baltimore therapist and professor at the Johns Hopkins University School of Medicine; Dr. Fran Ferder, a Franciscan nun and therapist who works with the Archdiocese of Seattle; Dr. David Finkelhor, codirector of the Family Research Laboratory at the University of New Hampshire; Dr. Glen Gabbard, director of the Menninger Clinic in Topeka, Kansas; Dr. John Gonsiorek, a Minneapolis therapist; Dr. A. Nicholas Groth, director of Forensic Mental Health Associates in Orlando, Florida; Mark Laaser, a former United Church of Christ minister and counselor in the Minneapolis-St. Paul area; Kenneth Lanning, supervisory special agent, Federal Bureau of Investigation in Quantico, Virginia; Dr. James Pedigo, director of the Impaired Professionals Program at the Joseph Peters Institute in Philadelphia; Father Kenneth Pierre, a priest psychotherapist in Minneapolis, Minnesota; Gary Schoener, director, Walk-In Counseling Center in Minneapolis, Minnesota; and Richard Sipe, a Baltimore-area psychotherapist and author of *A Secret World: Sexuality and the Search for Celibacy* (New York: Brunner/Mazel, 1990).

50   Quote from Dr. John Money comes from an article on child sexual abuse in the Catholic Church in the *San Jose Mercury News*, December 30, 1987.

51   Quote from Dr. Glen Gabbard comes from author's interview with Dr. Gabbard in October 1992.

51   Quote from Archbishop Daniel Sheehan of Omaha, Nebraska, comes from author's interview with Sheehan in August 1992.

51   Quote from Bishop Kenneth Untener of Saginaw comes from author's interview with Untener in Saginaw, Michigan, in September 1992.

52   Quote and anecdote from Mark Laaser come from interviews with Laaser in Minneapolis in September 1992.

52   Observations that men in the priesthood may not go through the same paces of psychosexual development as other men are based on interviews with, and research by, experts on sexual disorders and child sexual abuse cited previously in the notes for this chapter.

53   Observations about the seminary experience and the life-style of priests and their possible connection to immaturity, sexual repression and loneliness are drawn from interviews with some of the experts previously cited in this chapter. Observations are also based on interviews in 1992 with the following priests, ex-priests and experts, among others: Father Kevin Clinton of Mendota, Minnesota; Father Victor Clore of Detroit, Michigan; Bishop Thomas Gumbleton of Detroit; Eugene Kennedy, a Chicago psychologist; Father Anthony Kosnik of Marygrove College in Detroit; Dr. John Allan Loftus, a priest psychotherapist at Southdown treatment center near Toronto; Father Richard McBrien, former head of the Department of Theology, Notre Dame University; Pasqual Otazu, a former Benedictine monk in Miami, Florida; Tim Unsworth, author of *The Last Priests in America* (New York: Crossroad, 1991); Bishop Kenneth Untener of Saginaw, Michigan; and Father Tim Wozniak of St. Paul Park, Minnesota. Observations are based, as well, on a 1991 review of research titled *Consultation on Priests' Morale: A Review of Research*, produced by the National Federation of Priests' Councils.

54   The full title of the Kennedy report is *The Catholic Priest in the United States: Psychological Investigations*, by Eugene F. Kennedy and Victor J. Heckler (Washington, D.C.: United States Catholic Conference, 1972). Additional comments on the report's findings and its relevance to the priesthood today come from author's interviews in August and September 1992 with Eugene Kennedy and Dr. Sara Charles Kennedy in Chicago, Illinois, and St. Joseph, Michigan.

55   Quote from Richard Sipe comes from authors' interviews with Sipe in Timonium, Maryland, in July 1992.

55   Quote from the Reverend Margaret Graham comes from author's interview with Dr. Graham in August 1992.

55   Quote from Vincent Bilotta comes from an article, "Unholy Acts," published in *The New Yorker*, June 7, 1993.

56   Quote from Dr. Nicholas Groth comes from author's interview with Dr. Groth in September 1992.

56   Quote from Dr. Judith Becker comes from author's interview with Dr. Becker in September 1992.

57   Sipe's figures come from authors' interviews with him and his previously cited book.

57   The discussion of children being more vulnerable to trusted authority figures, particularly priests, is based on interviews with the following experts: Dr. Robin August, a psychotherapist in Miami, Florida (June 1992); Dr. David Finkelhor, director of the Family Research Laboratory, University of New Hampshire (July 1992); Gary Schoener, a Minneapolis psychotherapist; Gail Ryan of the Kempe Center in Denver, Colorado (August 1992); Anne Cohn Donnelly, executive director, National Committee for the Prevention of Child Abuse (August 1992); Mic Hunter, a psychotherapist in St. Paul, Minnesota, and author of *Abused Boys: The Neglected Victims of Sexual Abuse* (New York: Ballantine Books, 1990); Walter Bera, a Minneapolis psychotherapist; and Thom Harrigan, a Boston-area psychotherapist.

58   Schoener's anecdote comes from author's interviews with Schoener in Minneapolis, Minnesota, in September 1992.

58   Gail Ryan's quote comes from author's interview with Ryan in August 1992.

59   Quote from Mike Lew comes from author's interview with Lew in September 1992.

59   Quotes from the self-help book by a Protestant minister incarcerated for child sexual abuse come from a copy of the book provided by the minister. He requested anonymity.

60   General observations about the structure and workings of the Catholic Church are drawn from myriad sources, including the following books: *A Church Divided* by Terry Sweeney (Buffalo: Prometheus, 1992); *The Catholic Moment* by Richard John Neuhaus (New York: Harper & Row, 1987); *Tomorrow's Catholics, Yesterday's Church* by Eugene Kennedy (San Francisco: Harper & Row, 1988); *Report on the Church: Catholicism After Vatican II* by Richard P. McBrien (New York: HarperCollins, 1992); and *Archbishop: Inside the Power Structure of the American Catholic Church* by Thomas J. Reese (San Francisco: Harper & Row, 1989).

60   Specific observations about the reasons that bishops reacted poorly to reports of child sexual abuse by Catholic priests are drawn from the authors' interviews in 1992 with the following bishops: Cardinal Joseph Bernardin of Chicago; Bishop Matthew Clark of Rochester, New York; Bishop Thomas Gumbleton of Detroit; Archbishop Thomas Kelly of Louisville, Kentucky; Bishop Raymond Lessard of Savannah, Georgia; Cardinal Roger Mahony of Los Angeles; Bishop John McCarthy of Austin, Texas; Archbishop Daniel Pilarczyk of Cincinnati; Archbishop John Roach of St. Paul-Minneapolis; Archbishop Daniel Sheehan of Omaha, Nebraska; Bishop Kenneth Untener of Saginaw, Michigan; and Archbishop Rembert Weakland of Milwaukee, Wisconsin.

60   Observations about bishops' failures are also drawn from interviews in 1992 with some of the previously cited experts about child sexual abuse and abusive priests; with some of the previously cited priests; and with some of the previously cited experts on, or critics of, the Catholic Church and the culture of Catholicism.

61   Greeley's quote comes from an address he made in October 1992 to the first annual conference of Victims of Clergy Abuse Linkup (VOCAL) in Arlington Heights, Illinois.

61   Observations about the nature of a hierarchy and its fostering of abuse are drawn from interviews in September and October 1992 with Dr. Fran Ferder; the Reverend Marie Fortune, a United Church of Christ minister and executive director of the Center for the Prevention of Sexual and Domestic Violence; Mic Hunter; Mike Lew; and Richard Sipe.

62   Sipe's quote was from an address he gave to victims of abuse by priests in the Chicago suburbs in October 1992.

CHAPTER 4: SUFFER THE CHILDREN

65   The story of Tim Martinez is based on author's interviews conducted in Albuquerque, New Mexico, in August 1992 with Martinez; his mother, Rose; his father, Louis; his attorney, Bruce Pasternack, and private investigator Jerry Mazon. It also includes information culled from Sigler's personnel file from the Archdiocese of Santa Fe; depositions of Martinez, Sigler, Archbishop Robert Sanchez and Father Clarence Galli; Complaints, affidavits, briefs and motions filed in the case of *John Does I through X vs. Roman Catholic Church of the Archdiocese of Santa Fe, Inc., Jason E. Sigler, Bishop Arthur Tafoya and Clarence Galli*; news reports published throughout 1992 in the *Albuquerque Journal* and the *Albuquerque Tribune*; the arrest report of Jason Sigler for criminal sexual conduct with other youths (83-01690) from the Albuquerque Police Department and the plea and disposition agreement in that case filed in the district court, Bernalillo County, New Mexico.

Sigler, who is no longer a Catholic priest, refused to be interviewed on this matter.

68   Quote from Schoener is from author's interview with him in Minneapolis in September 1992.

70   The story of Bonnie Bonin is based on authors' interview conducted in Lafayette, Louisiana, in July 1992 with Anthony Fontana and Bonnie Butaud Bonin; personal letters, photographs and other private documents provided by Ms. Bonin; correspondence between Fontana and officials of the Diocese of Lafayette; and media reports published in the *Times of Acadiana* and the *Times-Picayune* (New Orleans), and the *National Catholic Reporter* in 1986. In a brief telephone interview, Bonnie's mother, Martha Butaud, confirmed Bonnie's account of their family's

close relationship with Engbers but denied calling her daughters "whores." She also said she has no recollection of Bonnie ever telling her Engbers was sexually abusing her. Shortly after Bonin filed suit against Engbers, the priest returned to his native Holland. He is deceased. There has been no action taken on her suit.

72   The story of Jennifer Kraskouskas is based on author's interviews with Jennifer, Lynn, Jackie and Tony Kraskouskas in Gardner, Massachusetts, in July 1992. It is supplemented by reports published in the *Telegram & Gazette* (Worcester, Massachusetts) in April 1990. Kelley, still imprisoned as this book was being completed, did not respond to requests for an interview.

75   The story of Ed Morris is based on author's interviews with Morris and his attorney, Jeff Anderson, in Chicago in October 1992. Pinkowski is deceased. Morris's suit was thrown out by Pennsylvania courts because the statute of limitations had expired. An appeal is being prepared.

CHAPTER 5: FALSE IDOLS

78   Father Ned is a pseudonym for a priest offender who agreed to interviews on condition of anonymity. His story is based on interviews in August and September 1992 with Father Ned; with officials in his diocese; with therapists in his area who know and have worked with him; and with friends of his in the priesthood.

80   General observations about how priests become involved in, or rationalize, child sexual abuse are drawn from interviews with experts on sexual disorders and child sexual abuse previously cited in the notes for Chapter 3, "Genesis." The observations are also drawn from interviews in July, August and September 1992 with the following therapists who treat abusive priests: Dr. Canice Connors, Sister Sheila McNiff and Father Stephen Rossetti of the St. Luke Institute in Suitland, Maryland; and Dr. John Allan Loftus of Southdown in Aurora, Ontario, Canada.

81   Father Martin is a pseudonym for a priest offender who agreed to interviews on condition of anonymity. His story is based on interviews in August and September 1992 with him and with his therapist.

84   Observations made by Dr. James Pedigo come from author's interview with him in August 1992.

84   Observations about Father Mark Lehman are drawn from interviews with the following people, some of whom are identified by pseudonyms at their request: Laura Reckart, Susan Lindley and Paula Anderson, all of the Maricopa County Attorney's office; Elizabeth Evarts and her son, J. P. Evarts; Patty Hanson (pseudonym); Dawn Barton (pseudonym) and her mother; and St. Thomas the Apostle parishioners Dennis Desmond, Kathy Desmond and Nancy Richards. Details are also drawn from police documents including Phoenix Police Department Re-

port no. 09-086927 and from court documents in the case of the *State of Arizona vs. Mark Allen Lehman* (CR-9100442 and CR-9105341).

Details of Father Mark Lehman's sexual history are drawn from a risk assessment of Lehman conducted in February 1991 by Robert Emerick and Dr. Tom Selby of the Adult Paraphiliac Assessment Team at Phoenix Memorial Hospital.

Lehman declined several requests for interviews for this book.

86   Father Charles is a pseudonym for a priest offender who agreed to interviews on the condition of anonymity. His story is based on interviews with him in October 1992.

87   Comments by Father Robert Kirsch come from his deposition in 1992 in the case of *Sandra S. vs. Father Robert J. Kirsch, Roman Catholic Church of the Archdiocese of Santa Fe, Inc., and St. Thomas Apostle Church in Abiquiu, New Mexico*. Father Kirsch did not respond to requests for an interview about this case.

88   Comments from and observations about Sister Georgene Stuppy are drawn from her depositions in May 1991 and August 1991 in the case of *Jane C. Doe vs. Sister Georgene Stuppy, Sisters of the Third Order Regular of St. Francis of the Congregation of Our Lady of Lourdes, the Church of Queen of Angels in Austin, Minn., and the Diocese of Winona (Minn.)*; from author's interviews with her alleged victim, who requested anonymity, in September and October 1992; and from personal letters Stuppy wrote to the alleged victim. The case was settled out of court in December 1992. Sister Stuppy declined to be interviewed about this case but gave the authors the following statement in February 1993: "I deny any allegations of wrongdoing."

88   Quote from Kenneth Lanning comes from author's interview with him in Quantico, Virginia, in July 1992.

89   Observations about Father James Porter are drawn from references previously cited in Chapter 1.

90   Observations about Father Paul Henry Leech come from police interviews with victims and their families in the case of the *State of Rhode Island vs. Paul Henry Leech* (no. 84-2495). Leech was sentenced to three years in prison in 1985, served his sentence and is no longer working as a priest. He declined repeated interview requests.

91   Details of the suicide of the Benedictine monk are drawn from an article printed in the *San Diego Union and Tribune* on August 2, 1986.

91   Details of the suicide of Monsignor William Reinecke are drawn from articles printed in the *Washington Times*, the *Washington Post* and the *Virginian-Pilot* in August 1992 and from author's interview with members of the Arlington County (Virginia) Police Department.

CHAPTER 6: THE SILENCING OF THE LAMBS

97   The discussion of the reasons why children remain silent after their abuse is based both on interviews with dozens of victims and interviews with the following experts: Dr. Robin August, a psychotherapist in Miami, Florida (June 1992); Dr. David Chadwick, director of the Center for Child Protection in San Diego, California (August 1992); Dr. David Finkelhor, director of the Family Research Laboratory, University of New Hampshire (July 1992); Dr. Dick Krugman, Kempe Center in Denver, Colorado (August 1992); Gary Schoener, a Minneapolis psychotherapist; Gail Ryan of the Kempe Center in Denver, Colorado (August 1992); Anne Cohn Donnelly, executive director, National Committee for the Prevention of Child Abuse (August 1992); Mic Hunter, a psychotherapist in St. Paul, Minnesota and author of *Abused Boys: The Neglected Victims of Sexual Abuse* (New York: Ballantine Books, 1990); and Mike Lew, a Boston-area psychotherapist and author of *Victims No Longer: Men Recovering from Incest and Other Child Sexual Abuse* (New York: Nevraumont, 1988).

The Lafayette psychologists' report is cited in the *San Jose Mercury News*, December 30–31, 1987.

98   The story of Calvin Mire is based on interviews in Lafayette, Louisiana, in July 1992 with Mire; his attorney, Anthony Fontana of Abbeville, Louisiana; and Lafayette attorney J. Minos Simon. It is supplemented by the extensive court records of the civil and criminal proceedings against Gauthe and the Diocese of Lafayette in 1985 and 1986, as well as reports in the following newspapers during 1986: The *Times of Acadiana*, the *National Catholic Reporter*, the *Times-Picayune* (New Orleans), the *Providence Journal*, the *Houston Post*, the *Dallas Morning News* and the *Daily Advertiser* (Lafayette, Louisiana) and the *San Jose Mercury News*.

Currently imprisoned, Gilbert Gauthe did not respond to requests for an interview for this book.

101   The story of Susan Sandoval is based on author's interviews in Albuquerque, New Mexico, in August 1992 with Sandoval; her attorney, Bruce Pasternack, and private investigator Jerry Mazon. It also includes information culled from the *Albuquerque Tribune* and the *Albuquerque Journal* throughout 1992; the 1992 depositions of Robert Kirsch and Archbishop Robert F. Sanchez in the case of *Sandra S. vs. Father Robert J. Kirsch, the Roman Catholic Church of the Archdiocese of Santa Fe, Inc., and St. Thomas Apostle Church in Abiquiu, New Mexico*; correspondence from Kirsch to Sandoval; and the evaluation of Kirsch prepared by the Servants of the Paraclete in January and February 1989. Kirsch did not respond to requests for interviews about this case. Sandoval's lawsuit was still pending as of April 1993.

103   Many researchers and therapists contributed to the discussion of repressed memory. They include Mike Lew, a Boston-area psychother-

apist. Information was also culled from Lawrence Daly and J. Frank Pacifico, "Opening the Doors to the Past: Decade of Declayed Disclosure of Memories of Years Gone By," *The Champion*, December 1991.

103   The story of David Clohessy is based on author's interviews with Clohessy in August 1992 and his attorney, Jeff Anderson in October 1992 and is supplemented by reports in 1991 and 1992 in the following newspapers: The *St. Louis Post Dispatch*; the *Kansas City Star; The Missourian; The Catholic Missourian*; the *Columbia Tribune*; the *News and Tribune* (Jefferson City, Missouri). Father Whiteley declined to be interviewed about this case. Clohessy's lawsuit is still pending, caught in a legal dispute over the constitutionality of Missouri's law governing the statute of limitations in sexual abuse cases like his.

Clohessey's parents, in a telephone interview in April 1993, confirmed his account of the family's close relationship with Whitely and David's estrangement from the family after he made accusations against the priest. But they insist the estrangement was his choice, that they believe his allegations and want to support him.

Clohessy's brother Kevin, the priest, also says the estrangement is as much David's doing as his own. He said in a telephone interview in June 1993 that he does not specifically recall the quote David attributes to him.

106   The story of Cristine Clark is based on author's interviews in Chicago with Clark and her mother in July 1992. Stefanich pleaded guilty, was sentenced to six months in jail, served his time and left the priesthood. Bishop Joseph Imesch of the Diocese of Joliet declined to comment on her case or her charges that the diocese had received reports about Stefanich prior to the end of her relationship with him.

CHAPTER 7: CASTING OUT LEPERS

112   Amy Hanson and Dawn Barton are pseudonyms given to the two girls in the Lehman story, both of whom are still minors. All other members of the families identified by those same last names have also been given pseudonyms. Anna Ramos is also a pseudonymn.

112   The narrative covering the investigation and trial of Father Mark Lehman is constructed from author's interviews in Phoenix, Arizona, in June and July 1992, with the following people, some of whom are identified by pseudonyms at their request: Laura Reckart, Susan Lindley and Paula Anderson, all of the Maricopa County Attorney's office; Detective Lou Marotta of the Phoenix Police Department; Elizabeth Evarts and her son, J. P. Evarts; Patty Hanson (pseudonym); Dawn Barton (pseudonym) and her mother; Barbara Topf, Dennis Desmond, Kathy Desmond and Nancy Richards, all of whom are St. Thomas parishioners or friends of the families involved in the case against Father Mark Lehman; Ann Malone; and Father Robert Skagen.

It is also constructed from police documents including Phoenix Police Department Report no. 09-086927 and from court documents in the case of the *State of Arizona vs. Mark Allen Lehman* (CR-9100442 and CR-9105341). The risk assessment was done by Robert Emerick and Dr. Tom Selby of the Adult Paraphiliac Assessment Team at Phoenix Memorial Hospital in February 1991.

Characterizations of St. Thomas the Apostle parish are drawn from previously mentioned interviews and from author's visit to the parish in July 1992.

123 Bishop Thomas O'Brien, through spokespeople and a diocesan lawyer, declined repeated requests for an interview. Sister Mary Louise Ante did not respond to repeated requests for an interview to discuss the charges made against her.

Father Robert Skagen said in a brief telephone interview in July 1992 that he could not comment on ways in which the parish did or did not act during the criminal investigation into Father Mark Lehman because there was civil litigation pending against St. Thomas and the Diocese of Phoenix. Diocesan officials, he said, had asked him not to discuss the case.

Father Skagen did, however, choose to rebut a few of the criticisms of his actions. He said he sat with the priest's family and supporters in court because those people had asked him to while the victims and their families had not. He said diocesan officials put constraints on his ability to reach out to the victims and their families.

He and Sister Mary Louise Ante were not uncooperative with Laura Reckart and Susan Lindley, he said, and characterized the women as hostile in their interrogations. "They were horrible," he said. "You can at least be civil, and these two women were not. Honest to God, I couldn't believe that any professional people could be this rude."

He added that he was unaware of any difficulty Patty Hanson experienced in finding work, praising her musical talent and saying that the one time he was called on to give her a reference, he gave her a laudatory one.

Ann Malone, contacted by telephone in July 1992, declined to grant an extended interview about her support of Father Mark Lehman. She said she does not recall the police ever visiting her house the night she held a farewell supper for the priest.

Father Mark Lehman, who has filed an appeal of his conviction and his ten-year prison sentence, declined repeated requests for interviews relayed to him in prison. His attorney at the time this material was being researched also declined to be interviewed.

Observations about the trial of Father George Bredemann are drawn from interviews with Cindi Nannetti of the Maricopa County Attorney's office and with the family of two brothers victimized by Bredemann.

Additional details about the trials and convictions of both Father Mark Lehman and Father George Bredemann were drawn from articles that appeared in 1990, 1991 and 1992 in the *Arizona Republic* and the

Phoenix Gazette. Father Bredemann, currently serving out a forty-five-year sentence in Arizona, declined to be interviewed about the details of his case.

123   For information on source of details and quotes pertinent to the Gastal family and their suit against the Roman Catholic Diocese of Lafayette, Louisiana, see notes for Chapter 2.

126   Information on Pasternack is based on author's interviews with him; with his investigator Jerry Mazon; his clients, Susan Sandoval and Tim Martinez. Further information on the attacks against him was taken from the *Albuquerque Tribune,* October 23, 1992. For specific information on the Sigler and Kirsch cases, see first note for Chapter 4 and third note for Chapter 6.

CHAPTER 8: THE CRUCIFIXION OF INNOCENCE

131   The story of Dennis Gaboury is based on author's interviews with Gaboury (October–November 1992); Vic Gaboury (November 1992); Beatrice Gaboury (November 1992) and supplemented by the media reports in the Porter case referred to in the notes to Chapter 1, "While God Wasn't Watching." The quote from Gaboury comes from a letter published in the *Sun Chronicle* (North Attleboro, Massachusetts) on November 1, 1992.

137   Information on the damage comes from authors' interviews with Gail Ryan, facilitator of perpetrator prevention programs at the Kempe Center in Denver, Colorado; Walter Berra, a Minneapolis therapist; Thom Harrigan, a Boston-area therapist; Dr. Gloria Malone, a Phoenix psychotherapist; Dr. Gayle O'Callaghan, a Baltimore psychotherapist; Dr. Frank Reichhold-Caruso, a Boston-area psychotherapist; and experts cited in specific quotes. See also, David Finkelhor et al., "Sexual Abuse and Its Relationship to Later Sexual Satisfaction, Marital Status, Religion, and Attitudes," *Journal of Interpersonal Violence* 4:4 (December 1989).

138   Quotes are from authors' interviews with Dr. Alexander Zaphiris, professor of Social Work at the University of Houston (September 1992); Mic Hunter, a St. Paul psychotherapist (September 1992); the Reverend Marie Fortune, executive director of the Center for the Prevention of Sexual and Domestic Violence in Seattle, Washington (September 1992).

139   The story of Christopher Schultz is based on reports published in the *Washington Times,* May 23, 1991.

139   The story of the Florida man who hanged himself is from Carl Cannon's series on child sexual abuse by priests published in the *San Jose Mercury News* on December 30, 1987.

139   The story of the Luddy victim is based on a lengthy report published in the *Pittsburgh Press*, August 28, 1991, and shorter pieces in the *Pittsburgh Press* and the *Allentown Morning Call* during 1991 and 1992. After pursuing his suit for four years while the Church fought to keep all information on Luddy secret, the victim gave up and dropped the matter in August 1992.

140   Information on the Porter victim comes from author's interview with Cheryl Bryant, another alleged victim of Porter.

140   The story of Gregory Riedle is based on a report in the *Allentown Morning Call*, October 11, 1987.

140   The story of the Seattle victim comes from an interview with Dr. Fran Ferder, a Franciscan nun and psychotherapist who works with victims of child sexual abuse in Seattle, and from the *Seattle Post-Intelligencer* (June 27, 1988).

140   The story of the San Diego woman is based on author's interview with the victim.

141   The quote from Mire—as well as the information on the marital status of the other boys abused with him—is based on author's interview with Mire in Lafayette, Louisiana, in July 1992.

141   Information on the marital status of the Porter survivors is based on author's interviews with eighteen members of their group based in North Attleboro, Massachusetts.

141   There is no clear statistic to indicate what percentage of sexually abused children grow up to become molesters. Even the statistics available on the percentage of abusers who were themselves abused are highly contested. A 1979 study by Nicholas Groth found that 32 percent of a group of 106 child molesters reported abusive experiences in their own childhoods. Researchers at Bridgewater Massachusetts Treatment Center found that 57 percent of the child molesters there had been victims of sexual assault as kids. For a full review of the literature, see David Finkelhor, *A Sourcebook on Child Sexual Abuse* (Newbury Park, Calif.: Sage, 1986).

141   Information on David Clohessy comes from authors' interviews with Clohessy, August 1992.

142   Quote from author's interview with Thom Harrigan, a Boston-area psychotherapist, conducted in September 1992.

142   The letter from the Phoenix girl is from court documents filed in the criminal case against Father Mark Allen Lehman from 1990 to 1992.

142   The therapist's quote is based on author's interview with the male victim's Phoenix therapist.

142   The information on the suicide case was published in the *Toronto Star*, February 11, 1990.

142   The story of the Kraskouskas family is based on interviews with Jennifer, Lynn, Tony and Jackie Kraskouskas in Gardner, Massachusetts, in July 1992. The advertisement cited was published in the *Telegram & Gazette* on Tuesday, April 17, 1990. Bishop Timothy Harrington did not respond to repeated requests for an interview.

143   The story of Miguel Chinchilla is based on interviews with Miguel Chinchilla; his mother, Rita; his brother Ignacio; and Chancellor Gerald LaCerra of the Archdiocese of Miami. LaCerra would not comment on the innocence or guilt of Father Castellanos. In commenting on the meetings between Miguel and diocesan officials, the only dispute between Miguel and LaCerra involved the videotaping of the first meetings. Father Castellanos declined the authors' request for an interview except to say, in February 1993, that Chinchilla's allegations are "totally groundless. The whole thing is absurd."

CHAPTER 9: CARDINAL SINS

153   The Adamson chronology—and all anecdotes, details and quotes within it—is constructed from articles that appeared between December 1988 and January 1991 in the *Minneapolis Star Tribune* and the *St. Paul Pioneer Press*. Information in the chronology was updated by author's interviews with attorney Jeffrey Anderson in October and November 1992. Adamson was never charged criminally. Most of the civil lawsuits against him were settled out of court for undisclosed amounts. One case went before a jury, which awarded the victim $3.5 million, a sum later reduced by the judge.

157   The story of Father Carmelo Baltazar is based on reports in the *Idaho Statesman* from 1985 to 1988 and the *San Jose Mercury News* (December 30, 1987). In 1985, Baltazar was sentenced to seven years in prison after pleading guilty.

157   Information on the Calabrese case came from the *Orlando Sentinel*, October 1992, and from author's interview with Dutchess County district attorney William Grady. Grady provided the author with a copy of his letter to Archbishop O'Connor. Neither O'Connor nor Grady will make public the archbishop's response.

158   Information about the Authenreith case was drawn from articles published in the *San Jose Mercury News*, December 30–31, 1987. Authenreith was never charged criminally but the families of his victims received a total of $3 million in compensation as the result of civil lawsuits.

158   Information about the Garcia-Rubio case was drawn from articles published in the *Miami Herald* on November 13, 22 and 25, 1988; and on March 6, 1989.

159   Information about the O'Connell case was drawn from articles published over several years in the *Providence Journal-Bulletin*, with the primary references appearing on June 6, 1983; June 24, 1986; July 30, 1989; and September 7, 1989. It is also drawn from police interviews and records and from court documents in connection with the case of the *State of Rhode Island vs. William O'Connell* (no. 85-1065-A and 1066 A). It is drawn, as well, from author's interview in July 1992 with a parishioner at O'Connell's church and author's interview in August 1992 with Father Jude McGeough. O'Connell was sentenced to one year in prison and two years in inpatient therapy.

160   James Seritella's comment was provided to the authors by Father Thomas Doyle, who attended the meeting. It has also been widely reprinted.

161   General observations about the ways in which bishops responded to child sexual abuse complaints and to the lawsuits that ensued are culled from authors' interviews with dozens of victims and their families; with prosecutors who have pressed charges against priests and attorneys who have filed civil suit against dioceses; and with therapists and other experts whom dioceses have consulted. Observations are also culled from the authors' examination of newspaper articles and court records relating to more than two hundred cases that they have uncovered.

161   Bishop Gelineau's response to the $14 million lawsuit stemming from the O'Connell case is described at length in an article from the *Providence Journal* published on September 7, 1989.

162   Narrative about Father Thomas Doyle and the writing of the Doyle-Peterson-Mouton report is constructed from author's interviews with Doyle at Grissom Air Force Base in July 1992 and from author's interviews in July 1992 with Judy Trosson, who typed the report, and Ray Mouton.

163   Quotes from the report come from a copy of it obtained by the authors.

164   Observations about the report's reception and fate are drawn from authors' interviews over June through November 1992 with Doyle, Mouton, several of the bishops cited in the notes for Chapter 3, "Genesis," and Mark Chopko, general counsel for the National Conference of Catholic Bishops.

165   Quote from Ray Mouton comes from author's interview with Mouton in July 1992.

166   Information about the personality and demographic profiles of American bishops and the way bishops filtered and reacted to complaints of child sexual abuse is drawn from interviews with the twelve bishops listed in the notes for Chapter 3; with therapists among those listed in the notes for Chapter 3 and Chapter 5, "False Idols," who have evaluated priests and their alleged victims for dioceses across the nation; from

priests in dioceses across the nation; and from many of the books previously cited in Chapter 3. The information is also drawn from authors' interviews over June-November 1992 with Eugene Kennedy, Chicago psychologist and Catholic scholar, in Chicago, Illinois, and St. Joseph, Michigan; with Father Richard McBrien, former head of the theology department at Notre Dame University; and with Father Charles Curran, a professor at Southern Methodist University.

167   Quote from Cardinal Joseph Bernardin comes from author's interview with Bernardin in Chicago, Illinois, in August 1992.

167   Quote from Bishop Kenneth Untener comes from author's interview with Untener in Saginaw, Michigan, in September 1992.

168   Anecdote about Archbishop Rembert Weakland's visit to a convent in the 1960s comes from author's interview with Weakland in September 1992.

170   Quote from Archbishop John Roach comes from author's interview with Roach in September 1992.

170   Quote from Archbishop Daniel Sheehan comes from author's interview with Sheehan in August 1992.

170   Quote from Bishop Thomas Gumbleton comes from author's interview with Gumbleton in Detroit in August 1992.

171   Quote from Archbishop Daniel Pilarczyk comes from author's interview with Pilarczyk in October 1992.

171   Anecdote from Father Bernard Bush comes from author's interview with Bush in August 1992.

171   Quote from Eugene Kennedy comes from authors' interviews with Kennedy in Chicago, Illinois, and St. Joseph, Michigan, in August and September 1992.

171   Absence of national coordination was verified in authors' interview with Mark Chopko, general counsel for the National Conference of Catholic Bishops, in Washington, D.C., in July 1992.

172   Information about Rome's lack of concern for, and cooperation in solving, the child sexual abuse problem is drawn primarily from interviews with the bishops previously cited.

172   Quote from Bishop Kenneth Untener comes from author's interview with Untener in Saginaw, Michigan, in September 1992.

172   Quotes from Father Stephen Rossetti come from authors' interview with Rossetti in July 1992 in Chestnut Hill, Massachusetts.

173   Details on Cardinal Joseph Bernardin's commission and its report are drawn from the author's interview with Bernardin in Chicago in August 1992; from articles that ran between October 1991 and November 1992 in the *Chicago Tribune*, the *Chicago Sun-Times*, the *New York*

Times and *USA Today*; and from a copy of the June 1992 report of the commission.

173   Details of the June 1992 meeting of the National Conference of Catholic Bishops are drawn from interviews with reporters at the meeting; from newspaper articles covering the meeting in publications nationwide; from author's interview with Dr. Fred Berlin in Baltimore, Maryland, in July 1992; from author's interview with Archbishop Daniel Pilarczyk in October 1992; and from authors' copy of Pilarczyk's statement to the news media following the conference.

174   Details of the November 1992 meeting of the National Conference of Catholic Bishops and, particularly, of the meeting between victims and bishops are drawn from author's attendance and reporting at the conference; from author's subsequent interview with Cardinal Roger Mahony; and from author's interviews during and after the conference with reporters David Crumm of the *Detroit Free Press* and Patricia Edmonds of *USA Today*. It is also drawn from authors' interviews during and after the conference with each of the members of the group that met the bishops: Fran Battaglia of North Attleboro, Massachusetts; Barbara Blaine of Chicago, Illinois; Cheryl Bryant of Sandwich, Massachusetts; Pat Burns of Arlington, Virginia; David Clohessy of St. Louis, Missouri; Frank Fitzpatrick of Cranston, Rhode Island; Dennis Gaboury of Baltimore; and Ed Morris of Philadelphia.

175   Information on the policy of the Diocese of Cleveland comes from author's interview with Santiago Feliciano in August 1992.

175   The midwestern bishop's "little Lolita" comment was repeated to author by the reporter, who wishes to remain anonymous, who spoke with the bishop.

176   Account of Bishop John McCarthy's handling of a 1987 case and his quotes about that case come from author's interviews with McCarthy in August 1992.

CHAPTER 10: UNSPOKEN COVENANT

178   The story of a Vatican official saying "Can't you just talk to the judges" made the rounds in Church circles in 1992 and was told in the closed-door executive session at the National Conference of Catholic Bishops' November 1992 meeting in Washington, D.C.

179   The section on Costello is based on authors' interviews with him in July 1992, as well as on the court records of the McCutcheon and Chleboski cases. McCutcheon was sentenced to twenty-five years in jail in 1986, a sentence reduced to probation on the condition that he enter inpatient therapy. Chleboski was tried in both Virginia and Maryland, found guilty and sentenced to twenty-two years in jail in Virginia and eight in Maryland. The *Washington Post* article mentioned was pub-

lished on February 28, 1991. Interdonato said in an interview in January 1993 that he did not remember the conversation described by Costello.

181   Dworin's quote and the story of Aguilar Rivera are based on author's interviews with Dworin and his partner Gary Lyon in Los Angeles in July 1992, as well as on reports that appeared in the *Los Angeles Times* from February through June 1988. Aguilar Rivera was charged with sexually abusing ten altar boys. He is a fugitive from justice, believed to be in Mexico.

181   The story of Detective Rodriguez's investigation of Father Salazar is based on an interview with Kenneth Wullschlager, associate district attorney of Los Angeles. Background on the Salazar case came from reports published during December 1986 in the *Los Angeles Times*, the *San Jose Mercury News* and the *Los Angeles Daily News*. Salazar pleaded guilty to molesting boys ages thirteen and fourteen and was sentenced to six years in prison in 1988.

182   The discussion of the furor over Maday is pulled from accounts published in the *Chicago Tribune* and the *Chicago Sun-Times* in spring 1992. The Greeley quote is from his editorial in the *Chicago Sun-Times* on June 14, 1992.

182   The story of Father Simms is based on accounts appearing in the *Baltimore Sun, Montgomery County* [Maryland] *Journal*, the Annapolis, Maryland, *Capital* (March 1988–March 1989). The Maryland states' attorney dropped the charges against Simms in 1985. An out-of-court settlement was reached in 1989 for an undisclosed sum. As of early 1993, Simms was working in the chancery of the Archdiocese of Baltimore.

183   The story of Dino Cinel has been widely covered in Louisiana newspapers, especially in the *Times-Picayune*. But the most thorough account was published in "Unholy Alliances," in *Vanity Fair*, December 1991. This section is based on the accounts that appeared in the *Times-Picayune* (May 1991–September 1992), *Vanity Fair* and on author's interview with Gary Raymond, the private investigator involved in the case.

184   The story of the prosecution of Father Leech is based primarily on author's interview with Craven in Rhode Island in July 1992. It is supplemented with newspaper clips from the *Providence Journal* (October 1985).

185   The report on 190 clerical child molesters was written by Annie Laurie Gaylor of the Freedom from Religion Foundation (Madison, Wisconsin).

185   The information on the Bredemann case—and the two other abuse cases used as comparisons—is pulled from the *Mesa Tribune* (July 23, 1989), the *Arizona Republic* and the *Phoenix Gazette*, also July 1989.

185   Information on the O'Sullivan case is from the *Boston Globe* (November 1984). In 1984, O'Sullivan pleaded guilty and was placed on probation for five years under the condition that he receive inpatient therapy and pay his victim's family $1500.

185   Information on the Weaver case is from the Cherry Hill, New Jersey, *Courier-Post* (March 1987).

186   Information on Brother Andrew Hewitt is from the Newark *Star-Ledger*, April 1989.

186   Information on the Andersen case is based on author's interview with Judge Cardenas in September 1992; prosecutor Mike Koski in July 1992; investigator Don Howell, July 1992; and the letters, reports and other documents in the court file of the case. Andersen did not respond to repeated requests for an interview about this case.

188   Information on the Henry case is based on author's interview with prosecutor Cynthia Ulfig and the court documents in the case.

188   Information on the McLaughlin cased was based on reports in the *News Herald* and the *Columbus Dispatch* (July 1989). McLaughlin was ultimately sentenced to eighteen months in jail.

188   Information on MacRae story from report in the *Keene Sentinel, Journal Tribune* (Biddeford, Maine) and *Boston Globe* in November 1988. In 1988, MacRae pleaded guilty to paying a Keene boy for sex and was sentenced to one year in jail. The sentence was deferred and he was sent to an inpatient therapeutic center.

189   Information on the South Florida case, which concerns Father Ernesto Garcia Rubio, is from reports in the *Miami Herald* in November 1988 and March 1989.

189   Information on the Noe Guzman story comes from the *Houston Chronicle*, October 1, 1992. Noe Guzman pleaded guilty to assaulting the girl and was sentenced to ten years in prison.

189   Cannon quotes from author's interview in September 1992.

190   Figure for advertising revenue loss from authors' interview with Richard Baudoin in Lafayette, Louisiana, in July 1992.

190   *Pittsburgh Post-Gazette* story and quote from author's interview with Eleanor Bergholz in August 1992.

190   Goedert's statement was in the *Chicago Tribune*, October 11, 1990.

191   Law's comment was printed in the *Boston Globe* and the *Boston Herald*, May 24 and 25, 1992.

192   Information on the situation at the *Providence Journal* was based on author's interviews with two members of that paper's staff, who requested anonymity. Asked why the *Journal* downplayed the story so

seriously, state editor Philip Kukielski said in an interview in March 1993 that it was displaying "customary caution" about an allegation that had not yet become formalized by the filing of criminal charges or a civil suit. Kukielski said the newspaper's concern that the accusations might be a hoax was one that attends many sensational stories that are difficult to corroborate. He said the *Journal* may have been more cautious than usual because the accused was a religious figure. "There was ostensibly a reputation to be preserved here," he said. "This was a person who had chosen a religious life."

192   Crumm quote taken from author's interview with him in August 1992.

193   Schoener quote taken from author's interview in September 1992.

193   Rossetti quote taken from author's interview in July 1992.

193   Valcour information taken from *Houston Post*, August 2, 1992. Feierman quote from interview with the *Rocky Mountain News* (July 5, 1987). Pedigo quote taken from author's interview in August 1992.

194   Sipe quote taken from authors' interviews in July 1992.

194   Loftus quote taken from author's interview in August 1992.

195   Schoener quote taken from author's interview in September 1992.

195   Information on the Diocese of Crookston is from the *Boston Globe*, the *Star Tribune* (Minneapolis) and the *St. Paul Pioneer Press*, July 1992. Information on Andersen sentencing from interview with Judge Cardenas.

195   Feierman's most recent assertion in this regard was made to the *Boston Globe* for an article published July 16, 1992. On that occasion, he said that only two or three graduates of the New Mexico program had ever gone on to act "inappropriately" again.

195   Sipe quote from authors' interview in July 1992.

195   Loftus quote from author's interview in August 1992.

196   The 1986 letter was included in the court file of Andrew Christian Andersen in Orange County, California.

196   Information on the Porter case—including Porter's tenure in New Mexico—is culled from the *Boston Globe*, the *Providence Journal*, the *Boston Herald*, the *St. Louis Post-Dispatch* and the Associated Press, May through December 1992. Information was also provided by Bruce Pasternack of Albuquerque and is part of the record of the lawsuit he has filed on behalf of four clients against the Paracletes. Information on the Perrault case was provided by Bruce Pasternack, an Albuquerque attorney, in an interview with the author in August 1992. Further information was culled from clips in the *Albuquerque Journal* and the *Albuquerque Tribune* in November and December 1992. Information

on Sigler's residence at the Paraclete center came from Sigler's personnel file from the Archdiocese of Santa Fe; depositions of Martinez, Sigler, Archbishop Robert Sanchez and Father Clarence Galli; complaints, affidavits, briefs and motions filed in the case of *John Does I through X vs. Roman Catholic Church of the Archdiocese of Santa Fe, Inc., Jason E. Sigler, Bishop Arthur Tafoya and Clarence Galli*; and news reports published throughout 1992 in the *Albuquerque Journal* and the *Albuquerque Tribune*.

196   Information on the Paraclete program in the late 1980s is taken from materials provided by the Order to judges, therapists and bishops. Information on the absence of restrictions on the movements of all priests other than those there by court order was provided by a guest at the center who wishes to remain anonymous.

197   The letter from the Paracletes was printed in the *Jemez Jonker* in September 1992 and posted on the door of the town's general store.

197   Information on the Fredette case is from the *Boston Globe*, August-September 1992.

198   Information on the Heck verdict is from the *Boston Globe*, August 2, 1991.

198   Information on the O'Malley-Bernardin confrontation is from the *Chicago Tribune* and the *Chicago Sun-Times*, September 1992.

198   The statistics on newspaper coverage were compiled by the authors, using computerized databases. The information on the reaction to the *Globe*'s coverage is from a column by the paper's ombudsman, August 10, 1992.

199   Archbishop Pilarczyk's quote is from author's interview in October 1992.

CHAPTER 11: BITTER FRUITS

200   Anecdote about the priest on a suburban street in Boston comes from author's interview in July 1992 with Father William P. Fay, dean of the College of Arts and Sciences at St. John's Seminary in Brighton, Massachusetts.

200   Anecdote about disillusioned Phoenix woman comes from author's July 1992 interview with Nancy Richards of Phoenix, Arizona, a former parishioner of St. Thomas the Apostle Church, where Father Mark Lehman served as a pastor before his indictment on child sexual abuse charges in 1991.

201   Details about Cardinal Bernardin's news conference and its contents are drawn from articles in the *Chicago Tribune*, the *Chicago Sun-Times* and the *New York Times*. Details about the personal effect of the

child sexual abuse crisis on Bernardin and on the percentage of time he spends dealing with issues related to the child sexual abuse crisis are drawn from author's interview with Bernardin in August 1992. The assertion that child sexual abuse complaints have cost his diocese millions of dollars is based on authors' knowledge of settlement amounts in the $400,000 to $500,000 range in just a few of the lawsuits against the diocese that have ended in court-sealed settlements. Detail about priests joking that there won't be pension funds left is based on authors' interviews with priests and their friends in Chicago, some of whom requested anonymity.

201   The cartoon described ran in the *Arizona Repubic* first on July 28, 1992, and then was reprinted along with a storm of angry letters from readers on August 8, 1992.

202   Andrew Greeley's quotes on the topic have appeared in the *New York Times* and *Vanity Fair*, among other publications. He characterized child sexual abuse by priests as perhaps the most serious crisis faced by the Catholic Church since the Reformation in his October 1992 address to the first annual conference of Victims of Clergy Abuse Linkup (VOCAL) in October 1992.

202   Characterizations of what the bishops say about the child sexual abuse crisis, how they reacted to it and their assessments of both its dimensions and its effect on the Catholic Church are drawn primarily from the authors' interviews with the twelve bishops listed in the notes for Chapter 3. These characterizations are also drawn from authors' interviews with priests; Mark Chopko, general counsel of the National Conference of Catholic Bishops; Father Thomas Doyle, coauthor of a 1985 report on the problem submitted to the Church; and magazine and newspaper articles from 1985 through 1992. These characterizations are further drawn from author's reporting at the November 1992 meeting of the National Conference of Catholic Bishops in Washington, D.C.

203   Assertion that price tags for lawsuits easily reach the $100,000 to $500,000 range is based on authors' interviews with victims of priests who have filed and settled lawsuits; on settlement amounts that have been made public or have been leaked to reporters for a variety of publications, including the *National Catholic Reporter* and the *San Jose Mercury News*; and authors' interviews in October and November 1992 with St. Paul attorney Jeffrey Anderson.

203   Characterization of the Catholic Church's greater vulnerability to lawsuits is based on authors' interviews in 1992 with two lawyers whose expertise is clergy malpractice: Robert W. McMenamin, of Portland, Oregon, and Jeffrey Anderson of St. Paul, Minnesota. It is also based on articles about clergy abuse in a variety of national publications including the *National Law Journal*.

203   For sources of details on the settlement amounts and other figures related to the Gauthe case, see notes for Chapter 2. The $20 million figure comes from "Unholy Alliances," *Vanity Fair*, December 1991.

203   Figures from the Doyle-Peterson-Mouton report come from a copy of the report obtained by the authors. Descriptions of how those figures were tabulated come from the text of the report and author's interviews with Father Thomas Doyle in July through October 1992.

204   Assertion that there is no way to know how much child sexual abuse has cost the Church is based on authors' interviews in June through November 1992 with attorneys who have sued the Church; bishops of different dioceses; and Mark Chopko, general counsel of the National Conference of Catholic Bishops. Assertion is also based on interviews in June through November 1992 with those Church critics and observers who do offer estimates and a critical examination of the flaws in their methods. Their estimates have appeared on TV newscasts and in newspaper and magazine articles nationwide from 1988 to 1992.

204   Reported settlement amounts for the cases in Orlando, Florida, and Springfield, Illinois, are drawn from articles that appeared in the *San Jose Mercury News* on December 30 and 31, 1987.

204   Assertion that most settlement amounts are not disclosed is based on authors' examination of more than two hundred cases they have uncovered.

204   Assertion that the Church may not even have a private record of its losses to child sexual abuse cases is based on the authors' interviews with Mark Chopko in Washington, D.C., in July and November 1992.

205   Number of lawsuits Jeffrey Anderson has filed comes from author's interview in December 1992 with Anderson.

205   Information on insurance is based primarily on authors' interviews in June through November 1992 with bishops in twelve different U.S. dioceses; Father Bernard Bush, a California priest who has helped dioceses nationwide formulate policies that would satisfy insurers' requirements; Mark Chopko; Robert McMenamin; and Jim Wojczynski, executive vice president of service programs for the Michigan Catholic Conference.

205   Chopko's observations are based on authors' interviews with him in July and November 1992 in Washington, D.C.

206   Financial figures for the Archdiocese of Los Angeles come from an article in the *Los Angeles Times*, June 14, 1992.

206   Amount for which the Diocese of Fall River settled with victims of Father James Porter was published in the *Boston Herald* in December 1992. The figure has been confirmed by the authors.

206   Characterization of the way the child sexual abuse crisis has affected innocent priests is based on authors' interviews in June through November 1992 with the following priests, bishops and friends of priests, among others: Father Jeremiah Boland of Chicago; Father Kevin Clinton of Mendota, Minnesota; Father Victor Clore of Detroit; Father John Dooher of Boston; Father William P. Fay of Brighton, Massachusetts; Martin Hegarty of Chicago; Father Bill Kelly of Hingham, Massachusetts; Archbishop Thomas Kelly of Louisville, Kentucky; Cardinal Roger Mahony of Los Angeles; Father Thomas McCarthy of Youngstown, Ohio, who serves as president of the National Federation of Priests' Councils; Father Thomas McDonnell of Boston; Father Jude McGeough of Providence, Rhode Island; Archbishop Daniel E. Sheehan of Omaha, Nebraska; Tim Unsworth of Chicago; Bishop Kenneth Untener of Saginaw, Michigan; Father Armand Ventre of Providence, Rhode Island; and Father Tim Wozniak of St. Paul Park, Minnesota.

207   Characterization of changes in the priesthood after Vatican II is based on books previously cited in the notes for Chapter 3. It is also based on authors' interviews in June through November 1992 with the priests and bishops cited in the notes for this chapter and with the following experts: Eugene Kennedy, Chicago psychologist and Catholic scholar, and Father Richard McBrien, former head of the theology department at Notre Dame University. It is based as well on a 1991 review of research titled *Consultation on Priests' Morale: A Review of Research*, produced by the National Federation of Priests' Councils.

207   Seminary enrollment figures come from author's interview in September 1992 with Father Robert Wister, executive director of the seminary department of the National Catholic Education Association in Washington, D.C.

207   The estimate of the decline in the priesthood—subject to considerable debate, in part because not everyone agrees on the definition of "active priest"—has appeared in numerous publications, among them Tim Unsworth, *The Last Priests in America* (New York: Crossroad, 1991), and literature distributed by the National Federation of Priests' Councils.

207   Description of recruitment tactics is drawn from a variety of articles on the subject published in newspapers and magazines nationwide, including the *Chicago Tribune* and the *Wall Street Journal*.

207   Characterization of the ways in which the priest shortage has transformed the life of priests is based on sources previously cited in the notes for this chapter.

208   Anecdotes about priests in the Boston-Providence area either being targeted with, or overhearing, derisive comments about priests as pedophiles come from author's interview in July 1982 with Father William Fay, dean of the College of Arts and Sciences at St. John's Seminary in Brighton, Massachusetts.

208   Anecdote about Father Jude McGeough comes from author's interview with McGeough in August 1992.

208   Anecdote about a Chicago priest comes from author's interview in August 1992 with Tim Unsworth of Chicago, author of *The Last Priests in America* (New York: Crossroad, 1991).

209   Quote from Father Dominic Grassi comes from author's interviews with Grassi in Chicago in September 1992.

209   Narrative of Father Dominic Grassi's family background, career and the changes he has witnessed in the reputation of the priesthood, particularly after the dawn of the child sexual abuse crisis, is based on author's interviews with Grassi in Chicago in September 1992. Text and purpose of the letter he and other priests read from the pulpit are taken from "The Cardinal's Commission on Clerical Sexual Misconduct with Minors," released by Cardinal Joseph Bernardin of Chicago in June 1992. Reference to the "October massacre" comes from interviews with other Chicago priests.

213   Figure of fifty-three thousand priests is rounded off from the statistics in the *1992 Official Catholic Directory* (New Providence, N.J.: P. J. Kenedy & Sons, 1992).

213   Priests' voting child sexual abuse their top item of concern comes from author's interview in August 1992 with Father Thomas McCarthy, president of the National Federation of Priests' Councils, and from materials sent to the authors by the conference.

213   Quote from Father Kevin Clinton of Mendota, Minnesota, comes from author's interviews with Clinton in August and September 1992.

215   Rossetti's quotes and the results of his survey are taken from the September and October 1992 editions of the Catholic magazine *Today's Parish*.

216   The anecdote about Gerardo Gamez is taken from an article that appeared in the *Houston Post*, September 29, 1992. The priest pleaded guilty and was sentenced to ten years in jail and to pay a $10,000 fine.

217   *Boston Globe* poll was published on July 26, 1992.

217   Quote from Eugene Kennedy taken from author's interviews with Kennedy in August and September 1992 in Chicago, Illinois, and St. Joseph, Michigan.

218   Anecdote about, and quote from, Archbishop Thomas Kelly is drawn from author's interview with Kelly in October 1992. Description of the "PrimeTime Live" broadcast is based on authors' viewing of that broadcast in July 1992.

218   Characterizations of American bishops' concerns about the child sexual abuse crisis are drawn from previously cited interviews with bishops in 12 different U.S. dioceses and from author's attendance at the

November 1992 meeting of the National Conference of Catholic Bishops in Washington, D.C.

218   Archbishop Robert Sanchez's estimate that 30 to 40 percent of his time in late 1992 was spent dealing with child sexual abuse complaints comes from his conversation with one of the authors at a news media reception at the November 1992 meeting of the National Conference of Catholic Bishops in Washington, D.C.

218   Archbishop John Roach's assertion that bishops mention child sexual abuse within five minutes comes from author's interview with Roach in September 1992.

219   Quote from Bishop Kenneth Untener comes from author's interview with Untener in Saginaw, Michigan, in September 1992.

219   The joke about the priest and the janitor was told to the authors by numerous people—including prosecutors and victims—over the course of their reporting from June 1992 to November 1992.

CHAPTER 12: A PATH TO REDEMPTION

220   See Fiore's columns in *The Wanderer* (St. Paul, Minnesota), 1991–92 and author's interviews with him. Fiore is an exclaustrated Dominican priest living in Madison, Wisconsin.

220   See Jason Berry, *Lead Us Not Into Temptation* (New York: Doubleday, 1992). Berry has also written numerous op-ed pieces for newspapers on child sexual abuse by priests. While he often insists that he is not confusing homosexuality and pedophilia, a major portion of Berry's book—which is subtitled *Catholic Priests and the Sexual Abuse of Children*—is devoted to what he characterizes as the rising number of gay priests and to a discussion of the purported gay life-style. In a September 17, 1989, piece on child sexual abuse in the *Washington Post*, he writes, characteristically: "Homosexuality is part of this darkened mindset."

220   Doyle comment is from authors' interview in October 1992.

222   The quote from Sister Michaels is from the *Toronto Star*, July 2, 1989. The other quotes are from the *Toronto Star*, December 15, 1990. The report from the Canadian bishops is *From Pain to Hope*, published June 1992 by the Canadian Conference of Catholic Bishops. They also published materials for study groups entitled *Breach of Trust, Breach of Faith*.

224   Sipe's quote is from his presentation to the First Annual National Conference of VOCAL—Victims of Clergy Abuse Linkup—in Arlington Heights, Illinois, October 1992.

224   More careful screening has become the insistent cry in dioceses all across the country. Comments on its effectiveness are pulled from interviews with the experts in child sexual abuse mentioned in notes to Chapter 3, particular Dr. Judith Becker, Dr. Fred Berlin and Dr. Nicholas Groth. Schoener quote is from author's interview with him in September 1992.

225   David Finkelhor, *A Sourcebook on Child Sexual Abuse* (Newbury Park, Calif.: Sage, 1986) reviews the literature on personality characteristics of molesters and provides information on the studies supporting the hypothesis that these characteristics are common to abusers.

226   In virtually every candid discussion with heterosexual victims and their supporters, as well as with bishops, the element of confusion between homosexuality and child sexual abuse creeps into the conversation—despite the repeated insistence of the experts with whom both sides consult that homosexuality is irrelevant. The father of one Chicago victim is convinced that high-placed homosexuals in his archdiocese are shielding active child molesters and ended one interview with a crack about how the problem is growing because seminaries have become "lavender palaces."

226   Regarding sexuality instruction to seminarians, the report to Joseph Cardinal Bernardin by his commission on clerical sexual misconduct with minors (June 1992), for example, recommends the creation in seminaries of "academic courses and components in their formation programs that deal in depth with psychosexual development, including both moral and deviant sexual behavior." In their explanation of the recommendation they call for discussions on how to be celibate and how to handle their sexual urges, but also on how to recognize how developing an emotional relationship with a child can escalate into "grooming"—touching, showing them pornography and engaging in sexual intercourse. The Kosnik quote is from author's interview in September 1992 in Detroit.

226   Quote from Mic Hunter from author's interview, September 1992.

227   Ratzinger quote is from the Ratzinger Report, a compilation of interviews the Cardinal did with Italian journalist Vittorio Messori, published in 1985. Ratzinger is widely considered to be one of the most influential voices in the Vatican.

227   The efforts of bishops to gain the power to laicize priests who molest was confirmed by Bishops Untener, McCarthy (Austin) and Pilarczyk in authors' interviews with them. In November 1992, just after they discussed the matter yet again at a closed session of the winter meeting of the National Conference of Catholic Bishops, Philadelphia archbishop Cardinal Anthony Bevilacqua returned to Rome to continue the lobbying efforts.

227   The quote from Pilarczyk is from author's interview, October 1992, when Pilarczyk was in his last month as president of the National Conference of Catholic Bishops.

228   Weakland's comments and quote are from author's interview, September 1992.

228   McBrien's column, distributed by the Universal Press Syndicate, appeared in many newspapers around the country. His quote below that is from author's interview in August 1992.

229   Information on the origins of celibacy is culled from a variety of literature. See, in particular: William Bassett and Peter Huizing, ed., *Celibacy in the Church* (New York: Herder and Herder, 1972); Vern Bullough and J. Brundage, *Sexual Practices in the Medieval Church* (Buffalo: Prometheus, 1982); Henry Lea, *History of Sacerdotal Celibacy in the Christian Church* (New Hyde Park, N.Y.: University Books, 1966); Uta Ranke-Heinemann, *Eunuchs for the Kingdom of Heaven* (New York: Doubleday, 1990); E. Schillebeeckx, *Celibacy* (New York: Sheed & Ward, 1968); also see relevant section in Richard Sipe, *A Secret World: Sexuality and the Search for Celibacy* (New York: Brunner/ Mazel, 1990).

231   Quote from Mike Lew from author's interview in September 1992.

231   This Vatican pronouncement, referred to as the Oath of Fidelity, was published in *L'Osservatore Romano*, the official Vatican newspaper, on February 25, 1989.

233   The Council of Trent was in 1545.

233   The pope's comment was made in Miami on September 10, 1987.

EPILOGUE: AMAZING GRACE

237   The profile of Jeanne Miller and account of her lawsuit and emergence as leader of the victims' movement are based primarily on the authors' extensive interviews with her in the Chicago area in July, August and September of 1992. The profile and account are supplemented by research papers, written recollections, letters and file documents provided by Miller; by interviews with Miller's romantic partner and housemate, Andy Kagan, and with some of Miller's associates, including Richard Sipe and Father Thomas Doyle; and by articles published in a variety of publications, most notably the *Chicago Tribune*.

237   Descriptions of events at the first annual conference of VOCAL/ The Linkup are drawn from author's attendance at that conference in October 1992.

243   Descriptions of the reactions of Father Walter Somerville and Marilyn Steffel to Miller's initial complaints about Father Robert Mayer come from an article in the *Chicago Tribune*, January 6, 1993.

244   Details of Father Walter Somerville's meeting with Cardinal Bernardin and Cardinal Bernardin's comments in that meeting were described by Miller and subsequently confirmed by Father Somerville in a brief interview in February 1992. Cardinal Bernardin declined to comment on specifics of the Father Robert Mayer case.

244   The account of Miller's telephone conversations one afternoon in July 1992 are based on author's visit with Miller at her home that afternoon.

247   Jeanne's dissertation is titled: "Pedophilia in the Priesthood: A Church in Crisis." It was copyrighted in 1988, then revised in 1991 as a manifesto for VOCAL/The Linkup.

247   The arrest of Father Robert Mayer and his subsequent conviction were reported by the *Chicago Tribune*, the *Chicago Sun-Times* and the Associated Press in stories spanning 1991 to 1993. Father Mayer and his lawyers continue to deny any of the wrongdoing alleged by Miller regarding her family's case and other families' cases. Those allegations prior to 1991 never led to criminal charges of any kind against Mayer.

249   Details of Miller's various meetings and correspondences with Cardinal Bernardin—and of his decision not to attend the VOCAL conference—are based on interviews with Miller and documents in her files. Bernardin's change of heart regarding the VOCAL conference was also described in a column in the *Chicago Tribune*, October 16, 1992.
    Cardinal Bernardin, in a telephone interview in April 1993, said he could not comment on any allegations against Father Mayer before the incident with Jeanne Miller's son, or on the immediate response to Miller's allegations, because he did not arrive in Chicago until a few weeks after the incident allegedly occurred. He said as well that he was not as directly involved in dealings with the parents at St. Edna's as were other officials in the diocese. "I was assured that the matter had been properly dealt with," he said. "In retrospect, it may not have been."
    In regard to the assertion by Miller and other parties that Cardinal Bernardin refused to prohibit or limit Father Mayer's contacts with children, or to mandate therapy for Father Mayer, the cardinal said: "I don't feel free to respond to that. There certainly were things done. Some of these would be covered by confidentiality. I want to emphasize—in those days, we did not have the setup we do now. It may not have been handled as well as it might have been."
    He confirmed that Father Mayer repeatedly denied any wrongdoing to him. He said he cannot recall details of the final, presettlement meeting in which he supposedly told Miller, "Trust us." He does not remember making that remark.
    He confirms all subsequent details of his meetings and relationship

with Miller. He said he did not attend the VOCAL conference because he had intended it to be a moment of pastoral healing and came to fear it would be contentious and bitter. He said his letter to Miller made it clear that she should feel free to contact him anytime in the future on other matters. As of April 1993, she had not.

An official with the archdiocese who attended the meeting with parents that Miller described said in a March 1993 telephone interview that he could not recall any of the specific remarks made by him or the other official there because the event occurred ten years ago. He added that archdiocesan officials consistently reached out to the hurt families but were persistently hampered in pursuing any action against Father Mayer because Miller and other parents did not want their children to be interviewed directly by archdiocesan officials.

INDEX